Forecasting Methods for Management, Second Edition
Steven C. Wheelwright and Spyros Makridakis

Decision Making and Planning for the Corporate Treasurer
Harold Bierman, Jr.

Corporate Financial Planning Models
Henry I. Meyer

Strategies in Business
Shea Smith, III, and John E. Walsh, Jr.

Strategies in Business

Strategies in Business

SHEA SMITH, III, B.S., MBA

Information and Planning Director
International Division
Monsanto Company

JOHN E. WALSH, Jr., B.S., MBA, DBA

Professor of Management
Washington University

A WILEY-INTERSCIENCE PUBLICATION

JOHN WILEY & SONS, New York · Chichester · Brisbane · Toronto

This publication is designed to provide accurate and authoritative information in regard to the subject matter covered. It is sold with the understanding that the publisher is not engaged in rendering legal, accounting, or other professional service. If legal advice or other expert assistance is required, the services of a competent professional person should be sought.

From a Declaration of Principles jointly adopted by a Committee of the American Bar Association and a Committee of Publishers.

Library of Congress Cataloging in Publication Data:

Smith, Shea, 1916–
   Strategies in business.

   (Series on systems and controls for financial management)
   " A WILEY-INTERSCIENCE PUBLICATION ."
   Includes bibliographical references and index.
   1. Corporate planning. 2. Business.
I. Walsh, John Edward, 1927–   joint author.
II. Title.
HD30.28.S58   658.4'01   77–25091
ISBN 0–471–80002–3

Printed in the United States of America.

10 9 8 7 6 5 4 3 2 1

SERIES PREFACE

No one needs to tell the reader that the world is changing. He sees it all too clearly. The immutable, the constant, the unchanging of a decade or two ago no longer represent the latest thinking—on *any* subject, whether morals, medicine, politics, economics, or religion. Change has always been with us, but the pace has been accelerating, especially in the postwar years.

Business, particularly with the advent of the electronic computer some 20 years ago, has also undergone change. New disciplines have sprung up. New professions are born. New skills are in demand. And the need is ever greater to blend the new skills with those of the older professions to meet the demands of modern business.

The accounting and financial functions certainly are no exception. The constancy of change is as pervasive in these fields as it is in any other. Industry is moving toward an integration of many of the information gathering, processing, and analyzing functions under the impetus of the so-called systems approach. Such corporate territory has been, traditionally, the responsibility of the accountant and the financial man. It still is, to a large extent—but times are changing.

Does this, then, spell the early demise of the accountant as we know him today? Does it augur a lessening of influence for the financial specialists in today's corporate hierarchy? We think not. We maintain, however, that it is incumbent upon today's accountant and today's financial man to learn *today's* thinking and to *use today's* skills. It is for this reason the Wiley Series on Systems and Controls for Financial Management is being developed.

Recognizing the broad spectrum of interests and activities that the series title encompasses, we plan a number of volumes, each representing the latest thinking, written by a recognized authority, on a particular facet of the financial man's responsibilities. The subjects contemplated for discussion within the series range from production accounting systems to planning, to corporate records, to control of cash. Each book is an in-depth study of one subject within this group. Each is intended to be a practical, working tool for the businessman in general and the financial man and accountant in particular.

ROBERT L. SHULTIS
FRANK M. MASTROMANO

PREFACE

In recent years formalized business planning has exploded into prominence. Books, periodicals, university courses, and management seminars on the subject have swelled to gigantic proportions.

In spite of efforts to make planning more productive, only rarely is the process truly effective. Books on the subject written by academicians have been too theoretical and those by business people too limited. The academician has lacked understanding of many of the real problems. The businessman has lacked breadth. This book, coauthored by a businessman and an academician, attempts to bridge the gap between these two poles.

The book is devoted to strategies because they are the most important and most difficult part of the planning process. They define the direction of a corporation. What follow after strategies are steps simply to make sure that the strategies are effectively implemented.

Information is the starting point. What strategies are practical possibilities are influenced by myriad internal and external business environment factors, both psychological and real. The first two chapters deal with these internal and external factors. The third chapter discusses how to manage the information, and the fourth chapter covers the human factors involved in developing and deciding strategies.

Then follows a series of chapters on five major kinds of strategies: product, customer, organizational, financial, and one that is just emerging on the business scene—public affairs. The last chapter deals with the key issues in designing and staffing the total process.

The book was written primarily for business practitioners—persons who develop business strategies—like chief executive officers, product managers, area managers, managers of international operations, and staff planners. It also has value, however, as a text for advanced university courses in management or as a supplementary book for a course in business policy, where cases are the basic means of instruction. For the business executive it offers a wealth of how-to-do-it approaches and only enough theory to provide perspective. For the student it offers a realistic view of strategies and planning and concentrates on theories that have practical application.

By the use of case illustration and direct examination of many strategies, this book seeks to broaden and deepen understanding and help the strategist develop new ideas, avoid costly mistakes, and save valuable time. Specifically it shows ways to set objectives and goals, to collect and manage useful and reliable information, to use the best analytic tools, and to develop strategies. In summary the approach is to suggest "how to do it."

We have received many good suggestions from Edward C. Schleh, President of Schleh Associates, Inc., on Chapters 3 and 5; Robert K. Mueller, Board Chairman of Arthur D. Little, Inc., on Chapter 4; and Merle Welshans, Vice President of Finance of Union Electric Company, and Elmer N. Funkhouser, Jr., Special Assistant to the Dean of the Harvard Business School, on Chapter 8. Professor Powell Niland of Washington University was also helpful in raising several searching questions.

Encouragement and financial assistance for much of this book came from the Research Committee on the Graduate School of Business, Washington University, and especially from former Dean Karl A. Hill.

We owe special thanks to Carol E. Hogan, who contributed secretarial assistance, and to Mrs. Jane Warren for helpful editing of several chapters.

For granting permission to use previous published material, we are indebted to Bruce D. Henderson, President of the Boston Consulting Group, *Business Week, Harvard Business Review*, Dr. Robert B. Stobaugh of the Harvard Business School, H. A. Pope & Sons, and Ralston Purina Company.

Despite the assistance rendered by the persons and organizations mentioned, we are responsible for the contents of the book.

SHEA SMITH, III
JOHN E. WALSH, JR.

January 1978
St. Louis, Missouri

Contents

Strategies in Business

INTRODUCTION

WHAT IS A BUSINESS STRATEGY?

No company can succeed without sound business strategies. Take MGM, the one-time film great. In the early seventies James T. Aubry, Jr., its chief executive officer, vowed to run it like a business and not an art form. Under his leadership the company made inexpensive films. This strategy was sound as far as it went, but it lacked balance. Business considerations were overemphasized; the art form was almost neglected. And MGM's budget movies were usually bad and of hardly any interest to anyone.

Another example, where poor business strategies have been vividly apparent, is the major American automobile companies. "They totally misjudged the small car market," said consumer pollster Albert Sindlinger, "they overproduced and overpriced." The American automobile companies, who had a glut of big cars during the oil embargo, were faced with a glut of small cars less than 2 years later. Some automobile company executives blamed excessive government interference, others blamed foreign car makers. But the basic problem was the major American car makers' inability to assess the car market correctly and to develop the right business strategies.

On the other hand the Maytag Company has provided illustrations of sound business strategies. In the past decade the company has earned about 13% on sales, nearly triple the average of its industry. Its organizational, product, customer, financial, and public relations strategies have been aimed at building and selling a high-quality washing machine at premium prices.

The illustrations just cited raise several fundamental questions. What is a business strategy? How should a sound one be prepared? How can a poor one be detected? We give our complete attention to the last two questions throughout this book. But first, let us make sure that there is an agreement on our use of the term.

It is easy to tell you that the word *strategy* is derived from the Greek word *strategos*, literally meaning "the general's art." It has been used in business since the end of World War II and can have many diverse meanings depending on the wish and attitude of the user.

Professors Learned, Christensen, Andrews, and Guth offer this definition:

> For us strategy is the pattern of objectives, purpose or goals, and major policies and plans for achieving these goals, stated in such a way as to define what business the company is in or is to be in and the kind of company it is or is to be.[1]

The Stanford Research Institute provides another:

> Strategy is the way in which a firm reacts to its environment, deploys its principal resources, and marshals its main efforts in pursuit of its purpose.[2]

Executives of one multinational corporation simply call business strategy the "game plan."

We add a final one that cannot be left out, for it represents our use of the term in the pages that follow. *We call strategy the routes with alternatives for reaching objectives and goals.*

We do not claim that our definition is better than anyone else's. The elements that make it up come in part from historical uses of the word, in part from Webster's *Seventh Collegiate Dictionary*, and in part from our work experiences. We know that our definition is brief. We also know that, unlike some other definitions, it is not aimed exclusively at the highest level of management. Our definition is broad, because we want it to cover several levels in a typical large corporation.

Much difficulty arises, we believe, when people use the term *strategy* without specifying at what level in the corporation it applies. For example, although no one questions its appropriateness at the corporate level, does it apply also to the divisional level, to the functional area level, to the department or section level? One might surmise from our definition that we would apply this term to all, but we would not. We would omit the department or section level, because in our view it does not represent the higher levels of management; as we see it, the art of the department or section head is not comparable to our historical military standard, the art of the general.

Whereas some authorities might refer to routes that need to be taken to achieve objectives and goals as tactics, we prefer to call them strategies or substrategies. Many explanations could be offered in defense of our choice. J. Thomas Cannon partially supports our view with this statement:

---

[1] Learned et al., *Business Policy*—Text and Cases Revised Edition, Richard D. Irwin, Inc., Homewood, Ill., 1969, p. 15.
[2] Unpublished definition from the Stanford Research Institute.

The principal distinction between strategy and tactics is that strategy determines what major plans are to be undertaken and allocates resources to them, while tactics, in contrast, are the means by which previously determined plans are executed.[3]

The primary distinction we make is that the term *tactics* is synonymous with implementation or execution, while *strategy* is a component part of planning.

Let us distinguish among corporate, divisional, and functional strategies by illustrations. We begin with corporate strategies, the type referred to in most of the definitions cited earlier. Originally the objective of the International Multifoods Corporation was to be one of the largest flour mills on the North American continent, which it now is. Its present objective is to increase profits and improve profit margins. The strategy or the routes with alternatives for reaching this objective have followed three lines: (1) a program of acquisition and internal development designed to guide Multifoods into selected, high-growth areas of the consumer food and away-from-home eating market and to reduce its dependence on thin margins on bulk bakery flour; (2) a strengthening of the top management team with outside executives and an increase in the responsibilities of long-term management employees; (3) a weeding out of operations and facilities with below-average profit potential.

So far, so good. Now let us take a look at one of the divisional strategies of the company. Consumer division executives were well aware that they could not break into the mass markets and take on the food-processing giants. "We were late getting in, and we knew it," explained James H. Kalestad, vice president and general manager of the division. The divisional strategy has been to move into small, specialized markets with good growth potential related to new life-styles, For example, to avoid the "potentially bruising confrontation with the Krafts and Bordens of the world," in 1972 the division acquired the Kaukauna Klub cheese operation, which dealt in the relatively uncrowded field of snack-type specialty cheeses.

Of the different functional strategies (production, finance, marketing, etc.) we have selected for illustration the marketing strategy of a company manufacturing replacement parts for American-made automobiles. Marketing executives keep a watchful eye on the "big three" of the automobile industry, for once these firms enter a foreign country a potential exists for a replacement-parts industry. Products carry private brand names rather than the company's trademark. They are sold in one standard grade at prices higher

[3] J. Thomas Cannon, *Business Strategy and Policy*, Harcourt, Brace & World, Inc., New York, 1968, pp. 15–16.

than competitors'; emphasis is on excellent design, high quality, and fast shipment.

Although classification of strategies by organization levels (corporate, divisional, and functional) is the primary scheme we use, we could have turned to many other types of classifications.

For instance, our primary classification could have been by time horizons, since in general time horizons of strategies are longest at the highest levels of management and progressively decline through subsequent levels.

In his penetrating book *Top Management Planning* George A. Steiner emphasized other ways to classify strategies: according to scope and importance (*master strategies* cover basic corporate objectives and means to pursue them, and *pure strategies* specify uses of resources in one area of activity); according to impact on sales and profits; according to whether the strategy in question is a response to an external force (such as the action of government or competitors) or originates within the company (such as reorganization for optimum use of executive talent); and according to whether the strategy deals with physical or nonphysical resources.[4]

Finally we could have taken an international perspective and compared business strategies by countries, using priority factors similar to those developed by the Japan Productivity Center and the University of California in comparing business strategies in Japan and the United States.

These different types and classifications of strategy clearly show that there are many ways of thinking about business strategies. With this comment we end this section, for we believe we have said enough in these few pages to give you the origin, some current usages and classifications, and our interpretation of the term.

[4] George Steiner, *Top Management Planning*, The Macmillan Company, New York, 1969, pp. 239–240.

CHAPTER 1

STRATEGY DETERMINANTS IN THE INTERNAL ENVIRONMENT

The internal environment of any business and the external environment in which it operates, when realistically appraised for the present and future, should determine strategies in business. We emphasize the phrase "realistically appraised for the present and future" because the internal and external environments are changing and will continue to change vastly and swiftly. From certain clues the environments provide, the most successful companies seem to be able to visualize the impact of change, and they develop strategies to take advantage of it. For instance, the growing world demand for minerals, the vast resources of unexplored terrains such as the Amazon basin, and striking advances in aerial survey techniques developed for military uses have led to Goodyear Aerospace Corporation's introduction of the side-looking airborne radar (SLAR) into the commercial market. Although we do not belabor the point now, we could add multiple instances to show that, as environments change, business strategies should change—for new problems and opportunities, new restraints and freedoms are created.

The *external environment*, which is the subject of Chapter 2, includes all the outside forces that affect either a company's sales of goods and services, its purchases, or both.

The *internal environment* includes all the resources of a company.

The moment the typical business executive enters his or her office or plant, he or she is absorbed in the internal environment, Although it is in front of executives' noses, all too often they don't suspect what depths it possesses. Change may upset them. It may be easier to develop fixations than to readjust concepts. For example, executives often think about a product by considering the raw materials in it, the way it is made, the functions it performs, the manner in which it is sold, or its customers' needs and expectations instead of by considering all of these things.

Theodore Levitt, in his excellent article Marketing Myopia," writes:

> The railroads are in trouble today not because the need was filled by others (cars, trucks, airplanes, even telephones), but because it was not filled by the railroads themselves. They let others take customers away from them because they assumed themselves to be in the railroad business rather than in the transportation business. The reason they defined their industry wrong was because they were railroad-oriented instead of transportation-oriented; they were product-oriented instead of customer-oriented.
>
> . . . Today TV is a bigger business than the old narrowly defined movie business ever was. Had Hollywood been customer-oriented (providing entertainment) rather than product-oriented (making movies), would it have gone through the fiscal purgatory that it did? I doubt it.[1]

If executives are to make sound decisions, they must have intimate knowledge of the key elements of the internal environment and their interrelationships and understand how changes in them may affect their choice of strategies.

This chapter does not deal with every element of the internal environment (such an undertaking would be long, tedious, and for our purposes unnecessary) but rather concentrates on key elements, the critical determinants of business strategy. These include the following:

- Corporate objectives and goals.
- Physical resources: financial, marketing, personnel, and technology (the latter including research and development [R & D], equipment, processes, materials, and communications and control systems).
- Policies, styles, attitudes, and moods of management.

---

[1] Theodore Levitt, "Marketing Myopia," *Harvard Business Review,* July–August 1960, p. 45.

CORPORATE OBJECTIVES AND GOALS

To understand why corporate objectives and goals are key elements in the internal environment, we must first know what they are. We immediately encounter a problem in semantics, for no general agreement exists concerning the exact meaning of these terms.

For the purposes of this book we define objectives as *statements of what corporate management wants to achieve* and goals as *more quantitative statements of anticipated achievement covering a set period of time, either short or long term*. These definitions are perhaps not as precise as some, but we feel that they are better simply because they are easier to remember.

When asked why objectives and goals are classified as key elements of the internal environment, we could quickly reply, "Because they make known where the company wants to go." We could list several other reasons: They establish a common business philosophy throughout the company; they motivate executives in the company to make decisions and take action; finally, they enable employees of a company to channel their energies and the available resources in fixed directions.

Executives who write corporate objectives and goals would probably admit that many are so general that they are almost worthless to subordinates and outsiders. Phrases like "maintaining X% growth of earnings," "being a good corporate citizen," and "being among the top hundred multinational corporations" are not very helpful in providing goals that employees can do something about.

By the same token, corporations' objectives are sometimes primarily negative, stressing what the company will not do or become—for example, "the Hart Company will not become a conglomerate." We admit that a few negative objectives can make clear the limits of expected corporate achievement. Still, negative objectives can cause a company to miss opportunities for highly profitable ventures and can foster negative attitudes toward new projects.

Finally some objectives are incompatible or contradictory. Much like theories of the English utilitarian philosopher Jeremy Bentham they often seem to provide "the greatest rewards for the greatest number" of executives, employees, stockholders, customers, and suppliers. It scarcely needs statement that attainment of objectives of this sort has been proved both mathematically and practically impossible. When one objective states that a company will become a major multinational company with significant positions in all parts of the world and another states that a dim view will be taken of investment in Latin America and the Asia–Pacific area and that projects in the countries of those areas will be limited to nominal, opportunistic investments, the objectives can be classified as contradictory.

When we began our discussion of vague, negative, incompatible, and contradictory objectives, we mentioned that they were almost worthless to subordinates and outsiders. Why, then, do corporate executives so often write objectives that have these undesirable qualities?

It is fair to say that executives who formulate corporate policy have a good knowledge not only of themselves but also of their superiors and peers. They know how difficult it is for a group of executives to reach a consensus. They know that unanimous agreement on objectives is all too frequently reached only when the objectives are so general, hackneyed, or commonplace that there is little room for dispute. They also know, as the framers of the U.S. Constitution knew, that general statements or objectives provide more flexibility in decision making, for they permit companies to pursue unforeseen opportunities. The corporate objectives of Ralston Purina (Exhibit 1.1) permit the company to engage in almost any kind of business. General objectives also allow for a latitude of interpretations at different levels of the organization and thus permit lower levels of management to use their own initiative.

Moreover, the general objective can be viewed as a tool of survival. If an objective is quite specific and proves to be a complete failure, one or more executives who formulated it can easily enough be held responsible. Much like the East Asian requirement that many executives put their seal or chop on documents so that no single executive can be held responsible, the general objective makes the search for a scapegoat exceedingly difficult. Frequently the scapegoat, if there is one, is the one who failed to carry out the general objective properly. Typical corporate executives indicate only why the company is in business and what it hopes to achieve. Goals specify, of course, when and to what extent the company hopes to fulfill its objectives.

Although objectives generally represent a consensus of executive power groups within the company, in the external environment there are ever-increasing numbers of government and pressure or social groups that can also affect the wording of objectives, contributing to vagueness and generality. For example, can you imagine the federal government's reaction to a company that would explicitly state an objective to restrain competition or the criticisms from special-interest groups of a stated objective to increase investment threefold in South Africa? The danger of sharp criticism and emotional reaction to specific written objectives is greatly magnified for the U.S.-based multinational company, which has to deal with both American and foreign gov-

Exhibit 1.1   Ralston Purina Company Corporate Objectives

Ralston Purina Company

CORPORATE OBJECTIVES

Our primary objective is to optimize use of our resources . . . to produce short- and long-term profit growth consistent with the balanced best interest of customers, shareholders, employees, suppliers, and society at large. To achieve these results, we must perform effectively in the following key result areas:

Customer satisfaction . . . Management development and performance . . . Employee attitude and performance . . . Social responsibility . . . Productivity . . . Innovation.

We recognize that the primary purpose of our business is to perform a necessary economic service by creating, stimulating, and satisfying customers. We must be a market-oriented company dedicated to the principle that, in order to supply the right product or service at the right time and in the right way, we need first to establish what the customer wants, where, when, how, and at what price.

Building on our base of protein and nutrition, we will remain diversified in our operations, multinational in organization, and global in outlook.

3

We dedicate ourselves to the principle of continuous self-renewal so that individuals, organization structure, products, facilities, and systems do not stagnate. We recognize that:

- People are the ultimate source of renewal. We will bring to the corporation a steady flow of able and highly motivated individuals and then provide positive, constructive programs of management development.
- Organizational structure must be flexible. We will evolve subject only to the yardstick of what is most successful and meets our requirements.
- We will continue to ask the question "What Next?" We must recognize and manage the accelerating rate of change.
- We will analyze assets and functions in which potential is diminishing in terms of contribution to earnings, cash flow, and tie-in value to other units in order to develop a course of action which may include disinvestment.

- We must maintain an environment which fosters individual effort, rewards initiative and encourages the free and open exchange of ideas; self-criticism and constant restudy are vital to the present health of the enterprise and are essential elements to future growth—we welcome challenging positions and opinions.
- We will maintain effective and simple systems and procedures to implement organizational structure, and we will evaluate them at regular intervals.
- Since the dynamics of an organization are related to motivation, conviction and morale, we will endeavor to make every employee know that his optimum efforts make a difference.
- We must be results-oriented, measured and held responsible.

- We must create a climate of technology, special knowledges, and services which induce in our customers a desire to buy our products and/or our services.

4

We will consistently and systematically strive to delegate decision-making authority intelligently to the proper lowest level without abrogating management responsibilities. We will measure qualitative and quantitative results through a simple and sensitive control system.

ernment and pressure groups. For example, you can safely assume that annual reports and press releases dealing with the objectives of many oil companies are read and analyzed by key people in government ministries in countries of the Middle East. Objectives that might have a tinge of what government officials in several of these countries call imperialism can result in quick and violent reactions. In short, objectives must be written with a keen understanding of political realities.

Do not infer from what we have said that executives of multinational corporations are usually crafty, cunning, and unscrupulous. Far from it. They are aware, however, that political factions that oppose their activities are quick to apply labels of censure and condemnation. They often seek, therefore, to state their objectives in a way that will not stir up sinister mental pictures.

We have put the case of formulating objectives and goals before you, and we feel that *it is time to show you what we consider to be a well-written objective.* It offends no particular country, it is specific enough to enable company executives to know when it has been reached, and it is broad enough to provide latitude for strategies:

We shall become a multinational company by selling at least one-third of our dollar volume to foreign countries, distributed throughout all areas of the world in approximate proportion to the following relative potentials:

Europe/Africa/Middle East	58%
Asia/Pacific	25%
Western Hemisphere (other than the United States)	14%
Russia/E. Europe/People's Republic of China	3%
	100%

We shall also have at least one "internationalist" in top management on the board of directors and have our stock listed on the following major exchanges: New York, London, Paris, Brussels, Amsterdam, Frankfort, Dusseldorf, Zurich, and Tokyo.

In case you are interested, the potentials expressed as percentages are based on the 1970 gross national products (GNP's) of these areas. For many businesses there are better measuring sticks than GNP, and in such cases they should be used. For instance, if your company is a supplier principally to the telephone industry, the number of telephones in service can be used. If your company supplies principally the automobile market, the number of automobiles in service would be a possible measuring stick. For covering a broad range of industry, however, GNP or GDP (gross domestic product) is a good order-of-magnitude measurement, and it is available for almost every country in the world.

What Corporate Objectives and Goals Should Cover

As we have hinted before, corporate objectives and goals can be placed in two main categories; there is no in-between. They are usually direct but sometimes indirect statements of what the company either will or will not be. The category for a given objective will depend on the answers to specific questions about how the company should pursue satisfactory growth and profit levels:

● Should the company become a conglomerate, remain as it is, or become something in between?
● Should the company be international or primarily domestic?
● In which businesses or product lines and in what domestic or world areas should the company try to maintain or achieve a dominant market share in the industry? And in which businesses should a lesser competitive position be accepted?
● What are the company's standards for deciding when to invest and when to divest? What is the desired return on investment and sales? How much money must be invested in present and future businesses for achievement of these returns? Can the funds be generated with present resources?

Diversification

When corporate executives raise questions about the possibility of becoming a conglomerate, the issue in a nutshell is diversification. As Murray S. Hoffman has written, "In a broad sense, a conglomerate may be defined as a diversified company, with major interests in several unrelated fields of endeavor."[2]

True enough, But if we leave the broad, general sense for a moment and look for specifics, we observe a striking difference between "traditional conglomerates," which acquire other companies to reach limited goals, and "acquisitive conglomerates," which grow primarily from continuing, aggressive, diversified acquisitions.

In recent years many conglomerate corporations, particularly the acquisitive conglomerates, had hard going:

---

[2] *The Making of a Conglomerate*, edited by Charles Gilbert, Hofstra University Year Book of Business, Series 8, Vol. 3, Published 1972, p. 2.

While per share earnings turned in a respectable performance through 1968, so did earnings of other large companies which were involved in fewer markets. In 1969 and 1970 the chickens came home to roost. The downturn in business activity combined with high leverage factors resulted in a negative multiplier effect on earnings and deficits appeared on many a conglomerate income statement. As has occurred before, the lions of one year became the goats of the next.

Whatever else the conglomerate may have to offer, there seems to be no evidence that diversification *per se* can curb the effects of the business cycle or that the whole is any larger than the sum of its parts. In fact, in many cases, it may be suspected that the conglomerate whole might just be something less than the sum of its parts.[3]

Still, these observations should neither distort nor exaggerate the real issue, *whether the company's assessment of itself and its industry requires an objective of diversification as a way of either avoiding extinction or courting growth.*

An objective of nondiversification is based on the assumption that a product or product line can survive for a very long time in its present form or with only minor changes. There are a number of representative products, such as Coca-Cola and Wrigley's Spearmint Gum. On giving the matter special attention, however, we perceive that such products are only a small percentage of the total. The great majority of products are continually changing in price, design, materials, and performance to meet competition. With a growing emphasis by companies throughout the world on R & D, new products are created in the laboratories and factories. The body of technical knowledge and know-how has dramatically expanded in size and substance. The result of all this is a shortening of most product life cycles. An illustration is the invasion of plastics into markets traditionally held by metal goods; plastic buckets have almost replaced metal ones in the American home, for they are lighter and less expensive.

The nature of the objective of diversification may be made clearer when we consider the various alternatives available. At the lower end of the scale a company may decide to produce primarily new models of present lines; such a plan has long been typical of the automobile industry. We placed this objective at the lower end of the scale because it can closely approach an objective of nondiversification. After all, how significant are a new grill design and tail light arrangement for different model years of a given make of automobile? We conclude that these changes are minimal. In fact there is a gray area, which we have struggled with but failed to isolate, where improve-

[3] Ibid., pp. 553–554.

ment of present models ends and introduction of new models in a present line begins.

An intermediate position on the scale is reached when a company decides to follow an objective of diversification but to stay within its present business. An example will illustrate our meaning.

From 1955 until 1966 Pet, Inc., followed the objective of broadening its product lines in the food-processing and food-marketing business primarily through acquisition but also through internal growth. In 1955 Pet entered the frozen food business by acquiring the Crystal Cannery Company, a processor of frozen fruit pies. By 1963 the newly acquired companies included Funsten, a processor of a variety of nuts; Laura Scudder, a processor of potato chips, corn chips, pretzels, cheese puffs, peanut butter, cookies, and mayonnaise; Musselman, a processor of applesauce, apple juice, apple butter, fruit gelatin, fruit drinks, frozen fruit, and berries; and Whitman, a processor of chocolates and assorted cookies. In addition, Pet broadened its product lines with the introduction of Sego, a liquid diet food. Between 1963 and 1966, Pet also acquired three other companies: Reese, a leading packer and importer of specialty foods; Stuckey's, a chain of roadside stores, restaurants, and snack bars; and Winebrenner, a processor of canned and blended fruit juices.

At a slightly higher point on the scale is the decision to follow an objective of diversification primarily within present business lines but with one or a few aberrations. For instance, although most of the products of Foremost-Mc-Kesson, Inc., are in the food, drug and health care, and chemical distribution lines, one division of the company as of 1973 was involved in 40 major housing developments from Hawaii to Chicago.

At the high end of the scale is the decision for a company to become a conglomerate, which we have previously defined and discussed. Diversification encompasses a large number of totally unrelated enterprises. For example, the operations of Gulf and Western Industries include mining and refining metals; producing chemical specialties; manufacturing and selling heat transfer units, pistons, seat assemblies, and other automobile parts; manufacturing and selling material-handling equipment, high controls, cigars, pulp and paper products, raw and refined sugar, and edible molasses; growing fruits and vegetables; breeding and raising cattle; financing consumer, industrial, and commercial loans; distributing and warehousing replacement parts for American and foreign made automobiles; publishing and distributing worldwide motion pictures, sheet music, and records; and designing and engineering support systems for the aerospace industry.

Diversification has its own special kinds of risk. When diversification is restricted to one product or product line, the company is more vulnerable to business failure resulting from technical obsolescence. Once old and new competitors in the same industry, competitors in different industries, or both make significant technical breakthroughs and thus seek to dominate markets, there is nowhere to turn. On the other hand the objective of diversification into many different lines that may be quite unrelated to those previously produced exposes the company to the totally different kind of risk of undertaking more than it can deal with.

A deep knowledge and understanding of any business are essential for success; most businesses today are complex and require executives to have expertise in several different areas. At times executives extend themselves beyond their capacity to absorb and understand all the businesses in which their company is engaged.

We are inclined to believe, for instance, that Owens-Illinois, primarily a manufacturer of glass bottles and cardboard containers, became overextended by attempting to operate a sugar mill and sugar cane plantation in the Bahamas. Operations were discontinued because sugar yields per acre were substantially below what was needed for profitable operation. Of course, if some new technology had been perfected to increase yield per acre, the operation would have made money; but is it plausible to assume that the expertise could be found for a product that differed widely from the company's normal lines?

The risk of undertaking more than can be dealt with reaches its culmination with the conglomerates. Let us consider the special case of Litton Industries. After earning $1.30 per share in 1971 and $1.85 per share in 1970, the company reported a $0.15 per share loss on continuing operations for the fiscal year ending July 31, 1972. At the next annual shareholders' meeting the directors were asked what had happened to earnings in 1972. They replied that the company had made a number of hard decisions, some resulting in significant writeoffs and others in one-time expenses requiring some short-term adjustments to the plans of the company.

The Rust Engineering division had lost money and was sold. Resource exploration activities in Canada and Nigeria were shut down, and electric motor operations were consolidated into one plant.[4] Like the pricing problems of the Cole Office Furniture division, cost-estimating problems of the

---

[4] Litton Industries Stockholder's report for the 6 months ending January 31, 1973. For background on Litton Industries, read *The Conglomerate Commotion* by the editors of *Fortune*, New York, Viking Press, 1970, pp. 113–115.

Ingalls Shipyard division, marketing problems of the Monroe Electronic Calculator division, and the production problems of the Royal Typewriter division which had occurred several years earlier, the serious mistakes were seemingly basic and often elementary ones of marketing, production, and control.

Whereas the problems of Litton Industries in recent years seem reasonably representative for conglomerates, it is generally recognized that Textron has been relatively trouble free. For the fiscal year ending June 30, 1972, the return on stockholders' equity was 19.7%, the highest among major conglomerate corporations.

Now, why can one company successfully diversify into unrelated industries through acquisition when others following the same objective have failed miserably? Let us look more closely at company objectives and how they were interpreted for the development of strategies.

There are, as a matter of fact, only a few major analogies between the objectives of Textron and those of other conglomerates. Most conglomerates, including Litton Industries, bought companies to push up their price/earning multiples and then bought more companies and earnings. Litton Industries did not make helter-skelter acquisitions like many other conglomerates, since a basic objective of the company was to create, develop, and offer to the markets of the future a flow of innovative products and systems resulting from the economies of technology and scale. Nevertheless Litton suffered from many of the same maladies as other conglomerates; operating problems of acquired companies eventually became almost insurmountable.

This quotation from *Business Week* comments on what Textron has done differently:

> Textron has devoted more attention to operating than to financial wheeling and dealing. Its debt load has been light, and it has concentrated on acquiring manufacturing companies with proprietary products and leading positions in medium-sized industries. To be sure, Textron has made some acquisition mistakes, weeding out over the years an ocean cruise ship (sold at a $6-million loss) and a chicken-producing business. But it has never been forced to make the kind of wholesale divestitures that have become commonplace for conglomerates desperate for cash or eager to dump losers.[5]

Moreover, while most conglomerates have decentralized management, the route or strategy Textron took to meet objectives was different. William B. Gisel, president of the Bell Aerospace division says:

[5] "Is Taxation Ready for Takeoff?", *Business Week*, October 7, 1972, p. 67.

Our real happiness with Textron is the way Providence [the corporate headquarters] manages, which is to say without interference. We submit our plans and list our financial needs. Other than that, we're left alone. It is a helluva lot different from Litton and others I've bumped into.[6]

We are keenly aware, as was Aristotle long before us, that reasoning from too few examples can lead to false conclusions. Our intent is not, however, to prove a point but merely to illustrate one. And that point is that objectives and goals only help to determine strategies, but in the last analysis strategies based on realistic assessments of the internal and external environments make the difference between companies that succeed and those that fail.

Internationalism

When corporate executives consider whether their companies should be primarily domestic or primarily international or become something in between, the issue is internationalism. Motivation to go international is currently strong. The United States Department of Commerce encourages companies to export goods and services abroad because of the ever-growing negative balance of payments. Large companies attempting to maintain historical growth rates may be forced by antitrust laws to seek expansion outside the United States. Market research reports point out that markets for goods and services outside the United States can in some cases be larger than markets within. Improvements in communication and travel and the expansion of world trade in general have given American business executives a greater sense of awareness of other countries of the world and have motivated them to conduct business in some of them.

Conversely the Japanese government, in view of its staggering positive balance of payments and the fear of protective tariff laws, now encourages Japanese companies to export capital and make investments overseas.

Expanding world trade and investment coupled with some involvement in it have led executives of many companies—perhaps you—to the false assumption that their companies have an objective of internationalism. To be certain, ask yourself, "Does my company look to all countries of the world for markets and sources of supply? Are our sales and investment patterns and our management policies such that our company is serving mainly our home market and exporting to foreign markets only when we have excess capacity

---

[6] Ibid.

for domestic needs and foreign opportunities come to our attention?" Only if you answer "yes" to the first and "no" to the second question can you safely say that your company has an objective of internationalism.

Keep in mind that the decision to place strong emphasis on international growth, when the company previously has had no or only minor international business, requires some major changes that should be reflected in the company's stated objectives. For instance, demands for new kinds of knowledge are vastly expanded. The company needs knowledge not only of the political risks and economic health and prospects of various countries but also of international finance, tariffs, competition, rules and regulations for processing orders, and so forth. Moreover, new devices for financial control are required. In sum major organizational changes are needed. Hence it is a serious mistake to adopt internationalism as an objective without concurrently formulating and stating objectives that will handle the problems that accompany such a decision.

Products and Product Lines

When top corporate executives consider in what businesses and markets their companies should try to establish or maintain dominant or lesser market positions, two issues are involved:

1   What products and product lines should we pursue?
2   Where should we sell them?

Corporate executives realistically understand that their company can seldom have the top position in every product and every product line. They must often be satisfied with lesser positions because they have no other choice. In setting objectives they must weigh carefully the advantages and disadvantages of producing and selling each product and product line.

The concept of the product life cycle can be an invaluable tool in the setting of objectives and, as you will see later in this book, in the development of strategies for products and product lines. We suspect that you already have some understanding of life cycles, for the concept is not new. In the 1920s Raymond Pearl applied it to biology. In the 1950s Irvin Kravis developed related ideas in the field of economics. In the early 1960s E. M. Roger's book, *Diffusion of Innovation*, dealt specifically with the product life cycle. By the mid-1960s scholars like Theodore Levitt and Raymond Vernon were suggesting ways of using the concept as an effective managerial instrument of competitive power and as a useful way of explaining flows of trade. Empirical research with the basic purpose of making the concept more scientific, more precise, and more meaningful has continued unabetted into the 1970s. John Smallwood writes:

> The product life cycle concept in many ways may be considered to be the marketing equivalent of the periodic table of the elements concept in the physical sciences; like the periodic table, it provides a framework for grouping products into families for easier predictions of reactions to various stimuli. With chemicals—it is a question of oxidation temperature and melting point; with products—it is marketing channel acceptance and advertising budgets. Just as like chemicals react in similar ways, so do like products. The product life cycle helps to group these products into homogeneous families.[7]

When reduced to its essentials, the life-cycle concept can be described like this: products, like people, are born, grow, mature, age or decline, and eventually die.

We have divided the product life cycle into only three stages: growth, maturity, and decline. (Most writers would add an introduction stage, which we have included as a part of the growth stage.) From empirical data about one chemical company, we have prepared a graph (Exhibit 1.2) that shows typical curves representing price, sales volume, profitability, and number of competitors over the stages of the life cycle of one product. At the outset prices are high, sales volume and profitability are low, and few or no competitors exist. Soon sales increase rapidly. Profits rise, and more competitors are attracted. Increased competition results in greater sales volume but lower prices and lower profitability. Over time sales volume begins to decline. Prices and profits continue to fall, and the number of competitors levels off and starts to decline.

The length of time a company can remain in business depends largely on its success in remaining an efficient, low-cost producer with a large share of the market. If a company is able to maintain this position, it may be able to stay in business profitably throughout the life of the product. If not, it frequently makes the decision to get out of the market.

The ideas we have just expounded are oversimplified; the delicately com-

---

[7] John E. Smallwood, "The Product Life Cycle: A Key to Strategic Marketing Planning," *MSU Business Topics,* Winter 1973, p. 29.

Exhibit 1.2   Stages in the Product Life Cycle

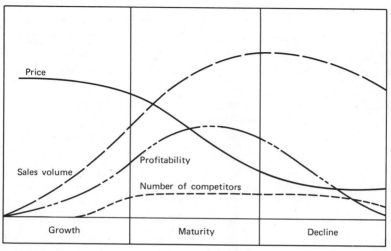

plex truth about product life cycles and related ideas cannot be told in a couple of paragraphs. In addition, before executives can apply the concept in even a broad, general way, they must be able to answer the following fundamental questions: What is a product? What is a stage? What changes occurring in the external environment could affect his products? What tests can be used to measure the validity of the concept?

These questions are often quite difficult to answer. Take, for instance, the definition of a product. One might say that an automobile is a product, but is this the best classification? Does it cover the numerous facts that ought to be considered? Should automobiles be classified by size, horsepower, body style, engine, function, manufacturer? Would these further divisions be clearly understandable, or would they be so simple as to be untrue to the essentially complex nature of most products? Victor Cook and Rolando Polli, in their attempts to cast product life cycles into workable models, have used rather detailed classification of products. In their research on cigarette life cycles, they divided the general product class—cigarettes—into product forms (e.g., plain tip and filter tip) and brands within the product forms (e.g., Philip Morris).

With scrupulous care they attempted to answer the other questions previously cited. What were the results? Overall 52% of the categories fit the product life cycle model either perfectly or quite well. One might ask, are such results good enough? We think the answer to that question depends on the requirements of management. Cook and Polli pointed out, however, that, although their original objective had been to show that product life cycles were too naive to explain much, after conducting the research they believed that the product life cycle had proved to be a surprisingly good model of sales behavior.[8]

Experience curves developed by members of the staff of The Boston Consulting Group, Inc., are useful tools to help executives decide on the objectives, goals, and strategies their companies should follow during the entire product life cycle but especially when the mature stage of a product life cycle is reached.

Like learning curves, experience curves appear as curves on a linear scale and straight lines on a log-log scale (Exhibit 1.3.) Unlike learning curves—which include only inputs of labor, materials and equipment, and processes—experience curves include all costs involved in getting a product to a user.

After making extensive studies of reports of the Electronic Industry Association, the Manufacturing Chemists Association, and statistical supplements to the *Survey of Current Business,* the staff of The Boston Consulting Group concluded that *costs appear to go down on value added at about 20–30% every time total*

Exhibit 1.3   Experience Curves

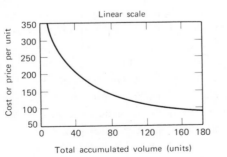
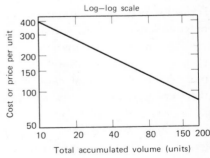

[8] Victor Cook, "MSI'S Research on Product Life Cycles" paper presented at a seminar on Product Life Cycles held by the Marketing Science Institute on September 6, 1969.

product experience doubles, both for the industry as a whole and for individual producers.[9] To put it in another way, every time accumulated production is doubled, regardless of the industry, cost declines from 20–30%.

To illustrate the concept just stated, let us look at experience curves for an industry (Exhibit 1.4) and for individual companies within an industry (Exhibit 1.5.) You will note that both graphs are shown with log-log scales, since it is easier to make projections with straight lines. The industry graph, since it provides information on average price per unit for a specific total accumulated volume, is helpful for an estimation of the average cost and possible profit margin for the product when future volume reaches a given amount. Once future profit margins are identified, product and product-line objectives and goals can be set. Conclusions of the following types can be reached:

1 All product lines will continue to be profitable.
2 Some product lines will continue to be unprofitable and should be phased out.

Exhibit 1.4   Integrated Circuits

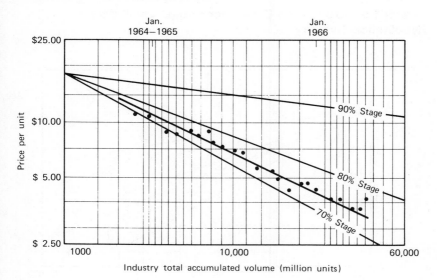

Industry total accumulated volume (million units)

[9] "Perspectives on Experience," The Boston Consulting Group, Inc., Boston, 1968, p. 12.

3 Some product lines are becoming marginal and should be subjected to further study before being phased out.

There is a final point to which we must draw attention. Barring a fortuitous technological or marketing breakthrough by another firm, the fastest growing producer in the industry will be the company with the lowest cost. The experience curve concept further implies that the fastest growing company is also the most likely to achieve a breakthrough, because only by constantly doubling experience can a company build up the knowledge that puts it in a position to achieve technological and marketing progress.

In addition to the concepts of product life cycles and experience curves, matrices are also helpful in the selection of objectives and subsequent strategies for products and product lines. From rigorous evaluations of technology, packaging cost, market share, advertising and sales effectiveness, and the location and attractiveness of the market served, present competitive positions and growth potentials can be determined.

The matrix is merely a device for pigeonholing products or product lines

Exhibit 1.5 Experience Curves for Companies Within a Hypothetical Industry

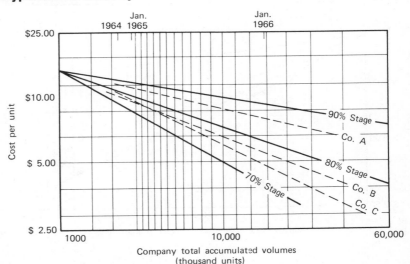

into categories, as in Exhibit 1.6. Note the perspective this matrix provides. It enables an executive to see clearly and quickly which products have the best opportunites for growth according to a combination of two criteria: growth potential and competitive position. And refinements can be made to the matrices. For example, The Boston Consulting Group has developed a growth market share matrix that uses circles with diameters proportional to the dollar sales or cash flow for each product. These circles make easy a visual comparison of the major products from which strategies are developed.

New developments—product lines that are still in research but have advanced to the point where glimmers of success can be seen—might also be subjected to matrix analysis. One such matrix might categorize developments into odds of success and the profits that may accrue if the development is successful. Another matrix might show the odds of success ranged against the estimated R & D costs to achieve success.

These and similar matrices are directed toward the development of clear-cut product or product-line objectives not only for domestic but also for worldwide operations.

From worldwide objectives, area or country objectives are derived. In a sense the methodology is similar to the division of overall U.S. product or product-line objectives into objectives by region or state. It differs markedly,

Exhibit 1.6   Illustrative Matrix

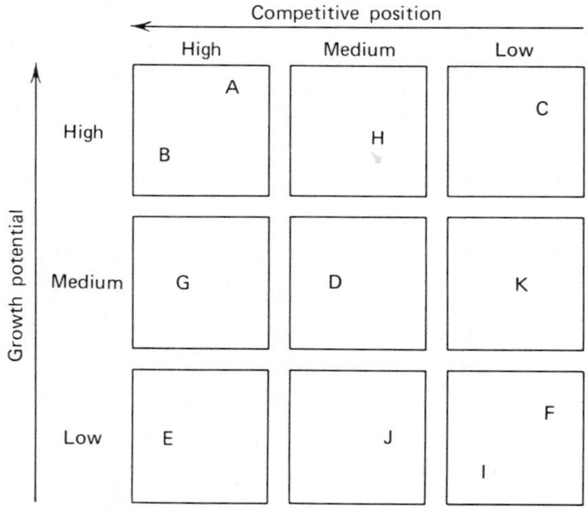

however, in complexity because of striking differences in culture. The company that dominates a field in a given country may not be the leader in the product or product line worldwide. This situation is not uncommon in Japan, for example. A company may have entered Japan early with technology for which it received equity; the Japanese partner may have successfully adapted the technology to the unique needs of the Japanese economy and thus aided the company in achieving a dominant market position there. In other cases, companies manufacturing in a foreign country may capture a dominant market position there with the help of host-government policies protecting local industry against imports.

Geographic Areas

After objectives have been established for products and product lines, the next step is to identify the geographic area where they will be made and sold. For solely domestic operations an abundance of reliable government and industry data available from many sources, excellent transportation and communications systems, and a common language and customs make the task of assessing manufacturing and sales potentials of states and regions not inordinately difficult. Of course, factors such as proximity to raw materials and sources of supply, to a pool of skilled or low-cost labor, and to principal markets must be carefully analyzed and weighed, but the task is readily manageable.

On the other hand the task for the international company is considerably more complex. It usually entails a thorough analysis of the different countries and areas of the world and economic, social, and political projections of from 5 to 15 years. We discuss these projections in more detail in the next chapter on the external environment.

Geographic sales objectives will be based in part on a company's present geographic distribution of sales. For instance, a common criterion for distribution of sales is sales potential. A U.S.-based international firm typically has from 70–90% of sales in the United States; a disproportionately large amount of remaining sales in Europe, Canada, and Latin America; and negligible sales in the rest of the world. Hence, its executives may decide to place emphasis on other countries to take advantage of some large, unrealized potential.

On the other hand the executives may decide that their products are useful primarily in developed countries, as in the case of safety glass for automobiles, and that the company should therefore concentrate only on the developed world areas—Europe, the United States, Canada, Australia, New Zealand, Israel, and South Africa.

Another key factor in determining where in the world either to make or sell products is the attitude of company executives to different countries and world areas. The attitude of executives is of course relevant to the domestic scene as well. The subject is covered in depth later in this chapter.

Financial Policies

Financial policies are usually based on historical company and industry customs and data. A few financial policies have been so critically important that for many companies they have been treated as major corporate objectives and goals. Typically, they are stated as follows:

> Specific goals toward which priorities are directed are after-tax returns of 10% on sales, 11% on assets, and 14% on equity.

For the most part financial policies are considered to be not objectives and goals but rather constraints on them. For instance, financial policies related to dividends, distribution of stockholders' equity, and debt-to-equity ratios limit the resources available for expansion, new projects, and acquisitions. Others related to desired returns on investment and sales determine in part how much money will be needed for future business, where and when investment funds will be generated, and when divestment is called for.

Obviously we cannot continue our broad discussion of how financial policies constrain and at times determine objectives and goals without looking at one financial policy in depth. Let us use as our example the debt-to-equity ratio. In the United States this ratio follows a set range for companies within different industries. Among major companies in the chemical industry in 1972 the range of debt-to-equity ratios was from 0.10 for DuPont to 1.05 for Dow Chemical. The average for the seven major companies in the industry was 0.53, and the most common debt-to-equity ratio was 0.46.

When we look at the operations of Dow Chemical more closely, we can easily see how the financial policy of high debt-to-equity ratio relates to company objectives and goals. One of Dow's basic objectives has been to be the technological leader for every product they manufacture. But this leadership requires major expenditures in research and development and new plants. In the 5 years 1968–1972 Dow Chemical has spent more than $1.6 billion on new plants. To pay for these plants the company borrowed heavily; its long-term debt increased from $84 million to $1094 million. If the company had stayed within the traditional range of debt-to-equity ratio for its industry, the basic objectives of technological leadership would have been unattainable. Dow executives took the position therefore that the best way to finance research and development and new facilities was to break from traditional debt-to-equity ratios and assume greater debt. They had two good reasons for selecting debt financing. First they were convinced that inflation was here to stay and that debts could be repaid with inflated dollars. Second they felt that new technology would provide returns on investment that would be considerably higher than interest charges on debt.

We would be negligent not to give debt-to-equity ratios wider consideration, for the ranges considered reasonable in the United States are not necessarily appropriate in other countries.

For an illustration we need look no further than the steel industry:

> The Japanese steel industry, like most other Japanese manufacturing, is financed with about 80% debt and 20% equity, nearly the reverse of the U.S. industry's ratio. Many shareholders feel the American ratio is cheapest, but U.S. steel producers argue that the heavy debt load gives foreign producers the advantage.
>
> Armco's executive vice-president, Harry Holiday, says this means the Japanese do not face a problem in getting funds to finance huge new integrated plants. For U.S. steel companies to attract that kind of financing, he maintains, they would have to earn 13% to 15% after taxes compared with 3% to 4% returns for the Japanese. They have not been able to do so and this is the reason no new integrated mills have been built in the U.S. In order to get the return needed, Holiday says the domestic industry has one choice: boost its prices.[10]

Because different financial policies for different countries and world areas can be relevant to corporate objectives and goals, we expand our discussion to profitability standards. Two questions have frequently been raised by executives of international companies. Should a separate set of return-on-investment (ROI) standards be established as a financial policy for operations in foreign countries? If so, what should these standards be? Executives asking these questions accept the premise that in general foreign investments carry more risk than domestic ones. Foreign risks may include:

[10] "The Steel Industry Negotiates to Survive," *Business Week*, May 15, 1971, p. 95.

1   More government interference and intervention.

2   Inflation that is both steeper and more difficult to cope with.

3   Higher currency-hedging costs because of devaluation risks.

4   Higher credit risks that require higher reserves for doubtful accounts.

5   Less efficient management.

6   Less efficient labor.

7   Unreliable market forecasts.

8   Unreliable estimates of engineering and construction costs.

9   Uncertain tariff rates.

With these risks taken into account, ROI standards can be set for countries and areas of the world. Argentina with high risks might have a standard of 24% ROI after tax, Canada with low risks only 12%. It may indeed be argued that such standards would simplify the formulation of objectives and goals, eliminating from consideration for investment countries and areas where unusually high rates of ROI are required. There are practical limitations, however, to the use of ROI standards. First of all the risks related to a specific project in a given country may be either considerably more formidable or less imposing than the general risk level associated with that country. For example, it is quite possible that a specific project with numerous other risks in Canada and additional incentives in Argentina might make an Argentine investment with a 15–20% ROI after tax more attractive than one of a comparable return in Canada. In addition, country-by-country ROI standards need to be continually changed as the political and economic environments change. Furthermore ROI isn't always the primary factor in investment decisions; foreign government action may limit the alternatives to investing now or perhaps forever losing the opportunity. And ROI is not the best means of judging the profitability of a foreign investment in which there is high debt leverage.

Despite the several limitations cited, the establishment of a financial policy of higher ROI for higher risk countries is a step in the development of geographic objectives and goals.

Let us proceed now to the question of when to divest. Since we discuss this question further in a later chapter, we simply mention several standards that have been useful:

1   Businesses with product or product lines earning less than the out-of-pocket cost of the net investment should be subjected to divestment analysis.

2   Businesses in which market share is less than one-third that of the leading competitors are vulnerable and suspect, especially in a rapidly growing market.

3   Businesses in markets growing at less than 10% annually are suspect.

4   Businesses that reflect a past pattern of diminishing market share are suspect.

5   Businesses in which a company's raw-materials costs are substantially outside company controls are suspect, particularly those in which the value-added component is small.

6   Businesses that by the nature of their products and byproducts yield toxic or potentially pollutive effects are vulnerable to statutory or regulatory control and are therefore suspect.

7   Businesses that by their very nature require disproportionate management attention are suspect.

In setting financial objectives, top management generally evaluates all the objectives relating to degree of diversification, products and product lines, and geographic areas, and uses financial standards as guidelines for arriving at some quantitative conclusions about where the company should be heading. Sometimes the initial effort in developing corporate objectives may suggest to top management a mediocre performance over the next 5 years under present strategies. Top management may well decide that it has resources that can and should be used to improve strategies. The summation of the forecasts from lower levels of the corporation may and usually does produce some very unreliable results. Top management must then try to identify the areas of inconsistency and return these forecasts for justification or revision by the persons who submitted them. Clearly, final financial objectives should be agreed to by the divisions or sections of a company and translated down to business group or profit center levels.

PHYSICAL RESOURCES

We may now turn to physical resources, the second key element in the internal environment determining business strategies. No extensive comments are called for. It is fairly obvious that financial, marketing, personnel, technology (including processes, R & D, equipment, and material), and communications and control systems constitute the key physical resources that determine strategies.

Although we recognize that physical resources can be a strength or a weakness, depending on their relationship to the external environment, we are using the term primarily to refer to something special, something that gives a company an edge over its competitors.

Financial Resources

The importance of financial resources, especially money, as a key determinant of business strategies is evident and very widely accepted. As a case in point, Juan T. Trippe, the founder of Pan American World Airways (Pan Am), always followed the strategy of pioneering usage of the newest airplanes. The company experienced few problems in buying the newest airplanes, because during most of its existence it had been profitable and its credit had been excellent. In recent years, however, Pan Am has ceased to be a money maker. The company lost $28.9 million in 1972 and more than $150 million from 1969 through 1972. As a result, funds available for purchasing planes have been severely restricted. In early 1973 the company had to cancel its tentative purchases of the new supersonic British–French Concorde; since it could afford only one new type of plane, it had to search for one that provided a higher rate of return. In brief the shortage of funds forced the company to change what had always been a basic strategy.

The amount of money available to carry out business strategies depends, as in the case of Pan Am, on how much can be raised internally and externally. A company's balance sheet provides a picture of financial resources as of a specific date. The income statement enumerates incomes, expenses, and profits or losses for an accounting period. The statement of sources and application of funds, sometimes called a statement of changes in working capital, complements both the balance sheet and income statement in disclosing changes in financial position; it summarizes the financing and investing activities of the company. All together, they are the best measures of internally generated funds and their use. When compared with competitors' financial statements, they suggest the funds that can be raised externally.

A company's current financial position—its debt, its equity, its working capital, its profitability, its return on sales and equity, and the funds generated internally—can be taken directly from the financial statements or quickly computed from data on them. For example, the funds generated internally are readily calculated as retained earnings plus depreciation less dividends.

On the other hand estimation of the externally generated funds available is more complex. First a decision must be made whether debt (bonds, mortgages, and so forth) or the sale of stock or both will be used. Whatever the final decision, banks and other financial institutions rely heavily on standards, especially ratios, to evaluate the amount of debt that will be permitted, the interest rate, payback period, and other conditions and, for new stock sales, the offering price.

Among the most important ratios used are price/earnings, debt to equity, current assets to current liabilities, net profit after tax to net sales, net profit after tax to net worth, inventory turnover, and ROI.

The price/earnings ratio, as a measure of the attractiveness of a company's stock, determines the extent to which that company can acquire others without dilution of stockholder earnings—in other words, through exchanges of stocks rather than cash purchases. This ratio of financial resources is also a key measure of a company's capacity for raising capital through stock issues.

The debt-to-equity ratio discussed earlier determines to what extent a company can raise money through funded debt. If its debt-to-equity ratio is lower than those of competitors, a company has a financial advantage that will last until the ratio is considered too high by investment institutions.

The remaining ratios can be summarized as follows: Current assets to current liabilities is a measure of how well a company can meet a sudden demand to pay all of its short-term creditors. Net profit after tax to net sales provides profit margins or profits per dollar of sales. Net profits after tax to net worth provides the rate of return on stockholders' investments. Inventory turnover provides a good approximation of how effectively a company is using its inventory.

We must place in a special category ROI, which is the all-important ratio of net profits to investment. Developed by Alfred P. Sloan, Jr., of General Motors, it is used by many leading corporations and lending institutions as the basic measure of management efficiency. It is based on this premise: any business that can always earn an adequate return on the total money invested will be successful, will have a sound standard for investment decisions, and will experience little difficulty in borrowing funds and getting credit.

We could add many other ratios—for example, assets per dollar of sales, net sales to accounts receivable—but there is no need to continue. Our purpose is merely to point out some of the more important ratios in the determination of a company's ability to attract external funds.

We do need now, however, to draw attention to some of the shortcomings and oversimplifications of ratio analysis. A review of a company's financial ratios is never enough. Astute bankers must also have at their disposal critical ratios of other companies in the same business. Moreover, they need ratios covering a time span sufficient for the determination of trends.

An illustration will help us here. Earlier we mentioned that Dow Chemical Company in 1972 had a 1.05 debt-to-equity ratio, the highest in the industry, When viewed alone, the figure doesn't mean much. For some companies a 1.05 debt-to-equity ratio might be completely ill advised. For Dow Chemical it has been highly satisfactory. The company increased its profit on sales at the compounded rate of 10% a year for the years 1964–1973 despite falling prices in the chemical industry. In addition the company increased dividends each year from 1961 to 1973.

While financial ratios do represent a quantitative measure of a company's ability to attract external funds, other factors must be considered. Admittedly other financial tools, such as analyses of working capital, break-even points, and cash flow, have been used in an attempt to improve financial analysis; although helpful, they too fall short of the mark.

In making loans and floating stock issues, bankers and executives of financial institutions must rely heavily on judgment. They must consider present conditions and trends in the economy, trends and growth patterns in industries, conditions within the securities market, and U.S. government monetary and fiscal policies. Certainly one crucial factor is the company's image, the way in which bankers and executives of financial institutions see and evaluate the company and its management.

Charles D. Ellis, vice president of Donaldson, Lufkin & Jenrette, Inc., points out several assets that contribute to a company's image but are not included in the left side of the balance sheet:

> . . . the brilliance of management, important patents controlled by the company, good will in its marketing relationships with customers, research development that might lead to sensational products in the future, or . . . the simple achievement of having developed a tremendously successful business.[11]

---

[11] G. Scott Hutchinson, ed., *The Strategy of Corporate Finance,* President's Publishing House, New York, 1971, p. 86.

We add two more contributors to a company's image, perhaps further elaborations of the brilliance of management: their reputation for being talented financial managers and astute negotiators.

We recognize that positive images are no doubt based on actual skills, and these skills in themselves should help a company raise money cheaply. The reputation or image, as we see it, has a synergistic effect, providing what might be called an important additional psychological advantage beyond the actual skills.

Let us recall what was said at the outset—money and other financial resources are a key determinant of business strategies. If business strategies are to be successful, financial resources must be evaluated with a minimum of preconception and ignorance. Do you know how many dollars of borrowing capacity your company has? Do you know your company's present debt-to-equity ratio? Do you know the debt-to-equity ratios of your major competitors? Do you know what your present debt-to-equity ratios ought to be in view of the company's image and competition? You must have correct answers to these questions when formulating strategies.

Marketing Resources

Marketing resources is a familiar term to executives but one that may connote different things to each of them. We have seen thoughtful writers devote whole books to attempts to make the definition clear. Because there is still much to cover in this chapter, we must limit our definition. *Marketing resources are the skills and physical assets that enable a company to develop, distribute, and sell products effectively to customers.* The skills include the selection of the right products and packaging at the right price, the generation of reliable market forecasts, the establishment of effective channels of distribution, and the proper balancing of the advertising, sales promotion, and direct selling effort. The physical assets include company-owned or leased transportation equipment, warehouses, and wholesale and retail outlets.

Changes in incomes, values, and life-styles of people bring about new needs for products and services. According to a study by the Stanford Research Institute on the growth of 400 U.S. corporations, the most important single contribution to success appears to have been an awareness of change—a recognition of "what's new." Conversely a basic cause of failure is the inability to assess the market properly for change. Companies attuned to change and new needs are continually eliminating and modifying some products and services and introducing new ones.

Until meat and poultry prices soared in 1973, the whole trend of refrigerator design had been toward increased freezer space. As more people buy home freezer units to store large quantities of beef and poultry, they will need less freezer space in their refrigerators. The result will be a growing market segment for a modified refrigerator, perhaps one with just enough freezer space for an ice-cube maker and for a few days' supply of frozen foods.

Similarly, as the demand for frozen foods grows (it is expected to double in the next decade), there will be a need for new designs of frozen-food merchandising equipment and a trend for supermarkets to use warehouse facilities for frozen-food storage and distribution.

Along different lines, Bausch & Lomb, Inc., a leading manufacturer of ophthalmic products and scientific instruments, developed in 1971 a new plastic contact lens, called "Soflens," to meet users' needs. Normally, contact lenses require several refittings and even then cause discomfort. The new lens can absorb moisture from the eye and is pliable enough to conform to eye contour. Thus it is more comfortable, easier to fit, and will not pop out. The market for "Soflens'," although limited to people with nearsightedness and astigmatism, still represents potential sales of several million pairs.

The illustrations we have been citing should make clear how skills in analyzing product and market requirements can lead to new products, new emphases, and subsequently new marketing strategies.

The right product must often meet more than functional needs. Its design and packaging may have to satisfy esthetic needs as well. Finally the product must be priced right. We shall explain the last point by using an example.

The best quality home refrigerator might be constructed to last 13 years and sell at retail for $529.95. A model similar in size, design, and other features might be built to last only 7 years and sell for $429.95. Which is the better buy? One can see that, if only depreciation costs are considered, the most expensive model costs approximately $41 a year, while the other costs approximately $61 per year.[12] Still, the lower priced model might be the right one for a young married couple plagued with an array of payments or to people in high income brackets who want the newest features and seldom keep a refrigerator more than 7 years. In brief, determination of the right

---

[12] "Marketers Give Their Views on Product Tactics," *Marketing Communications,* September 1967, p. 69.

price, like selection of the right packaging and product, requires knowledge of how customers buy.

We think the basic mistake of companies that are fundamentally correct in forecasting change is their inability to make reliable long-range market projections or forecasts; all too often projections extend well beyond actual growth.

As a general rule of thumb, assessments for a fiscal or calendar year are usually dependable. Beyond one fiscal year inaccuracies begin to appear and over time seem to take off like a rocket. The whole process usually begins with the individual salesrepresentative, who makes reasonably accurate sales forecasts for a fiscal or calendar year but misses the mark completely on long-range sales forecasts. Perhaps the biggest stumbling block is lack of objectivity. Most individual salesrepresentatives confuse what they hope to sell with what is realistic. Other salespersons, we think a much smaller number, with higher political aspirations, feel that unduly high sales projections show that they wholeheartedly support their superiors' wishes or designs. Sometimes, of course, they simply seek to avoid criticism. Often the blame for overly optimistic sales forecasts can be placed on the manager who, instead of returning them or making corrections, submits them to superiors.

We believe that none of the previously mentioned situations would exist for long if salesrepresentatives and managers were penalized in some way for poor projections. But most of them are certain that, even if sales projections are substantially too high, no one will check on their figures because there is a good chance that managers and salespersons in most large companies will be in different positions, even different companies, when actual sales figures are available for comparison with long-range projections. They are usually right. What they overlook is, of course, the effect unrealistically high sales projections have in the setting of objectives and the formulation of business strategies.

Channels of distribution, vital marketing resources that can be constraints or determinants of corporate strategies, can be part of either the internal or external environment. When retail outlets or distribution centers, or both, are owned by the manufacturer, as in the case of French Shriner Shoes, or are strongly under manufacturer control through dealer franchises, as in the automobile industry, we have arbitrarily considered them to be part of the internal environment. When channels of distribution are independently owned and operated, we consider them part of the external environment.

William H. Newman has summed up well the advantages gained through the wise selection of channels of distribution in these comments:

The big U.S. companies, for example, are strong partly because each has a set of dealers throughout the country. In contrast, foreign car manufacturers have difficulty selling here until they can arrange with dealers to provide dependable service.[13]

The ability to balance properly advertising, sales promotion, and direct selling efforts along with the other skills just covered is the hallmark of companies like Procter & Gamble, Kimberly-Clark, and General Foods, which share a reputation for having outstanding marketing resources. Procter & Gamble, although primarily in the soap and detergent field, has through its unique marketing skills been successful in selling disposable diapers. Kimberly-Clark has skillfully used mathematical correlation techniques in forecasting worldwide sales for its Kleenex line. General Foods has applied its knowledge, resources, and facilities in markets to enable its Jell-O to capture 70% of the U.S. market for packaged gelatin desserts and its coffee line (Maxwell House, Yuban, and Sanka) to account for more than a third of all coffee sold.

Yet even these companies can make serious mistakes in using their marketing resources. The reason is plain enough. The strength of market resources, like that of any other resources a company has, can be appraised only by their relationship to the external environment. Different marketing resources are required for different product and product lines. Take, for example, General Foods' experience with its Gourmet Foods line from 1957 to 1960. In brief, General Foods' marketing resources were highly adapted to widely advertised, high-volume, low-priced, packaged consumer products emphasizing popularity, convenience, and value. The company had not previously sold luxury, expensive, and exotic food specialties.[14]

Executives of the company have admitted that the experiment with Gourmet Foods was a mistake from the outset. The Gourmet Foods general manager, Joseph B. Stark, called it "an adventure into the unknown." The company plunged into the product line without considering its own strengths and weaknesses. Indeed management even seemed to forget basic marketing approaches. For example, they failed to establish priorities for market objectives, conduct market tests, gain an idea of the size of the market, or provide an adequate advertising and promotion budget. The company limited itself to restricted channels of distribution and an inflexible price policy in selling

---

[13] "Shaping the Master Strategy of Your Firm," *California Management Review*, Spring 1967, pp. 80–81.

[14] Thomas L. Berg, *Mismarketing*, Doubleday & Company, Garden City, New York, 1970, p. 57.

Gourmet Foods. Despite some changes in strategy, Gourmet Foods failed to be profitable and the entire line was dropped.

Enough has been said now about marketing skills as a dimension of market resources. To discuss the advantages of excellent physical assets (transportation equipment, warehouses, wholesale and retail outlets) is unnecessary, for these advantages are widely accepted. We are ready then to turn to personnel resources.

Personnel Resources

A major point that frequently appears in books and articles on personnel and organization and in company annual reports is that the people in an organization with their widely varying skills are the essential corporate asset. This idea is set forth vigorously by David Packard, president of Hewlett-Packard Company.

> Again I find I am mentioning people as the key to future, simply to re-emphasize the fact that the future for all of us is determined more by what our people do than by how many dollars we spend. This is the philosophy which we try to carry out through our entire company, feeling that personnel problems are among the most important in building toward the future. We have a strong personnel program but no personnel department. We feel that personnel problems are the prime concern of all executive levels and therefore attempt to keep all our people looking ahead in this area.[15]

In a sense we have brought out the importance of skills of people in finance and marketing in the two previous sections and will continue with this theme in subsequent sections. What we do in this section is focus our attention briefly on how the proper mix of people, their interrelationships with each other, and their teamwork determine or constrain strategies. A company's strategies should reflect characteristics of the personnel resources or people in the organization from the president to the workers.

For instance, are the workers unionized? Is the union unusually strong? Does the union seek to usurp management functions? Are the workers primarily men or women? Are they skilled or unskilled? Are they from a partic-

[15] David Packard, "What the Chief Executive Should Be Doing," *Assuring the Company's Future Today,* M. J. Dooher, ed., General Management Series, Number 175, American Management Association, New York, p. 31.

ular cultural or racial group? Are wages paid hourly, by incentive, or both? Answers to these questions can seriously affect manufacturing strategies and in turn influence corporate strategies.

The problems General Motors had experienced with its highly automated Vega plant at Lordstown, Ohio, clearly show the importance of a team effort. General Motors' decision to highly automate the plant was a strategy designed to offset the low labor costs of foreign cars. Such a strategy required, of course, the fullest cooperation of workers and company management. The results from the beginning were just the opposite. From October 1971 to January 1972 workers filed more than 5000 grievances, assembly-line tasks were not completed, and even several acts of sabotage were committed.[16] All the actions cited directly and indirectly led to reduced productivity and output.

Many questions can be raised regarding supervisors and staff. Are first-line supervisors technically or nontechnically trained? How well are they able to identify aptitudes of workers? Are they unionized? Is supervision close or loose? Are there few or many industrial and manufacturing engineers? How closely do they work with their supervisors?

Many more questions can be raised regarding plant managers and manufacturing executives. To what extent are broad policy matters delegated to subordinates? To what degree does coordination exist between finance, marketing, and production executives? To what degree are there compromises among these functional-area executives in reaching corporate strategy decisions?

To continue developing the idea of the importance of people working as a team, from the worker to managers and across functional areas, involves a complete review of organization, which is not our purpose, It is sufficient for our purpose to have briefly noted here what perhaps is a primafacie case— personnel resources are determinants of business strategies.

Technology

"Technology" cannot be easily defined. As we try to think through its meaning, we recall that the term has been defined principally in two ways: as the application of science to industry and commerce and as the entire body of

---

[16] Charles B. Camp, "Paradise Lost, Utopian G.M. Plant in Ohio Falls from Grace under Strain of Balky Machinery Workers," *The Wall Street Journal*, January 3, 1972, p. 24.

ideas, methods, and materials used in the development of products. Within the framework of these two general definitions, however, authors frequently seek a greater precision in the use of key words.

We are concerned in this section with the knowledge and skills of people in R & D, engineering, and manufacturing and with the methods, equipment, and materials for manufacturing and testing products. We try to show through several illustrations that strengths in technology are or should be determinants of the best strategies, while weaknesses are or should be constraints.

Consider the example of the Warner-Jenkinson Company, a leader in many segments of the food-flavoring and food-coloring industry. To reach its objectives and goals, the company has relied heavily on a strategy of technical exactness. The gifts, aptitudes, skills, and training of many people and the laboratory equipment at their disposal ensure that the strategy will be carried out. A 30-member, hand-picked, in-plant taste panel acts as the final authority for flavor and quality of raw materials. Highly trained home economists in turn evaluate the flavor of foods containing company products. Skilled technicians in company laboratories use mathematical techniques and testing equipment to control the quality of ingredients at all phases of production.

Consider next the example of Warner & Swasey Company, a leader in many segments of the machine tool industry. To reach its objectives and goals the company has relied heavily on a strategy of concentrated efforts in R & D. During the recession of 1969 and 1970 annual expenses were cut $10 million, and yet R & D expenditures remained high and in some areas were intensified. Their recently developed 1-SC, a turning machine featuring a 12-station turret mounted on a separate carriage that provides full lateral and longitudinal motion, has given the company an advantage over competitors selling less modern turning machines.

Consider what the "conquest of taconite" has meant to the U.S. iron and steel industry in its effort to fight foreign imports. After many years of painstaking research the industry found a way of using billions of tons of low-grade taconite deposits that remained after the natural ores of the Iron Range had been depleted. Without doubt this process has enabled companies like U.S. Steel to follow corporate strategies that would have been impractical if large quantities of iron ore had had to be imported.

Many companies in other industries have an advantage of special skills and knowledge in R & D. In highly technical industries, such as pharmaceuticals, development of new products through R & D is a prerequisite to survival. Companies that have only limited R & D programs have been able to acquire through licenses and purchases the technology they need. Regardless of how technology is acquired, it defines to what extent strategies of product diversification can be applied.

Consider finally the following examples, which reflect the importance of manufacturing skills and equipment and raw materials in the determination of strategies for three companies in three different industries.

The number of numerical-control machines Warner & Swasey used for its own plants increased by 60% from 1968 to 1971; 20 more machines were purchased in 1971, bringing the total in use to 110.[17] As a result the company was able to reduce costs and increase flexibility of operations.

The Big Three of the automobile industry—General Motors, Ford, and Chrysler—have purchased robots to replace men for special kinds of assembly-line jobs. Since costs are critically important in determining strategies in the automobile industry, company executives were alive to the advantages of a spot-welding robot that could do the work of two men but would seek no salary increase, fringe benefits, or pensions.[18]

Weyerhaeuser, a leading wood-products manufacturer, now uses an increasing share of raw materials from managed new forests rather than natural old-growth stands, for log sizes are more nearly uniform and more adaptable to high-technology sawing. Productivity per man-hour at the mill is higher, and the volume of the log going into high-value commercial products is increased sharply. Even the amount and kind of wood chips and byproducts can determine whether the company should manufacture kraft or sulfate pulps, paper goods, or bleached or unbleached production. Each option fixes in what market the pulp will be sold and suggests the marketing strategy to use.[19]

Since a company's plant, equipment, and processes are fixed elements in the short run, they are often constraints on the numbers and kinds of items that can be produced. A poor plant location and obsolescent production facilities, for example, can only result in higher production costs and thus limit strategy alternatives. Even so, although technological resources are important, they can never be the sole determinant of corporate or even production strategies.

As a case in point, Company C produced plastic molding resins. A new plant under construction was to come onstream in 8 months, doubling pro-

---

[17] Warner & Swasey Corporation 1971 Annual Report to Stockholders.

[18] "Robots Replacing Men in Assembly Lines," *St. Louis Post-Dispatch,* February 25, 1973.

[19] Weyerhaeuser Corporation 1972 Annual Report, pp. 19–20.

duction. In the meantime the company had a much higher volume of orders than it could meet. In a strategic sense manufacturing's task was to maximize output to satisfy large, key customers. However, the plant's production control system was set up as it had been for years to minimize costs. As a result long runs were emphasized. Although costs were low, many customers had to wait, and many key buyers were lost. Consequently, when the new plant came onstream, it was forced to operate at a low volume.[20]

We do not have space to go more extensively into technological resources in this chapter, although we readily admit that they have been a vital internal resource for many companies. It is enough for now that the meaning of the term be understood and that technology be recognized as a key determinant of business strategies.

Communications and Control Systems

Two resources that have a critical impact on strategies are the personnel, materials, and equipment that constitute a company's communications and control systems. Perhaps it is axiomatic, but both systems depend on timely, complete, and accurate information. "Certainly one of the strongest arguments for decentralization in companies which have adopted the divisional form of organization has been the expressed need to have line operations executives as close as possible to the sources which generate the day to day information needed in guiding the business end," writes Wilbur B. England.[21]

While businessmen continually point out that the collection and interpretation of facts are the fundamental ingredients for all good decisions, these tasks themselves are difficult and complex.

A survey conducted by the Savage-Lewis Corporation more than a decade ago is relevant to the problems of communication that exist in industry today:

> Here's what the survey showed: vice presidents understand only 67 per cent of the message from the board of directors or top management. At the level of general manager, the amount of the same information surviving is down to 56 per cent.

---

[20] Wickham Skinner, "Manufacturing—Missing Link in Corporate Strategy," *Harvard Business Review,* May– June, 1969, p. 137.

[21] Wilbur B. England, *The Purchasing System,* Richard D. Irwin, Inc., Homewood, Illinois, 1967, p. 121.

As it reaches the plant manager, the level drops to 40 per cent. Among fore-men, it dips to 30 per cent, and finally, among workers, the rate of understanding is 20 per cent.[22]

This quotation is highly germane to the basic idea of this section— communi-cation systems are determinants of business strategies. The more progressive companies recognize this point and give special emphasis to the proper and timely use of information.

For example, Esso Research & Engineering Company, a unit of Exxon Corporation, has had for many years a technical information division. At the core of the division are 15 senior scientists who have had several years of prior experience in the company's research projects, both as team members and as directors of project teams. These men are supported by a group of junior scientists and library technicians, who investigate background literature for specific projects and prepare reports and abstracts. Their prime job is to stimulate the many other technical people in the company, trying to help them use their time more effectively by acting as intermediaries between the technicians' problems and the available information.[23]

Let us turn to control. As we use the term, we mean the process by which managers ensure that resources are obtained and used effectively in the ac-complishment of the organization's objectives and strategies.

One example taken from the operations of International Telephone & Telegraph Corporation should be sufficient to show how control systems af-fect strategies. According to Harold S. Geneen, the president and chairman of the board, his staff of specialists go at will to and through any and all of the company's operations. They teach, train, monitor, and improve operations. They provide a clear professional review with the managers and higher-ups if needed on a day-in, day-out basis. Through such a system of control the company is able to get the feedback it needs in determining strategies that are realistic and effective.[24]

[22] "Communications: How Much Gets Through?" *The Management Review,* American Manage-ment Association, March 1961, p. 35.
[23] Ted Stanton, "Fishing for Facts. Firms Add Specialists to Handle Rising Tide of Scientific Papers," *The Wall Street Journal,* December 20, 1960, p. 1.
[24] "Management Must Manage," address by Harold S. Geneen, Chairman and President, ITT, before the Investment Group of Hartford and the Connecticut Investment Bankers Association, February 15, 1968,

POLICIES, STYLES, ATTITUDES, AND MOODS OF MANAGEMENT

The third key element of the internal environment that determines business strategies is the policies, styles, attitudes, and moods of top management; in many cases this element may be the most important.

Broad company objectives remain consistent, but specific policies can shift appreciably, particularly during changes in the economic cycle. When business is good, the chief executive officer (CEO) is usually much more receptive to risk-taking proposals than in cyclical downturns. These changes in management policies are difficult to detect from lower echelons unless the corporation has a well-organized, effective communications system, and few companies do for this kind of information. The result is a decrease in efficiency because time is devoted to the wrong tasks or too much time is used on tasks with low priorities.

A change in policy can also be so subtle and gradual that top management is not conscious of the change, and lower levels of organization are completely ignorant of it. Perhaps no pronouncements will be made. Only after several weeks or months will the lower echelons in the company realize what has happened. In the meantime thousands of man-hours may have been wasted on projects that will be rejected by the company's management.

The styles of top management might be defined as the broad customs, ideologies, and plans for corporate operations and behavior. Styles can be categorized as centralized or decentrailzed, growth or profit, intuitive or systematic, task or power, present or future, formal or informal, and so on. One thing is certain. Styles of top management are known by executives within a corporation and recognized by competitors and other interested persons or organizations. Styles of top management not only affect the behavior of people in an organization but also without doubt shape the corporate strategies.

Here is a fragment of an article from *Business Week* that shows the problems created when there are differences in top management styles and that suggests the impact of style on corporate strategies:

When Spencer Love founded Burlington Mills in 1923, he envisioned it as a loose amalgram of successful textile firms that would reap the benefits of combined size but would sacrifice nothing in local autonomy over daily operations. But as the company grew into Burlington Industries, the world's largest textile manufacturer, a number of executives in its New York operation felt that the far-flung empire required more centralized management. The result has been a continuing war between the division-oriented executives in the South and centralized management advocates in New York.

Last week, the advocates of the divisional approach scored a clear victory by forcing the resignation of President Ely R. Callaway and selecting Horace C. Jones as his successor.

Even before assuming the presidency, Callaway had incurred the enmity of many divisional overlords by attempting to unify all BI activities in the home furnishings field under the Burlington House Label. The symbol of their discontent became the building of the same name on New York's Avenue of the Americas, which some derisively referred to as "Ely's palace."

. . . The division managers continued to fault him for his "flamboyance." They particularly resented his pushing for the creation of a centralized $15-million research center outside Greensboro, N.C. It closed after only five years because it was "ineffective."

The advocates of decentralized management are much more comfortable with one of their own in the saddle. Jones, 57, is a former president of Burlington's Lees Carpets Div. and, in their view, well grounded in the divisional view-point and not tainted with the centralized management mania.[25]

We could continue indefinitely with examples of style and its effects on strategy (Beech Aircraft's preference in the past for growth over profits, Hewlett-Packard's emphasis on present rather than future problems). But space does not permit a full treatment, and for our purposes it is enough to point out that, in dealing with the future internal environment, executives must judge how the style of management will change. Much depends, of course, on the age level of present top management. If there is a compulsory retirement policy, it is easy to forecast when top executives will be gone. It is another matter, however, to predict who or what kind of executives will replace them. If the company is earning even a small profit, normally the style of management will be perpetuated. Executives of the same mold will tend to replace those who have retired. If the company is unprofitable and has a set of strong, responsible, outside board members, a new top-management team will probably be named. Changes of this kind generally bring about a substantial change in management style.

There is another point to which we must draw your attention. By taking a good, long look at projected changes in society and the business environment and reasoning about them, you should be able to predict in some measure what management styles will be appropriate to meet future external requirements. In the early 1950s astute businessmen and academicians predicted that many companies would have to give more attention and emphasis to

[25] "Callaway Loses the Burlington War," *Business Week*, March 10, 1973, p. 42.

international operations if traditional growth levels were to be continued. A single train of reasoning involving a few inductions and deductions should have led the typical business executive with ordinary common sense to the hypothesis that the orientation and style of management would have to change significantly.

On this point we can enlarge further. Isn't it possible to predict today the orientation and style of management of the next decade or two? We think so. We know the CEO of the corporation of the future will be different from the counterpart today. People are demanding now, and they will continue to demand with increasing fervor, that business objectives include not only profitability but also service to society and ecological responsibility. The growing emphasis on the use of quantitative techniques, behavioral sciences and the computer in the curricula of business schools suggests that the CEO of the future will be part behavioral scientist and part operations researcher.

What remains to be discussed is what executives often consider exceedingly important—the attitudes and moods of top executives. These feelings are seldom, if ever, known to the scholar or outsider. They may not be known by insiders. They are usually known by experienced executives familiar with the history and traditions of a company and its disappointments and failures. Often, they serve as barriers to action.

For example, the CEO of one company was wholly opposed to doing business in Japan. Because of his World War II experiences he deeply distrusted them. Since his company had developed technologies in certain electronic product lines, the Japanese sought a joint venture. Their proposals never reached the CEO. His subordinates, knowing his bias, took no action, even though they recognized the potential profits in a joint venture.

Admittedly, even the most intelligent people seem capable of holding extreme feelings of bias and disregarding plain facts, and the absence of strong ties between countries and people, as in the example just cited, makes the preservation of delusions easier. The resulting attitudes of key executives should be recognized and allowed for when strategies are being developed.

Finally, moods, like attitudes, are states of mind but shorter in duration and more open to change. A top executive in a good mood is often more receptive to suggestions and even to widely divergent points of view. Certainly, moods of optimism and pessimism can rise and ebb according to a top executive's physical and emotional condition. Many people hold the opinion that executive moods are too short lived to affect corporate strategies truly, but from our experiences we are profoundly convinced that the moods of top executives do have a decided impact on strategies.

CHAPTER 2

STRATEGY DETERMINANTS IN THE EXTERNAL ENVIRONMENT

Whether they object to Charles Darwin's term or not, executives are inescapably involved in their companies' continuing "struggle for existence." As Darwin put it, "Every single organic being may be said to be striving to the utmost to increase its numbers; . . . each lives by struggle at some period of its life."[1] The survival of businesses and institutions, like that of plants and animals, depends on their ability to adjust to change in their external environment. However, whereas plants and animals adjust while change is taking place, businesses must adjust beforehand. As we have hinted in the previous chapter, an inability to anticipate change and adjust for it is one of the major causes of business failures. Further, businesspeople and administrators not only react to change but also are able *in part* to control it—to facilitate favorable changes and to restrain or prevent unfavorable changes.

In the last chapter we defined the external environment of a business in one sentence. While that definition is all right as far as it goes, more elucidation is necessary. We will therefore further define this broad, complex term by specifying what we believe are its five key elements:

● Competition.
● Technology.

---

[1] Charles Darwin, *The Origin of Species,* Great Books of the Western World Series, Encyclopaedia Britannica, Inc., Chicago, 1952, p. 34.

- Socioeconomic factors.
- Geopolitical considerations.
- Government.

We suspect that many executives consider these key elements of the external environment to be more important than those of the internal environment. The late Chester I. Barnard, former president of the Bell System of New Jersey, believed that "at root the cause of the instability and limited duration of formal organization lies in the forces outside."[2] We investigate and evaluate each of these five key elements with a view to plotting the future.

COMPETITION

We must admit that competition is one of the socioeconomic factors in the external environment. But competition is so crucially important in the determination of strategies that we have taken the liberty of listing it as a separate element and discussing it first.

On the eve of the Battle of Waterloo, Lord Uxbridge asked the Duke of Wellington what his plans were for the morrow, because, he explained, he might suddenly find himself Commander in Chief and would be unable to frame new plans in a critical moment. The Duke asked, "Who will attack first tomorrow—I or Bonaparte?" "Bonaparte'," replied Lord Uxbridge. "Well," continued the Duke, "Bonaparte has not given me any idea of his projects; and as my plans will depend on his, how can you expect me to tell you what mine are?"[3]

Perhaps this story is apocryphal. Nevertheless, it makes an important point. Although not stated in the story, Wellington's objective was to defend Brussels from an attack by Napoleon's army. Wellington knew the terrain and the capability of his forces, and he could foresee all of his alternative strategies. Still, the best strategy for him to take depended on the actions of Napoleon, his competitor.

Similarly in business, if executives realistically know the strengths and weaknesses of their own companies, they are able to see the degrees of free-

[2] Chester I. Barnard, *The Functions of the Executive,* Harvard University Press, Cambridge, Mass., 1956, p. 6.
[3] Philip Guedalla, *Wellington,* Harper & Brothers, New York, 1931, p. 294.

dom available for strategies. If they can also foresee what moves competitors
are going to take or contemplate taking, they can develop the best strategies
to negate or ward off the competitors' actions.

Surveillance of competition requires the examination of different areas of
competitors' organizations, activities, and results. The most important areas
are the following:

1 Share of the market.

2 Costs and prices.

3 Financial results, trends, and positions.

4 Research and development activities.

5 Management.

6 New projects, expansions, divestments, and contractions.

Share of the Market

what are the underlying factors that lead to development of PIMS?

On May 31, 1973, Dr. Sidney Schoeffler, then manager of plans evaluation,
General Electric Company, and co-director of the PIMS project (Profit Impact of Market Strategy) at the Harvard Business School, pointed out to
members of the Council of International Planning, Development, and Marketing Research Directors the following research findings:

> When companies have less than 15 percent of a market, they are hardly ever
> profitable. When they have more than 35 percent of a market, they are hardly
> ever unprofitable.[4]

Before these findings were made public, most businessmen knew intuitively
that a large, sustained share of a market was a guarantee of profits and
perhaps the most meaningful measure of marketing success or failure. If a
company had a 10% increase in sales but lost market share, it was obviously
losing ground to its competitors. On the other hand, if a company had a 10%
decrease in sales but a 25% increase in market share, it was gaining ground
on its competitors. As a result of the PIMS project executives now have some
clear, quantitative guidelines. When a company producing a single product
line has a market share decreasing toward the 15% level, either a total, all-

[4] Preceedings from the Council for International Planning, Development, and Marketing Research Directors, May 31, 1973, Cambridge, Mass.

out company effort to increase sales is urgently needed, or a hurried search for a prospective buyer or merger partner is called for.

The stumbling block to using the PIMS standard is that information on individual companies' share of the market is often difficult to obtain. Some companies use their sales force to gather information on competitors' market share. Others subscribe to services of marketing research agencies or search for information in published sources. There is no need to detail how market share information is obtained. The point is that, although gathering this information is difficult, there are methods for doing so. Certainly, there is no excuse for a company not to make the effort, for the value of this information is plain to any dispassionate eye.

Costs and Prices

In the last chapter we discussed the usefulness of experience curves for predicting a company's patterns of long-range total cost and profit. Now we discuss how they can be used in an analysis of competitors. Domestic competitors' costs can usually be estimated with reasonable accuracy, but foreign competitors' costs are more elusive, because often labor rates do not reflect bonuses and fringe benefits, which can be substantial. Costs can, however, be roughly estimated from the prices of foreign competitors' products, for in the long run prices of products parallel costs.

According to the research of the Boston Consulting Group, "prices follow the same pattern as costs if the relationship between competitors is stable." The research also points out that prices tend to parallel costs in competitive and rapidly growing technological industries. On the other hand, prices will not parallel costs when one of many producers competing in a very rapidly growing market, finding that his costs meet two conditions, decides to lower prices. The two conditions are that marginal costs be lower than marginal revenues at the time of his decision and that he be able to lower his costs (for instance, by increasing market share) faster than he is lowering prices and faster than industry costs are decreasing.[5]

We don't need to indicate at great length the advantages of being able to predict competitors' costs and thus estimate their pricing patterns. One might say that having such information would be analogous to Wellington's having obtained knowledge on the location and battle plans of major segments of

[5] "Perspective on Experience," The Boston Consulting Group, Inc., Boston, Mass., 1968, pp. 19–21.

Napoleon's army. To begin with, the ability to anticipate accurately next year's prices of competitors' products helps executives to set prices for their own products in such a way that market share may be retained or increased. Predictions of competitors' prices, coupled with reasonable forecasts of demand and its elasticity, also constitute the basic information for the selection of those pricing policies that will contribute to the maximization of profits and return on investment (ROI).

To put the matter in an even broader prospective, the ability to predict with a reasonable degree of accuracy competitors' costs and prices over 5 or 10 years gives executives of a company major advantages in the formulation of their own longrun strategies.

Financial Results, Trends, and Positions

From our point of view it is clearly very helpful for executives of a company to obtain and examine in depth competitors' balance sheets, income statements, and detailed breakdowns of financial results by area and major product groups. We are not, of course, suggesting clandestine methods to obtain these financial statements. Not only are such methods frowned upon, but also they are not required. Except perhaps for small companies and privately owned and operated companies, these documents can usually be found in annual reports, prospectuses, and security analysts' presentations.

It is not difficult to see that financial ratios can be computed and meaningful inferences drawn. For example, an evaluation of a competitor's current and historical turnover ratios (sales/investment) and profitability, along with changes in product mix, provide measures of the effectiveness of competitors' product-line strategies. An evaluation of liquidity ratios and a cash flow analysis, when considered along with dividend policies, indicate when capital expenditures may be expanded or curtailed and when additional financing may be sought. Price/earnings ratios indicate the reputation a competitor has with investors. Finally, administrative, engineering, and research expenses, when shown as ratios to sales and compared with the number of employees in each area, indicate how efficiently manpower is being used. These are not isolated examples. Numerous other ratios could be cited that, when properly analyzed, provide insights into competitors' present and future operations.

While most information used to evaluate competitors' financial results, trends, and positions is available in their published financial documents, additional pieces of necessary information must frequently be gathered elsewhere. Sales and categories of expense such as administrative, engineering, and research are readily obtainable from income statements, but the number of employees in each category is not. These numbers do appear frequently, however, in competitors' recruitment literature ("Join the engineering department of the Wilkens Company, where 326 men and women work together . . . "). Sometimes research organizations like the Conference Board conduct surveys on personnel profiles, as illustrated by this grouping of middle- and top-management jobs within the UniRoyal organization:

1   The lower middle management group. This includes members of the factory managers' and regional sales managers' staffs and also the district sales managers. There are about 850 employees in this group.

2   The upper middle management group. This is relatively broad. It includes not only the factory managers and the regional sales managers but also the heads of the operating functions in the divisions and the heads of many divisional and corporate staff departments. There are approximately 220 employees in this group.

3   The top management group. This group is limited to the general managers of the operating divisions, key members of the corporate staff, and the corporate officers. It comprises about 20 persons.[6]

We believe that the task of obtaining competitors' financial and related information is becoming easier, for the custom of corporations' withholding such information seems to be disappearing in the United States; we believe that this trend will continue. There is even some improvement in the availability of financial information on some foreign competitors. Nevertheless, a perceptible gap still exists in quality and detail between the financial reports of most European companies and those of U.S. companies. With the exception of some of the more progressive international companies, such as Sony Corporation, most Japanese companies either issue no financial reports in English—and sometimes even none in Japanese—or offer only unreliable or uninformative reports.

---

[6] Ruth Shaeffer, "Staffing Systems—Managerial and Professional Jobs," Conference Board Report 558, Conference Board, New York, New York, 1972, p. 69.

Research and Development Expenditures

Analysis of competitors' research and development expenses as a percentage of sales and the number and kinds of their patents issued leads to conclusions not only on the efficiency of their research and development (R & D) but also on the special features that will differentiate their products.

Domestic competitors seldom keep secret the amounts they spend on R & D. Most publicize this information as a form of advertisement, a way of improving their public image as progressive companies. But they never fully define R & D expenditures. Thus we feel certain that they frequently include any expenses even remotely related. Taken singly, R & D figures for one company may not be very helpful, but despite their limitations they do provide reasonably good, although admittedly rough, approximations of comparisons among competitors.

Similarly, the number and kinds of patents issued to competitors are at best only broad indicators of the productivity of their research. A more fundamental question is the intrinsic value of these patents. How serious a threat do they pose to other companies' processes and products? An answer can sometimes be found in the number of foreign countries in which competitors seek patents for specific processes or products. Much expense is incurred when worldwide protection is sought for a process or product. It is safe to assume that competitors will not seek such protection unless they believe that the benefits will far exceed the costs.

How can one gather information on patents worldwide? Some companies give this information in their annual reports. For example, this statement appeared in the Standard Oil of Indiana 1972 annual report: "Our scientists were awarded 325 patents and applied for 385 others."[7] Sometimes the U.S. Department of Commerce provides information of this sort on some products. Some private companies, like Der Went in Great Britain, provide worldwide patent search. For multinational corporations worldwide patent search is almost a necessity—at least with reference to major competitors in different areas of the world. The reasons are simple enough. When governments of developing countries grant a patent on a product, they usually substantially increase tariffs for similar products. Thus an important market can be lost when a competitor receives a patent. In addition, if a competitor is receiving numerous patents in a foreign country, you need to find out why and whether a market potential is there that has not been properly evaluated.

[7] Standard Oil of Indiana, 1972 Annual Report, p. 18.

Management

It is unrealistic not to try to learn as much as possible about competitors' management—at least that of the most important competitors, for this knowledge can provide clues to what strategies they will use and where and when they will use them.

Often the extent of knowledge available on competitors' management can be a mere shadow of what is known about one's own management. Usually there is little direct contact; thus what information can be gathered must by necessity be second or third hand. Collecting information calls, therefore, for implacable doggedness along a path beset with contradictions and myths, as well as realities; one must carefully examine the point of view of sources and check for partiality. These tasks are time consuming and can be costly. Still, we believe that the time and money spent are amply justified if the shadows can be made more solid.

The proper study of competitors' management should begin with an in-depth appraisal of their chief executive officer (CEO). Notice that we did not say the president or chairman of the board. While it is true that in most companies the person having one or both of these titles is in fact the CEO, there are exceptions. Although he remained on the board of directors after stepping down from the board chairmanship in 1960, Edgar J. Queeny was still the CEO of Monsanto Company until his death in 1968. He was the key person, the one whom other executives didn't cross, the one who was able to get his decisions accepted and put into action.

The information that should be included in an in-depth study of the CEO is not easy to pin down. We think it should include personal information such as the CEO's nickname, age, physical description, early background, education, military service, and hobbies and, if he is married, information about his wife and family. Some will dismiss this kind of information as details of little consequence. We admit that any one bit of information in itself doesn't mean much, but, when taken together, these clues can be helpful. If you can know something of a person's experiences, you can see his point of view, his values. A person's value are never quite separable from his style of management; they will always leave their mark on his business decisions.

An in-depth study should also include as much as possible about the CEO's work experience, or "track record," and his style of management. Does he have a technical, marketing, financial, or accounting background? What are his strong points? Is he good at obtaining money? Is he good at marketing certain kinds of products? Is he good at cutting costs? What kinds of policies has he been committed to in the past? We could raise more questions but will stop now, because the importance of answers to this kind of question is obvious.

Finally the proper study of competitors' management should include information on other key executives for very much the same reasons previously mentioned. For practical reasons in-depth studies such as suggested for the CEO are generally not required; they are perhaps too costly for the value of the information gathered. Much of the personal data beyond perhaps age and education can be omitted. Emphasis should be given, however, to work experience and style of management. Personnel changes must also be pointed out, for such changes can indicate the acceptance or rejection of different management styles. The resignation or early retirement of oldtimers and the elevation of other executives can even indicate major changes in strategies. For example, when Dow Chemical placed key people in its reorganized geographic divisions in 1966, a major change in its corporate strategy was implied. There was to be a strong international thrust. In the next 10 years this implication became a reality; Dow's international business grew faster than that of any other major chemical company, expanding from $327 million and 25% of total company sales to slightly more than 2.5 billion dollars and 46% of total company sales.

New Projects, Plant Expansions, Divestments, and Contractions

On October 8, 1973, the president and CEO of the 7-Up Company announced that a $300,000 plant producing 7-Up extract for bottling operations in the European Common Market, Scandinavian countries, and countries in the British Commonwealth would be built in North Dublin, Ireland. Similar information on other companies' new projects, plant expansions, divestments, and contractions frequently appears in business, financial, and trade publications and in inconspicuous places in the financial section of newspapers. This information should be of vital interest to their competitors. The reason is plain. The capacity and location of competitors' new plants suggest how much emphasis will be given in a geographic area for a particular product. In the case of companies producing a wide range of products, the building of new plants and old plant expansions by competitors frequently indicate on what specific products these competitors are concentrating their efforts.

On the other hand, divestments, sales of plants, or contractions in output indicate areas of deemphasis. For emphasis, by closing their large power transformer plant in St. Louis, the Central Moloney Division of Colt Industries, Inc., dramatically showed that this product would be eliminated from its line. Moreover, since other divisions' plants in Arkansas and Florida producing a variety of small distribution transformers were not affected, a reasonable assumption might have been that greater emphasis would soon be given to these products.

We wish neither to distort nor to exaggerate the advantages of monitoring competitors' new projects, expansions, divestments, and contractions, but consider the hypothetical case of a company that gathers and summarizes by product line the information just discussed on all of its competitors. The company would have an up-to-date record of industry capacity and an indicator of market share. Next, if company executives were to analyze these data along with industry demand and estimates, they would have a fairly accurate picture of future supply and demand. They could then predict with reasonable accuracy future price trends.

Finally one should not forget that competitors are often good customers for raw materials, supplies, or component parts. The RCA Corporation has manufactured picture tubes for color televisions for many of its competitors. This example from among many is enough to show that information on competitors' expansion or contraction of product lines can facilitate assessments of potential in certain categories of sales.

TECHNOLOGY

The intensified search by companies, government, and private research institutes throughout the world for raw materials, new products, new or modified machinery, and improved processes and methods has resulted in rapid changes in technology. The U.S. Steel Company, for example, estimates that 15% of current shipments consist of new or improved products that were not on the market before 1960. The percentage would be substantially higher in growth industries, such as plastics and electronics.

While technological advances have their advantages, they can also represent a serious threat to companies and industries they are lagging behind. Companies must therefore not only view their own technology as a subject of constant study but also survey the external environment for technological developments that offer opportunities for rapid growth or threats to present products. Such a survey should include competitors' R & D patterns, but it should also cover relevant technology in other industries and technology developed by government-sponsored or private research institutions.

In non-Communist Europe the technological developments in many industries, especially those that are capital intensive, have been primarily in machinery and processes. As a case in point, perhaps the greatest single contribution to flat glass production has been the float process developed by Pilkington Brothers of England. This technology has cut product costs in half and reduced investment costs by two-thirds. We need hardly recount the basic oxygen steelmaking process, which was developed in Europe in the early 1950s. These two processes are only two in a long list that could be mentioned if space permitted.

On the other hand it is broadly though not precisely true that the United States has been dominant in the creation of new products for military and civilian markets. In developing an antitank missile-guidance wire for the army, U.S. Steel Corporation developed a wire the thickness of human hair that has a tensile strength one-third greater than that of any previously in existence, that will stretch without breaking when the projectile is fired, and that can be coated for electrical conductivity and insulated for the prevention of short-circuiting; 2½ miles of this wire weigh only 1 pound. To meet the daylong and year-round demand for seasonal goods alone, new products developed in the United States have included artificial turf, high-intensity lights, all-weather tennis court surfaces, and inflatable bubbles to shield swimming pools and tennis courts.[8]

Closely related to new products are the technologies that result in the development of new raw materials, The more than 60 basic plastic materials available today with a wide range of properties come quickly to mind. Less obvious are the changes in basic raw materials like steel, which today is stronger, lighter, harder, and tougher but doesn't look much different from steel made decades ago. Such innovations represent a serious but undetected threat to the users of traditional raw materials, because new raw materials are frequently developed outside of the users' industry.

A basic trouble with rapid technological change is that companies making the major breakthrough find that the time available to make use of their advantage is continually being shortened. Here is the picture drawn by Barton Biggs, a managing partner of Fairfield Partners. For many industries we think it is an accurate one.

---

[8] "Business in Brief," The Chase Manhattan Bank, N.A., April 1973.

Five years ago, the innovative company with a breakthrough product into a new, uninhabited market could expect at least several years of very high earnings growth, while it exploited the field with monopoly pricing and no real competition. Examples would include DuPont, with synthetic fibers, and Xerox, with copying machines.

Today this lead-time for exploitation has shrunk drastically. In fact, the innovative firm is often lucky if it gets its investment back before a raft of competitors with similar products are buying their way into the market via price cuts. In no time at all, the new product has become a technological commodity with all the connotations of oversupply, price competition, and cyclicality that the word "commodity" implies.

Again DuPont is an example. In 1939 it began selling Nylon 6/6, a product which took four years and $27 million from discovery to commercial introduction. It was 15 fat years before a competitor's nylon was on the market. In 1965 DuPont introduced Corfam, which required considerably more time and money—nine years and $60 million—to develop. But in less than two years, several competing products were being offered at lower prices. Recovery of the investment is problematical.[9]

To enable companies to keep abreast of technological improvements in raw materials, products, equipment, and processes, technological forecasts are most helpful. For instance, a study by Battelle Institute of Geneva on the world market for herbicides concluded that: after 1990, 50% of the herbicides used in 1976 shall have been replaced by new products; markets will grow from $3.15 billion in 1975 to $5.1 billion in 1985; herbicides for corn, wheat, vineyards and orchards offer the best opportunities in Europe and soya and cotton in North America; maize in North America and sugar beet, rice, and potatoes in Europe will have the poorest growth.[10]

Forecasts, such as the one just cited, point out new fields that should be considered for entry and old fields for diversification or phaseout. They can also provide guidelines for research programs by indicating research areas that scientists consider important and that present high odds of success.

Technological breakthroughs can be forecast with a considerable degree of reliability, because raw materials, products, equipment, and processes that will be commercially important in 5 or 10 years are already being analyzed by scientists, engineers, and designers. The Delphi method, which will be explained in more detail later in this chapter, or some modification of it offers a way of estimating when a technological breakthrough will occur and when it will be commercially important.

[9] Barton M. Biggs, "Competition vs. Growth," *Barrons,* October 28, 1968, p. 5.
[10] *Information Chimie,* February 24, 1977, p. 13.

There are limits, however, even to the best techniques of forecasting technological breakthroughs, especially when one wants to know when specific technology will become commercially useful. Take the atomic fusion process, for example. Atomic energy would have great commercial value if technological problems could be solved. There has been progress, but how much more time will be required cannot be known. Still, many important capital investment decisions must be based on judgments of this sort. Certainly, if atomic energy by the fusion process were to be available commercially within the next 5 years, many companies would delay their present plans for building power plants. If it were known to be unavailable for 20 or 30 years, these companies would not delay their present plans.

SOCIOECONOMIC FACTORS

The definition of the broad, rather vague term *socioeconomic factor* can lead us into very complicated discussions. A simple dictionary definition will not serve, and a formal definition would require a book. To explain what we mean by the term, we must therefore turn to an informal definition and identify the following examples:

- Population.
- Education.
- Occupation.
- Income.
- Health.
- Crime.
- Pollution.
- Leisure time.
- Attitudes, values, and habits.

Within and among these socioeconomic categories, cause and effect are frequently interchanged. For instance, the steeply declining birth rate in the United States (cause) has resulted in smaller families (effect). A family with fewer children (cause) has a higher per capita income (effect). With higher per capita incomes and fewer children to rear (cause), the families can spend more time and money on leisure (effect). Similarly education (cause) qualifies a person for an occupation (effect), and occupation (cause) yields an income (effect).

The factors cited have several things in common. First they can be described as measures of the quality of life. Second they are dynamic, not static. Third they are categories of information from which businessmen and businesswomen make estimates of future market demands for new and old products and services.

The world *population* is now about 3.6 billion. A continuation of present growth would bring the world to around 6 billion by the year 2000. The average rate of increase is 2%, but averages can be misleading. The more affluent countries and the more affluent people in these countries show a decided trend toward zero population growth. The underdeveloped countries and the poor and ignorant in the developing countries continue to add to the population explosion. Even now, possibly 50% of the people of the world are underfed or poorly fed. How does this affect business strategies? More seafood will come from oceanside farms. Clams and scallops that reach maturity in 4 or 5 years under normal conditions will mature in 18 months in indoor warmwater plants.[11] Moreover, seaweed can be grown in the effluent from these shellfish.

In *education* we shall see an increasing proportion of students finishing high school and enrolling in universities. Training will continue throughout a person's career. The emphasis on education will mean not only more buildings but also more electronic teaching devices, a greater use of TV.

Two of the basic changes in *occupation* include continuing movement of people from rural to urban areas and a marked increase of women and blacks in the urban labor force, especially in service industries . What are the business implications? Food processors interpret the increase in the number of working women as a greater demand for convenience foods and for facilities for eating out.

Increasing *incomes* in major segments of the economy—especially in the building trades, organized labor, and the federal government—mean greater discretionary income for these groups and suggest greater emphasis on travel and self-improvement and on cultural and recreational activities. On the other hand many nonunion white-collar workers, elementary and secondary school teachers, and university professors find their salaries not keeping up with inflation and their discretionary income declining. These people may therefore no longer represent a market for some products that they traditionally used to purchase.

In the *health* field great strides have been made in transplanting body

[11] "Seafood Firms Sprouting Off California," *St. Louis Post-Dispatch,* January 20, 1974, p. 119.

organs and in treating diseases such as cancer. Better health means longer life, which suggests the extension of retirement ages and the growth of industries that sell products for the aged.

Crime has been increasing, particularly in the cities, for the past two decades. It determines in no small measure where factories, stores, and offices will be built. The general trend has been a movement of commercial enterprises from high-crime areas. Nevertheless, the increase in crime can represent an opportunity for some enterprises. It serves as a stimulus to producers of alarm systems, outdoor lighting, police equipment, and so forth.

Air, water, and sound *pollution* have received so much attention that they hardly need comment here. We only want to point out that attempts to decrease all kinds of pollution have given rise to myriad new companies and to new business opportunities for companies already established.

Increased *leisure time* has resulted in explosive gains for sports such as bowling, tennis, and skiing. On the other hand rapidly increasing prices for some leisure items—movie admissions, for one—may indicate shrinking demand coupled with high fixed costs. Nevertheless the overall demand for recreational goods and services is growing, and this field offers many opportunities for the business executive who is able to discern them.

The 1960s have seen major changes in *attitudes* toward women and minority groups. Other notable changes have taken place in traditional work *values*. Employees are seeking intellectually satisfying experiences; they are frequently avoiding unpleasant work. These two examples are enough to show that manufacturing executives must acknowledge changes in attitudes and values to formulate strategies that are in touch with the real world. Along with attitudes and values, *habits* are also changing. A greater reliance on information from TV rather than from magazines has caused some paper manufacturers to close mills producing coated and uncoated printing and publication papers. Although Kimberly-Clark retained its Kimberly Mill, the company indicated a change in emphasis for its coated printing and publication papers, toward prestige and specialized publications and commercial printing.[12]

One need not be a clairvoyant to see the threats and opportunities generated for businessmen and businesswomen by the various socioeconomic factors and the manner in which these factors determine future sizes of markets and shifts in market demand—in brief, how they determine strategies. Why, then, haven't corporate planning methods been more successful? W. W. Simmons,

---

[12] Kimberly-Clark, Annual Report 1971.

former director of exploratory planning for IBM Corporation, offers this explanation:

> We have forecasted, trended, and studied the movements of every one of our internal activities. Detailed expenses in every category. Forecast by product, product line, market, industry, geographic area, you name it. The increasing use of the computer has made it easier and easier to provide such data and, believe me, we have. In general, corporate planning has concerned itself with a consolidation of all of this data, into what we have called a corporate plan. In my estimation, the missing ingredient has been the external trends and changes which have had a marked effect on all of us.[13]

Mr. Simmons goes on to make it clear that when he is mentioning external trends he means changing value systems, increased use of computers, increased leisure time, the burst of communications, the rising tide of education—to put it briefly, most of the factors we have termed socioeconomic.

GEOPOLITICAL CONSIDERATIONS

For the company operating purely domestically, state and regional forecasts based on reasonably accurate data generally suffice. Executives can use them to evaluate present and future socioeconomic factors (population movements, changes in the types of consumers, per capita and disposable income, the workforce, and industrial and commercial developments) with reference to particular states and urban and rural areas within the states and regions. From these evaluations they can make decisions regarding factory, store, and office locations.

When companies move into international operations, their problems become strikingly more complex. Important information is frequently lacking, and a search for it can be frustrating and can result in the misdirection of energies. Nevertheless, consider what importance for investment decisions and developing strategies a forecast in the early 1960s would have had that merely pointed out that the European Economic Community (EEC) would be astoundingly successful. Consider the importance of knowing today where and when other regional blocs will emerge.

Similar kinds of forecasts about countries and areas are equally important.

---

[13] W. W. Simmons, "Forces for Change," Talk to the Toronto Chapter of the North American Society for Corporate Planning, February 18, 1971.

For example, which country or area in the world will become another Japan? Will Brazil continue its rapid economic progress and ultimately become the Japan of Latin America? Does India, with its enormous population and market potential, offer widespread business opportunities? Or do its social and economic problems and political leanings represent obstacles that cannot be overcome? What is Taiwan's future? Has it already had its "golden years"? Will it gradually be taken over by the Peoples' Republic of China or remain relatively independent? Country and area forecasts help multinational companies to determine in what countries and areas of the world they should operate and the amount of resources that should be allocated to a country or area.

In making an international forecast, the analyst usually establishes rough measures of area potentials and compares them with actual sales and investment. In the hypothetical case of a company manufacturing a wide line of industrial products, many of which are used by electrical power plants, top management may be wondering in what parts of the world the company should concentrate its efforts. We believe the following table would be exceedingly helpful:

Present and 1980 gross national product (GNP) figures provide a rough measure of the present and future potential of the broad industrial line of products; energy production provides a rough and adequate present and future potential for products that serve electrical power plants. Even a casual look at

	Percentage of Total 1980 Potential		Percentage of Total Present	
Area	Energy Production (Billion kWh)	GNP	Sales	Investment
United States	43	42	55	75
Western Europe	31	30	20	15
Middle East	1	2	1	0
Asia/Pacific	14	14	7	2
Latin America	3	6	12	5
Canada	6	3	4	3
Africa	2	3	1	0
	100	100	100	100

the table would lead one to conclude that Western Europe should be the prime target and Asia/Pacific the next most important area of concentration.

In a similar way country forecasts enable executives of multinational companies to analyze overall present and future business climates in foreign countries. One popular type of forecast is the country-rating system, originally developed for evaluating the present climate for investments but more recently adapted to forecasting. Some such systems are quite simple, others unusually complex. Typically a country is rated according to such basic factors as market size, growth potential, and investment climate and any other factors pertinent to the particular company. For instance, one multinational company includes in its country ratings a "comfort factor," determined by friendships developed with government officials and businessmen in the country, a common history, a common language, racial and religious similarities, proximity to the United States, good train and plane facilities, good roads, quick and efficient postal and telegraph services, and safety of food and water. We go into the format of country-rating systems in more detail later in this chapter.

As tools for evaluation, country-rating systems have their limitations. While they can contribute to the development of country strategies, they are useless for strategy decisions on specific products because they deal with the broad risks in a country, not particulars such as production costs of the product, selling prices based on the market for the product, and the like.

GOVERNMENT

We touch only briefly on local and state government, because their overall influence on business strategies is generally substantially less than that of the federal government. Their greatest impact comes from legislation on taxation and business incentives, which unquestionably helps to determine in what cities and states the start of new industries or expansions of old will take place.

Of the influence of the federal government's legislation, regulations, policies, and institutions in forming and altering business strategies, we could quote numerous instances related to procurement for the armed services, pollution, housing, minority hiring, traffic, currency problems, and so on. Considerations of space compel us, however, to confine ourselves to three taken more or less at random.

The first concerns an antitrust suit against IBM.

In September, 1973, International Business Machines Corporation was held in U.S. district court in Tulsa to have violated Section 2 of the Sherman Act in an anti-trust suit brought by Telex Corporation, which was initially awarded a $352.5 million judgment.

The decision, handed down by Judge A. Sherman Christensen, a senior U.S. district judge from Salt Lake City, found that the world's largest maker of computers had monopolized and attempted to monopolize the market for peripheral devices for its own computer products between 1969 and 1972. It was the first anti-trust case that IBM had lost, and the company said it would appeal the decision.[14]

The implications of this decision on the industry and on IBM's strategies, if IBM loses its appeal, were expressed by one analyst:

This decision changes the future rules of the game in the computer industry, but that doesn't mean the rules will be more favorable to companies like Telex. IBM can take radically new actions to maintain its position that aren't prohibited by the law. For example, it can come out with radically new products that are more difficult to copy.[15]

The second concerns the direct impact that the federal government's consumer protection activities have had on the profits and strategies of Pet, Inc. The company's 1970 Annual Report states:

The sales and earnings figures would have been even higher had it not been for the loss of SEGO sales from the time of the cyclamate ban until the cyclamate-free SEGO products were introduced in the March quarter. As a result of the ban, an extraordinary item of 32 cents per share was charged against earnings for costs incurred in disposing of SEGO products containing cyclamates.[16]

The third concerns amendments to the Social Security Law passed by the U.S. Congress in 1972 (HRI), which stress the interest of the federal government in guiding U.S. hospitals toward achieving new economics, especially in the planning and construction of new facilities. The results of the government action have been for hospital administrators to change their strategies and to seek better planning and housekeeping through the services of professional consultants.

[14] "IBM Loses Antitrust Action for First Time as Telex Corporation Is Awarded $352.5 Million," *Wall Street Journal,* September 18, 1973, p. 3.
[15] *Ibid.*
[16] Pet, Incorporated, 1970 Annual Report.

With our brief examples and comments we make several points. Activities of government at all levels have been multiplied. These activities are important in the formulation of business strategies. The trend will probably continue, but there are signs (for instance, state and local revenue sharing) that suggest more decentralization.

The influence of government is a worldwide phenomenon that has marked effects on business in general and on multinational company strategies in particular. To substantiate our view, we offer the following list of developments and trends evident in the governments of many countries, especially those in the free world:

- The search for an international monetary system that will meet the financial needs of the countries of the world while constantly maintaining a realistic relationship among world currencies.
- The trend for worldwide antitrust laws. Perhaps laws will develop that will be something in between the strict, rigid ones of the United States and the lax, flexible ones of Japan.
- The development of new tax systems, possibly patterned after the TVA tax system developed by the EEC countries.
- The movement toward protectionism that has been clearly visible in recent years. Perhaps this movement is only a temporary aberration in what has been a longrun trend toward trade liberalization. The direction individual countries ultimately take will have a profound effect on corporate strategies.
- The fear of economic domination by a handful of multinational companies that has haunted governments, particularly those of the developing countries. Some governments have already passed legislation to control multinational company activities. On the other hand some of these companies are seeking legal status under international laws and regulations. How governments will react to multinational companies in the future will determine in large measure these companies' organizational strategies.

Our discussion of the five key elements of the external environment has been broad and long. Admittedly the importance of each factor depends on the nature of the business and the nature of the industry. In evaluating the external environment, executives cannot escape the first step of determining what the critical elements and facets of these elements are in their business and what impact they will have. One multinational corporation in the pharmaceutical, foods, and plastics business considers the following to be key elements in its external environment that could have the greatest impact on its strategies.

Competition

- An increase or decrease in the size of competitors through mergers, acquisitions, and divestments.
- The building of larger production units for decreasing unit costs.
- The extent of forward and backward integration.
- The number of competitors who have gone multinational and the extent of their multinationalization.

Technology

- Major breakthroughs in the medical field (immunization controls, cardiovascular management, obesity control, preventive and diagnostic management).
- Effective, low-cost, safe, oral or implantable contraceptives.
- Ecologically benign crop improvement systems.
- The development and acceptance of fabricated vegetable protein foods.
- Widespread use of recyclable or consumable disposables (containers, etc.)
- Increase in the use of engineered composite products.
- Materials with greatly improved performance and resistance to failure.
- Increase in the development and use of nonwovens.

Socioeconomic Factors

- The population explosion with its influence on food, birth, control, pollution, and resources.
- Increasing affluence.
- Changes in peoples' attitudes and values concerning what constitutes a good life.
- Increase in leisure time.
- Shifts of people (unemployment, regional migrations, shortage of engineers, etc.).

Geopolitical Considerations

- EEC expansion.
- Japan's emergence as a superpower.
- Diminishing isolation of Peoples' Republic of China.
- "Takeoff" by Brazil.
- The growing power position of the Middle East as a result of its petroleum resources in a world that is experiencing a shortage of these resources.

Government

- Regulation of multinational corporations.
- Economic nationalism,
- Government actions to safeguard public interest in the use of products and services.

HOW TO DEVELOP FORECASTS OF THE EXTERNAL ENVIRONMENT

Knowing what the important elements in the external environment are and how they affect strategies is only the beginning of the task. These activities merely identify where attention needs to be focused; they don't indicate how a forecast is to be developed. Let us turn to that now.

The two most common methods of forecasting the external environment are:

1   Monitoring the forecasts of others and deciding what parts are relevant.
2   Conducting independently one's own forecast.

Of the two methods the first is more frequently used because it is more practical. We are inclined to believe, however, that most companies use both methods.

For example, future supply and demand for crude oil unquestionably play an important role in the decisions that oil company executives make today. Although the U.S. government, research institutes, banks, and the oil industry have prepared extensive literature on the subject, an oil company might augment what has been printed by conducting research and making forecasts on shale oil rights, economic processes for producing synthetic liquid fuels and lubricating oils from coal, or in-depth studies of its own current and potential oil reserves.

Monitoring the Forecasts of Others

Books, articles, bulletins, videotapes, video cassettes, and special services all devoted to the study of the future are numerous and rapidly proliferating. A new term has even been created to describe professionals in the field. They are called "the futurists," their subject "futurology." Their differing backgrounds, experience, and points of view naturally color their writings. Some futurists, like authors Herman Kahn (*The Year 2000*) and Alvin Töffler (*Future Shock*), give the reader a panoramic view of the future; others, like David A. Schulz, who wrote *The Changing Family: Its Function and Future,* deal with specialized fields. Still, each provides a picture, as accurate and unbiased as possible, of changes in one or more elements of the external environment in the near, immediate, or distant future.

We do not dwell on the contents of individual books, for too many have been written. Many of the sharpest perceptions and critical reviews of futurists' books have appeared in the *Bulletin* and *The Futurist,* both published by the World Future Society, Washington, D.C. These two publications also contain superior articles on forecasts.

Magazines like *Fortune, Business Week,* and *Time* and newspapers like *The New York Times* and the *Wall Street Journal* occasionally carry articles on the future external environment. A quick scanning of *The Reader's Guide to Periodical Literature* or of indexes provided by publishers should enable one to locate articles of interest.

Of the many organizations that provide services we list 12 we have found helpful:

1 The Hudson Institute.
2 The Futures Group.
3 Predicasts, Inc.
4 The Institute for the Future.
5 Stanford Research Institute—Long Range Planning Service.
6 Arthur D. Little—Service to Management and Investors.
7 Battelle Memorial Institute.
8 Business International.
9 Yankelovich, Skelly & White.
10 The Institute for Strategic Studies.
11 The National Planning Association.
12 The Bureau of National Affairs.

While all of these make laudable contributions, none claims infallibility. No organization or group of organizations is equipped to deal with the subtlety and variety to be found in the complex external environment. Just as we have constructed manageable, not complete, models in our discussions of the internal and external environments, so must the professionals who provide futuristic services. Their models are of course, considerably more detailed and quantitative than ours; by using computers, they have access to econometric and sophisticated mathematical techniques for developing quantitative models. Still, to compensate for elements or subelements that have been omitted or incorrectly weighed, the professionals typically establish only a range of likelihood.

The services provided sometimes overlap, but most organizations have special areas of expertise.

We think *The Hudson Institute,* located in Croton-on-Hudson, New York, does especially good research on socioeconomic trends for the intermediate and longrun future and provides useful evaluations of foreign areas and countries. It is, moreover, a pioneer in the development of scenarios, which are discussed in depth later. *The Futures Group,* located in Glastonbury, Connecticut, currently offers forecasts in more than 70 basic categories (political developments, currency values, and so forth), and the quality of these forecasts is evaluated and classified. For example, if a client submits a list of corporate objectives, the Futures Group will submit a report that enumerates forecasts of elements related to these objectives. *Predicasts, Inc.,* located in Cleveland, Ohio, has for domestic companies perhaps the most extensive coverage of forecasts by industry and for international companies quantitative forecasts of GNP and population for countries of the world. *The Institute For the Future,* with facilities in Menlo Park, California, and Middletown, Connecticut, is noted for its application of Delphi techniques and even computerized studies to business and government and for its development of new techniques for technological and industry forecasting. The *Stanford Research Institute* (Menlo Park, California), *Arthur D. Little* (Cambridge, Massachusetts), and the *Battelle Memorial Institute* (Columbus, Ohio) are well known for their numerous studies of future technology and industry trends. The Stanford Research Institute has published more than 500 long-range planning reports on all types of operations all over the world. Arthur D. Little typically confines its research forecasts to a range of 1 to 5 years. Only occasionally does it develop a 10 year or longer forecast. Battelle and Little have both been leaders in the development of input-output analysis for the improvement of business and industry forecasts. *Business International,* in New York City, has been prominent in international business as a developer of concepts and techniques in area and country forecasting. *Yankelovich,* also in New York City, is best known for its work in social trends and for its development of a laboratory test-market technique designed to forecast a company's share of the market for a new product. *The Institute for Strategic Studies,* located in London, has made its reputation with its assessments of military might and balances of military power, although it has also done highly dependable political and economic forecasting. The institute primarily gathers responsible research of others, and its associates meet with experts in the field rather than conduct extensive research of their own. The strength of *The National Planning Association,* in Washington, D.C., is its long-range economic and demographic projections for national, regional, state, and metropolitan areas. It also does thorough analyses of public programs and their future implications. *The Bureau of National Affairs,* also headquartered in Washington, D.C., has been reporting and interpreting the interaction of government and business since 1933—for instance, the applications to business of the Consumer Product Safety Act—through a variety of special reports and services. Its forecasts, as one might expect, cover principally short terms, from 6 months to several years.

All the organizations mentioned provide written reports and publications. All have either a published topical bibliography or card catalog files of their work. All conduct some type of training program, seminar, or forum.

We do not imply that only the organizations we have cited are important and effective. We only affirm that they have been most helpful to us. The Conference Board, in cooperation with the Opinion Research Corporation, has published an excellent report, titled "Perspectives for the 70's and 80's," but Conference Board publications in general provide coverage on many subjects other than the external business environment. Some organizations have not been included, because they specialize in forecasts for single products. Finally, some organizations have not been included, simply because we have had no experience in using their services.

Let us mention just one more organization as a reference source. *Future Search,* begun by the Institute of the Future in 1971, has served as an archive and repository of English-language forecasting literature, a data bank, and a computer-based library and distribution center for future information and literature.

Conducting Forecasts Independently

While we believe that the organizations cited and numerous others have enabled their clients to keep reasonably abreast of some of the literature and special topics of research, nevertheless perceptible gaps in the general literature remain, and much information on the external environment relevant to decisions made by a particular company is nonexistent or difficult to find. It is therefore frequently necessary for companies to conduct their own forecasts. They can either contract for the services of an outside organization to conduct forecasts or conduct their own. When using the sevices of an outside organization of their choice, they need to do little more than set up the scope of work and negotiate terms and conditions. We will concentrate our attention on the alternative of conducting forecasts independently.

After the critical elements and subelements of the external environment have been identified, the next step is the selection of the right methodology, which in turn depends on the kind of information desired. We think the following methodologies, some developed by professional forecasting organizations and others by companies with which we have been associated, are sufficient for most forecasts:

1   The Delphi Method.
2   Input-output Analysis.
3   Country-Rating Systems.
4   Impact and Cross-Impact Analysis.
5   Books of Threats and Opportunities.
6   Reports and Scenarios.
7   *Ad-Hoc* Task Forces and Committees.

Like the clubs in a golfer's bag, these methodologies have different uses. The first three listed are best suited for broad forecasts of elements in the external environment; the last four are best suited for putting broad forecasts into a practical context.

The Delphi Method   The Delphi method, developed by Norman Dalkey and Olaf Helmer, might appropriately be called a composite of experts' estimations. Called Delphi, because like the Greek oracle it has been employed to obtain opinions on what the future holds, it can be used to seek a consensus of opinion among experts on any subject.

The first step of the Delphi method is the selection of a subject or topic, perhaps an estimate of consumer expenditures for sporting goods over the next 3 years. The second step is to select a panel of experts. Naturally much care must be taken. The experts should:

> (1) be on the frontier of understanding in their own discipline, (2) have interdisciplinary interests, (3) see the correlation between national and international, present and future developments, (4) acknowledge the necessity of approaching the task as free as possible of fixed positions and self-fulfilling prophecies, and (5) seek by all means possible to do more than repackage what has already been said.[17]

Once the panel is selected, the method has three additional features:

> (1) anonymity, (2) iteration with controlled feedback, (3) statistical group responses. Anonymity is achieved by using questionnaires, where specific responses are not associated with individual members of the group. This is a way of cutting down on the effects of dominant individuals and reducing group pressure. Iteration consists in performing the interaction among members of the group in several stages; typically, at the beginning of each stage the results of the previous stage are summarized and fed back to members of the group, and they are then asked to reassess their answers in the light of what the entire group thought on the previous round. Finally, rather than asking the group to arrive at a consensus, the group opinion is taken to be a statistical average of the final opinions of individual members. The opinion of every member is reflected in the group response.[18]

The result is a group estimate that offers a reasonably good level of validity. In case this procedure seems too complex, Olaf Helmer offers this simplified version:

> Have each member of the panel independently write down his own estimate, reveal the set of estimates but without identifying which has been made by whom, and debate openly the pros and cons of various estimates; then have each person once more write down his own (possibly revised) estimate and accept the median of these as the group decision.[19]

---

[17] "Perspective for the 70's and 80's—Tomorrow's problems Confronting Today's Management." A special report from the Conference Board, p. 3.
[18] *Ibid.,* p. 3.
[19] Olaf Helmer, "Systematic Use of Expert Opinion," paper presented to AFAG Board Meeting, November 1967.

We think the Delphi method is well suited, but not limited, to specifying likely occurrences and impacts of all elements of the external future environment. Moreover, it provides a sharpened perspective on what the right issues and questions are. It has been used in a variety of ways, from the identification of future military procurement decisions to the development of a program to reduce the rate of violent crimes in the United States. Because of its flexibility and capacity for forecasting what problems will arise, the Delphi method can be used with many of the other methodologies we have listed.

Input-output Analysis   Originally input-output analysis was developed by economist Wassily W. Leontief as a tool for reckoning with intermediate sales and purchases in the American economy—that is, the inputs and outputs—that carry goods and services from industry to industry, from manufacturer to distributor, and on to their final purchaser in the market. Input-output analysis is, in the words of Leontief, "a way of looking under the hood at the inside workings of the economic system." [20]

To see the potential of input-output analysis for determining the increase or decrease of sales from one industry or sector to others throughout the economy, one needs to understand it. Let us therefore consider an example provided by Daniel A. Hodes, an economist for General Telephone and Electronics. Hodes wanted to determine the expected increase in the sale of radios to the automobile industry if demand for automobiles were to increase the next year by $100 million.

Using Leontief's input-output table—a matrix containing 81 vertical and horizontal listings of major industry groups, which incidentally has been published by the Office of Business Economics in the U.S. Department of Commerce—Hodes focused his attention first on the radio, TV, and commercial equipment cell in the horizontal row, which shows the distribution of the outputs or sales of that industry to the other 80 plus intraindustry sales. He then focused his attention on the motor vehicle cell in the vertical column, which showed the distribution of inputs or purchases, and constructed a chart (Exhibit 2.1). Notice that three numbers are shown. The first one, 158.8, means that the radio, TV, and communications equipment industry sells $158.8 million worth of products to the motor vehicle industry. The second, 5.23 in the lower left-hand corner of the cell, is the input-output coefficient.

[20] Wassily W. Leontief, "The Structure of the U.S. Economy," *Scientific American,* April 1965, p. 25.

Exhibit 2.1 Input-Output Analysis: An Illustrative Example

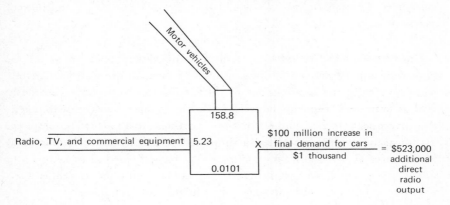

This coefficient tells us that, for each $1000 of output (sales) shown in the column by the motor vehicle industry, $5.23 worth of equipment is required for radio, TV, and communications. The last number, .0101 in the lower right-hand corner of the cell, is called the inverse coefficient. Not used in the solution to the illustrative problem posed by Hodes, it expresses for the radio, TV, and commercial equipment industry that portion of the industry's total output required directly and indirectly to meet one unit of final demand by the motor vehicle industry. For example, if the final demand for automobiles was forecasted to be $20 billion, the demand for radio, TV, and commercial equipment generated would be $202 million or $20 billion times the inverse coefficient (.0101). The methodology we have just described can be used to forecast the implications of increased automobile sales on other industries throughout the economy. Hence, input-output analysis can also provide indications of what new businesses might have the best growth potential for a company.[21]

The input-output approach can be used by large, multidivisional or multinational companies to indicate the flow of goods among divisions or subsidiaries and then to final users. *Inputs* would be the dollar value of goods each division or subsidiary purchases from other divisions and subsidiaries and would include the value added in the form of labor, depreciation, interest expense, and taxes. *Outputs* would include the dollar values of goods each

[21] Daniel A. Hodes, "Input-output Analysis: An Illustrative Example," *The Journal of the National Association of Business Economics,* Summer 1965, pp. 35–37.

division or subsidiary sells to other divisions and subsidiaries and to outside customers. The *input-output table* would be a graphic display of the flow of goods.

   Country-Rating Systems   Country-rating systems can be useful for measuring the attractiveness of countries and areas of the world for investment now or in the intermediate or distant future. As we have previously said, a country will typically be rated according to market size, growth potential, investment climate, and other factors pertinent to a particular company. To illustrate, we have prepared a simplified system with two fundamental factors, market size and business climate. We have divided these factors into subfactors, to which we have assigned weights obtained from a modified Delphi approach. Our country-rating system might look as follows:

Market-Size Factors	Weight
Gross national product	15
Industrial production	15
Population (total)	8
Urban population	8
Energy production (billion kWh)	4
	50

Business-Climate Factors	Weight
Political stability	20
Discrimination against and controls on foreign owners	10
"Comfort factor"	10
Inflation rate	5
International liquidity (total reserves)	5
	50
Grand total	100

Our next task is to use this system to evaluate countries and areas. Each country will have a number. One hundred points represents a perfect score, and so West Germany might currently have a rating of 92 and South Korea 46. We could next evaluate the potential of a country by using trend-line analysis and the Delphi method, so that as we assign numbers to countries for the year 1979, West Germany might receive an estimated rating of 94 and South Korea 63. We could quickly see not only what the absolute rankings of countries are but also how they have changed with respect to other countries.

Country-rating systems are helpful for determining in general where funds should be allocated for investment, but they are not helpful in determining which specific projects should be selected.

Impact and Cross-Impact Analysis   Impact analysis is a methodology for assessing the effect on business activities of events occurring in the external environment. Although impact analysis is applicable to such broad questions as the effect of a 10–15% reduction of heating oil allocations to the ABC Company or divisions within that company, it is particularly relevant to specific projects.

Let us take a hypothetical case, a proposal for the manufacture of hydraulic valves in the São Paulo area of Brazil. The first step in any analysis would be a listing of significant elements of the project that would contribute to its success or failure, usually within a 10- to 12-year period. We might have put our hypothetical project in Paramus, New Jersey, or Canton, Ohio, but we have selected the Brazilian location because it makes more vivid the impact of events occurring in the external environment. Let us assume that our significant elements include market demand, production-cost savings, prices, competitive position, new capital requirements, and degree of management control. These elements are inevitably affected by events occurring in the external environment, over which, unfortunately, the company has little or no control, especially in foreign countries. A major step in impact analysis is, therefore, the identification of the critical events. In the case of Brazil, they would typically be something like this:

1   Gross national product reaches $100 billion.
2   Tariffs on valves are lowered from 38% to 10%.
3   The radical left wing gains control of the national assembly.
4   Necco Valve, Ltd., a major competitor in the UK, becomes a second producer of valves in Brazil.
5   Brazil passes a law requiring majority Brazilian ownership for the metal-fabricating industry, which includes the manufacture of valves.
6   A new concept for a common market of Latin American countries replacing LAFTA (Latin American Free Trade Area) is implemented, this time successfully.

We are now ready to construct a matrix with the significant project elements shown as row headings and the events shown as column headings. What remains now is the determination, by means of a modified Delphi method, of the probability of occurrence of each event or alternatively its timing—in brief, the assignment of an impact value to each of these events. One can use a numerical scale ranging from zero to plus 10 for favorable impact and zero to minus 10 for unfavorable impact. These values are entered in the matrix and thus provide a composite, quantitative view of the impact of each event on key project factors and the total impact of all of these events (see Exhibit 2.2).

The impact analysis just described can be carried a step further; we can determine the interactions among events. When we do, we are conducting a cross-impact analysis. Originally conceived by Ted Gordon and Olaf Helmer of Rand Corporation and later further developed by The Institute for the Future and the Monsanto Company, cross-impact analysis enables one to identify reinforcing or inhibiting events and to uncover relationships between events that initially appear unrelated or only weakly connected. Since cross-impact analysis has been patented, we are not at liberty to discuss it in detail. In substance, it requires knowledgeable individuals or experts working on a project to assign probabilities to each event and then to assess the impact of events on each other. When all events have been cross-impacted, the values are fed into a computer, and a table of new probabilities is calculated. The results are usually depicted as probability curves over time and are compared with those reached by the group independently of the computer. These comparisons are useful in that they show inconsistencies in group decisions.

Exhibit 2.2   Impact Analysis Events

Key Project Factors	1	2	3	4	5	6	Total
Market demand	+ 8	0	− 6	0	− 2	+ 2	+ 2
Production-cost savings	+ 8	0	− 2	0	− 2	+ 2	+ 6
Prices	+ 2	−4	0	− 6	0	+ 2	− 6
Competitive position	− 4	−2	0	− 4	− 2	+ 4	− 8
New capital requirements	0	0	0	0	+ 4	0	+ 4
Degree of management control	0	0	− 2	0	− 8	0	−10
Total	+14	−6	−10	−10	−10	+10	−12

Books of Threats and Opportunities Once significant events have been noted and weighted and perhaps impacted and cross-impacted, the analysis should then logically turn to specific action programs that set forth who will take action and when. A methodology we have used, found helpful, and thus recommend is the compilation of a Book of Threats and Opportunities. Let us illustrate by taking from the book of an engineering company a typical page, in this case one that deals with the severe shortage of engineers graduating from college in 1976. The page would look like this:

Event A severe shortage of engineers graduating from college by 1976.

Threat Company may not be able to fill requirements for technical personnel beginning in 1976 and for many years thereafter because of the shortage. If starting salaries are very high, they will affect salary levels of all of the lower echelons of technical personnel and substantially raise costs.

Strategy Begin now to build up a backlog of technical personnel so that requirements will be substantially reduced during "shortage" years.

Action

	What	Who	When
1.	All divisions of company submit requisitions for hiring new technical personnel covering the next 4 years and concurrently indicate estimates of salary expense for these 4 years.	Division general managers	Due in 45 days
2.	Review results and decide on a hiring plan for new technical personnel over the next 4 years, with the highest number hired in the immediate year and a decline thereafter.	Chief Executive Officer and Personnel Director	Decision within 2 months from completion of step 1
3.	Revise training programs for new technical employees to absorb a surplus of engineers for 1 to 3 years.	Personnel Director	Completed by June of this year
4.	Compare results with targets for acquiring new technical personnel.	Chief Executive Officer and Personnel Director	September 1 each year for next 4 years

Reports and Scenarios   Every executive whose business it is to study the external environment knows that his work cannot end with a mere scanning or even the development of something comparable to a Book of Threats and Opportunities. More detail is required. Conclusions must be substantiated and courses of action recommended. Comprehensive reports provide this detail, for when properly prepared they explain and interpret events and their interrelationships. Generally these comprehensive reports should cover broad observations of the external environment in order that significant events may not be omitted. On the other hand, depth of coverage is also required for events of critical importance. Take, for instance, the illustrative forecast of a severe shortage of engineers graduating from college by 1976 just cited. Many companies would undoubtedly have required greater depth of coverage in their reports to obtain answers to questions like these: How acute will these shortages be? When will the pinch be felt? How long will the shortage last?

The scenario, made famous by Herman Kahn of the Hudson Institute, is a special kind of report that makes predictions of the future lifelike, interesting, convincing, and hence more readable. The scenario treats events forecasted in the external environment as though they have actually occurred and describes business activities under these new environmental conditions. Scenarios may take various forms. Sometimes they appear as future annual reports or the remarks of the CEO of a company at an annual stockholders' meeting. Sometimes they may center on a particular industry, such as agricultural equipment, and describe what changes have taken place in agriculture around the world and how these changes have affected the sales, profit margins, product lines, competitive positions, and organizational structures of companies in the industry. All scenarios seek to help executives sharpen their discrimination and see the consequences of change.

Ad-Hoc Task Forces and Committees   In reducing the discrepancies between conceived and actual external environments, companies must of course rely primarily on individual employees and staffs to gather facts, often detailed facts, and on line executives to use these facts and their broad perspective to make final decisions. *Ad-hoc* task forces and committees, when used properly, can also be strikingly effective.

One giant company in the electronics industry depended on a director of exploratory planning to identify key future events in the external environment of countries that were major customers. This staff executive, a sort of Henry Kissinger in a gray flannel suit, spent 2 months traveling around the world, visiting England, Holland, France, Switzerland, West Germany, Italy, and Japan. He talked with professionals—men who had published reports, articles, and books on the future external environment of these countries— and asked them hundreds of questions. The substance of his talks and his observations and conclusions were promptly documented. Upon returning home, he convened an *ad-hoc* task force made up of key company employees with expertise in engineering, manufacturing, marketing, finance, and research. For several weeks this task force met and reacted to his conclusions. Finally they reached a consensus on what they believed would be the major impacts on the company of the events he was forecasting. A set of recommendations was drawn up and sent to the CEO of the company for action.

Whether a single executive makes forecasts of changes in the external environment for his company or these forecasts are made by an outside organization, *ad-hoc* task forces and committees should play an important role. They are especially useful for evaluating (1) the relevance of the forecasts, (2) the omissions and errors, and (3) the impact of forecasted events on the company. Their analyses, conclusions, and recommendations are necessary inputs for those who must make final decisions.

Even when companies attempt to bring about or retard change in the external environment, the need for *ad-hoc* task forces and committees continues, for their work may provide top executives with realistic maps of the external environment.

Take, for example, General Electric Company's program in public affairs, which deals with the attitudes and behavior of people and organizations that affect General Electric's operations. The company established a public-issues committee, composed of outside board members and one corporate senior vice president. This committee then organized a staff to help identify major pressures on the company. The staff subsequently developed a list of major pressures classified by function (e.g., marketing , finance, and production) and instigated for the most part by labor and government. Then the threats that these pressures might present were added. A fragment from a section on the pressures in the marketing function might look like this:

Pressures

● To avoid excessive market share and profits for any one company.

- To control the activities of conglomerates in order to prevent them from selling "low" to win market position or selling "high" to raise profits.
- To eliminate reciprocity, which tends to shut out competition.

Threats

- Price controls.
- Dismemberment of large corporations.
- Limitation on numbers of businesses, share of market, or both.
- Excess profit tax.

Next, the staff brought together an *ad-hoc* committee of 10. This committee first determined the impact of the pressures and threats on company sales and profits. Next the members of the committee determined to what extent actions would be taken by the following 14 groups: consumer groups, share owners, government, unions, workers, managers and professors, small businesses, minorities, women, college students, environmental groups, populists, academic critics, and "moralists,"

The committee now had two sets of ratings, one that reflected the most important pressures and threats to the company and another that reflected the extent to which action would be taken by important pressure groups. A public-affairs program was then developed to deal, as effectively as possible, with those pressures and threats that received the highest composite score. Top-level executives in the company were assigned the job of finding ways to overcome or neutralize each of the key pressures and threats. In a sense these executives were to direct the company's counterattack.

Putting Forecasts of the External Environment to Use in Present-Day Decision Making

Proper surveillance of the external environment cannot be achieved unless those who make the final decisions put forecasts to use in present-day decision making. We argue that it is in this final but crucial step where many companies fail. The stunning realization that the United States is short of oil, natural gas, electric power, chrome, nickel, and cobalt seems to have caught many executives by surprise. While the oil and electric companies have been stressing shortages for the future, we point out the actions taken by many American industries.

Electric utilities and applicance makers, for instance, are still strongly promoting the extravagant use of their products (1977), seemingly oblivious to what their own researchers told them.

Even now, when wise Americans seek smaller cars to conserve fuel and money, American automobile makers have huge inventories of big cars. They have for the most part ignored consumer interest in small, efficient cars and consequently have lost much of the small-car market to foreign competitors.

None of the foregoing explains why many CEOs of companies have ignored competent forecasts. One basic reason may be the lack of credibility of staffs who develop the forecasts. Many are looked upon as poor businessmen who suffer from a lack of hard-line business experience. Therefore, the judgment behind their forecasts and conclusions is often seriously questioned.

Another reason is that forecasts frequently suffer from what the late Alfred North Whitehead called "the fallacy of misplaced concreteness," and CEOs know this. When forecasts reason deductively about the future external environment, they nearly always leave out something or rather many things, both things they forget and things they don't know, and thus their conclusions are unsound. For example, how many forecasts of future fuel supplies anticipated the possibility that the Arab nations would join together and stop exports of oil to the United States during the Arab–Israeli conflict of 1973? We suspect that very few, if any, did. Nevertheless this action has had a significant impact on the U.S. economy.

A final reason is that many executives are so busy keeping today's problems under control that they have little time to worry about tomorrow . It is a rare CEO who will allocate much of his time today to decisions whose results will not be fully realized for many years. Of course, they will allocate some funds and people for forecasting, because futuristic research is popular now, and they feel that they may be missing something if they ignore it. They will give some attention to shortrun forecasts. They are not inclined, however, to make present decisions from longrun forecasts.

We can only surmise that either these chief executives have developed a picture inside their heads of the extent of change in the external environment without experts' opinions or, like plants and animals, they will adjust when changes are not a forecast but a reality. In either case they expose their companies to great risk. For the past has shown that companies that lack competent information on the future often face defeat by unforeseen competition. According to a study in 1956 by the Stanford Research Institute on the growth of 400 U.S. corporations the most successful companies—those that increased sales by 400% in a decade—seem to be aware of change, to visualize its impact on their business, and to place their companies in a position to take advantage of it.[22]

[22] William E. Hoskins, "Company Planning in the 1960s," *Forest Products Journal,* November 1960, pp. 577–579.

CHAPTER 3

INFORMATION SYSTEMS STRATEGIES

To say that one must have reliable information on the internal and external environment for successful decision making is perhaps selfevident in the sense that its opposite is immediately seen to be false. Slightly less obvious is the need for a mechanism for the continual gathering, refinement, processing, interpretation, and distribution of reliable, relevant, and timely information. Business executives fulfill this need by setting up information systems.

The information they need includes that found in specialized, internally generated performance reports like production variances and cost efficiencies, financial reports like profit and loss statements and balance sheets, and action reports like quarterly deviations from managers' objectives. But this chapter deals primarily with the type of information often referred to as "intelligence," acquired through surveillance of the external environment. We have given greater emphasis to intelligence for several reasons. First this kind of information is typically required for unstructured decisions for long-range planning at top corporate levels, whereas specialized, internally generated reports are more often needed for more structured decisions. Second this kind of information is frequently more difficult to obtain. And third it requires greater testing for verification.

When we use the word *system* in the sections that follow, we are talking about the sets of interrelated and integrated elements or parts through which the company may accomplish objectives and goals.

IMPORTANCE OF INFORMATION SYSTEMS

Why are information systems important? Many explanations can be offered. First, changes in the external environment are occurring so rapidly today that the time available for analysis and decision making has markedly decreased. Consider the tire industry. The earliest tires were made of solid rubber. With the introduction of pneumatic tires material and basic structure changed very little until after World War ll. Since then the material used in tire cord, for example, has undergone a succession of changes: from cotton to rayon, from rayon to nylon, from nylon to polyester, from polyester to fiberglas, and from fiberglas to steel wire or DuPont's "Fiber B." In tire construction radial and belted tires now widely in use represent a major breakthrough. The financial implications of rapid change are clear. Companies in the tire and fiber businesses must react quickly or face staggering losses or even bankruptcy.

Second, the costs of capital equipment in most industries have risen rapidly, in part because of material and wage increases and in part because of new technologies and supplementary equipment. Consequently the acquisition or expansion of facilities represents a major business decision. The danger of rapid obsolescence of capital equipment is a paramount risk that in recent years has narrowed the tolerance for error, especially in highly capital-intensive industries. Take the oil industry, for example. A new process for manufacturing 100,000 barrels of synthetic crude oil a day from coal would require a plant costing in 1974 from $600–$700 million. With plant costs so high, few companies can afford to make mistakes on estimates of markets or the availability and costs of coal and natural crude oil.

Third, when a company becomes multinational, as more and more American companies are doing, their information needs balloon. In addition to information on the United States, they require precise, immediate, accessible information on the economy, government, and culture of from 1 to 124 countries so that they can properly examine business risks and opportunities. Moreover, key data on the developing countries of South America, Asia, and Africa are usually hard to obtain and verify.

Fourth, intense competition requires companies to manage information efficiently, and information systems provide line executives in companies with a tool for making better decisions and thus gain an advantage over competitors, or at least for keeping themselves from losing ground.

INFORMATION SYSTEMS AND THEIR RELATIONSHIP
WITH SYSTEMS FOR STRATEGY AND PLANNING

Few companies treat the handling of information as a major function of business like marketing, production, and finance. Information gathering is typically fragmented and thus inefficient. Accounting departments usually operate independently of management information systems (MIS) departments, which in turn are usually independent of corporate or divisional planning staffs. To our knowledge no major company has centralized its entire information function under one executive, and perhaps they are not yet capable of doing it. Still, top corporate planners need efficient information systems that provide the proper blending of information from line and staff executives to provide key inputs for the setting up of well-defined objectives and goals.

Systems within the human body provide a convenient way to explain the relationship that should exist between information systems and strategy and planning systems. The former are like the nervous system, the latter like the brain. An efficient arrangement of the two systems and the disposition of their parts as seen through x-ray eyes might look like Exhibit 3.1.

The stages through which information passes within the system are:

1   Gathering of raw information.
2   Processing of raw information.
3   Interpretation of processed information.
4   Distribution of processed information.

All these stages have one basic purpose—*to help the line make better decisions.*

In speaking about gathering raw information we must begin with questions that companies need to have answered about their external and internal environments: How rapidly is the economy growing? What is the present rate of inflation? What are the prospects of changes in the rate of inflation for the future? What will the effects of government planning activities be on our company? How strong are government controls at different national, regional, and local levels? What are the prospects for increased or decreased taxes? How available are land, water, fuel, and electricity? What demands will society make on companies? What types of products do consumers prefer? What are the trends in consumer taste? What are competitors' reported and actual capacities and plans for expansion? What products or services do they offer? What are their strengths and weaknesses? What are our company's

Exhibit 3.1 Relationship of an Information System to a Strategy and Planning System

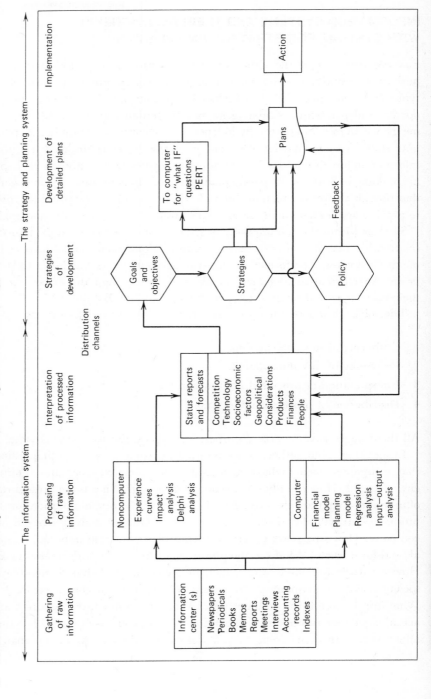

strengths and weaknesses? What happens to our cost structure when demand increases or decreases?

Typical sources include newspapers, periodicals, books, radio and television programs, memos, reports, proceedings of meetings, interviews, accounting records, and indexes. Considerable judgment is required in the selection of relatively sound sources; there is always the possibility of bias. One wouldn't depend on the *Daily Worker* for an accurate picture of labor conditions in a country or the publications of the public relations department of a company for a review of that company's strengths and weaknesses. Never is information more likely to be distorted than when a publisher or sponsor wants to prove something.

After sources have been initially screened and raw information has been gathered, the information itself must be scrutinized. Even the most reliable sources occasionally contain unclear or distorted information. They may lack detailed data or indulge in overstatement. Reporters, columnists, and news commentators must write or say something that will interest the reader or listener and hence may be tempted to create news where there is none.

Once raw information has been sifted, verified, and classified, bits and pieces must be fitted together—much as a jigsaw puzzle is assembled, except that some of the pieces of information are always missing. It is by this process of fitting information together that one can derive a picture of reality. The picture represents the *facts* that are sent to decision makers to assist in their development of objectives and goals.

The role of those who obtain and process information does not end with their presentation and dissemination of the facts to decision makers. Although they are not the ones who make decisions on objectives and goals, they are still accountable for the appropriateness and accuracy of the information they provide. Walter Lippmann has noted with keen perception that information suppliers must be unbiased in providing information to decision makers in the diplomatic service:

> . . . the power of the expert depends upon separating himself from those who make the decisions, upon not caring in his expert self, what decision is made. The man who takes a line and meddles with the decision is soon discounted. There he is, just one more on that side of the question. For when he begins to care too much, he begins to see what he wishes to see and by that fact ceases to see what he is there to see.[1]

He fails to point out, however, that the role of the information supplier is to

[1] Walter Lippmann, *Public Opinion*, The Free Press, New York, 1965, p. 291.

supply timely, useful information to the decision maker, and the information supplier cannot relieve himself of accountability.

In the planning and strategy system in our diagram, observe the feedback loop. From objectives and goals, strategies and policies are formed and plans developed. These detailed plans are then relayed to the information system.

MAJOR PARTS OF AN INFORMATION SYSTEM

The guideline for the design of the system is a thorough understanding of who the key decision makers are and what decisions they must make. These facts determine what raw information will be sought and how and by whom it will be gathered, processed, and distributed.

A system within which these activities can be carried out effectively will require three basic components. We believe that an *information center*—containing published sources of information, abstracts, and reports from internal sources and from various networks for specialized types of external information—constitutes the first essential part of the overall system. *Computers and computer models* are the second. Various *media for information distribution*—including memoranda, newsletters, and face-to-face discussions—constitute the final essential part.

THE INFORMATION CENTER

Companies have not one but many information centers (the accounting department, the patent department, the company library, departmental report files, etc.). In every company, large or small, each employee might be rightfully called an information center. Some companies have tried to coordinate the activities of their many information centers; we suspect that more have tried to reduce the number of centers or to consolidate them into one. The results of the latter efforts are usually disappointing, for like tentacles of a hydra most of the eliminated centers soon reappear.

We seriously doubt the practicality of a single information center that both holds and distributes all information within a company. Such a center could not possibly be current on all the problems of line executives. We do believe, however, in the advantages offered by a principal information center that maintains an index of the various kinds of printed information and their location within the company and that arranges for the distribution of information to those who need it.

A company library that houses a central collection of technical and non-technical materials might possibly serve as a principal information center. For giant corporations with small libraries in divisions located throughout the United States and the world, a center such as we have briefly described could greatly reduce duplication of published materials.

Several practical problems threaten, however, the effectiveness of a principal information center. First some individuals deliberately withhold information so as to eliminate competition in their quest for personal advancement. We are inclined to believe that, despite pressure from above, they would probably not provide much information. Second some information must be classified as confidential, and some managers would seriously question the ability of employees of a principal information center to handle confidential information properly. Finally the information center would most probably be outside the mainstream of activity. The staff would be faced with the difficult problem of determining what kind of information would be most important to decision makers. Later we discuss ways of solving some of these problems.

Published Sources

Publications are the most abundant sources of information and probably most important for current news. They may also be the most costly item on the information budget for many companies, particularly those that have not developed a complete information system.

Substantial savings can be made merely by eliminating duplicate subscriptions to periodicals or services. Single subscriptions can be widely shared in the following manner:

1 All employees are requested to indicate areas of interest, such as international affairs, marketing, finance, purchasing, production, personnel, and so forth.

2 They should then specify the periodicals and services they wish to receive regularly. They should frequently review their request lists, since new publications are constantly being added, and old ones are dropped.

3 Once a week the requested numbers of copies are made of the tables of contents of all periodicals received during the week.

4 These copies are sent to people in accordance with their requests.

5   Each individual indicates on his copies which articles he wishes to review and returns his copies to the information center.

6   The information center reproduces and distributes the articles for those who have requested them.

The process described does make articles available about 2 weeks later than if they were received by direct subscription. A 2-week delay is usually not, however, very important for most people involved. In addition to monetary savings the system offers two other advantages. It saves time by presenting the employee with a single page per magazine rather than the entire publication to be scanned for articles of interest. The system also automatically provides copies for filing of any articles that turn out to be sufficiently interesting.

The process we have just cited for periodicals can also be used for books. Lists of books on specified subjects can be circulated to people who have indicated an interest. When a person circles and initials a title on the list and returns the list to the information center, the book is loaned to him.

Abstracts

Whether companies should prepare abstracts from more extensive printed information is a repeatedly raised question in intelligence work. Many consultants have strongly urged client companies to make abstracts, and several companies have considered and in some cases adopted methods for abstracting. Experience to date suggests that abstracts are perhaps best suited to special purposes and narrow areas of interest, since expert judgment is usually required for the selection of the most important or essential material on a particular subject. A company seeking to prepare abstracts on many different subjects would probably find that, on the one hand, the cost of the required variety of experts would be prohibitive and, on the other hand, abstracts prepared by amateurs would be grossly inept.

After all, abstracting is an art. Even experts are unable at times to meet the needs of all readers. A reader's interest in any subject can be so varied that no one can predict what will be found valuable in a collection of information. A magazine article on Hoechst in Germany, for instance, may mention the name of the individual who has recently been promoted to advertising director of Hoechst's cosmetics business. This information may be the only news of interest to one reader, but it would probably not be considered of sufficient importance to be included in an abstract.

Let us return to the point we casually made about abstracting's being justified when reader interest is specific or narrowly defined. Now available from outside services are abstracts of forecasts of technological developments, market estimates for specific lines of products, and economic forecasts for specific countries. Such abstracts are useful for substantiating or rejecting individual bits and pieces of information that companies have gathered. When the abstract not only provides useful data but also rates the reliability of that information, it contributes a key dimension for decision makers.

Internal Sources

Most companies possess not only a vast reservoir of information but also the potential for gathering it. Relatively few companies have, however, developed systems for effectively using internal sources, Two companies that have developed such systems are DuPont and IBM, perhaps the most successful companies in their industries. Field salespersons are critical to any internal information system. They are in a position to develop and update certain information on the companies upon which they call and to report other information they consider valuable. A well-designed form that indicates clearly what information is wanted can help field salespersons. Moreover, a printed sheet, sometimes called a "watchlist," that sets forth topics on which more information is needed by the company can be a supplementary guide. Salespersons can be motivated to gather information if they are properly supervised and led to understand that their job advancement depends on it. But care must be taken that additional burdens, such as information gathering, do not prevent them from carrying out their primary objective of making sales. One solution would be to reduce their span of control or have a staff person do the paperwork.

In large corporations it is not uncommon for two different groups to conduct research and report on exactly the same subject—sometimes simultaneously, sometimes sequentially—without knowing about each other's efforts. Hence, to be effective, an information system for internal reports must keep people in the organization aware of past, current, and anticipated research.

These requirements are difficult to fulfill. Usually either there is little interest on the part of the group generating reports to notify others about their work in progress, or their research may be confidential. The problem of confidentiality can be alleviated in part by a classification system whereby some reports are available for review only with the approval of a designated individual.

Copies of internal reports should be deposited at some central location, such as an information center, and indexed. The index should be widely distributed so that people in the organization can easily determine what reports have been written in the past on a particular subject.

One novel approach to stimulating interest to others' research might be the establishment of an "information coordinating committee" composed of one person, the one most concerned with information or research, from every major group or division within a company. Each person would be responsible for keeping the others advised on his division's activities and providing the information center with a copy of all internal reports. But such a committee should be voluntary.

Another approach might be to have the information center screen each regular internal communication for references to reports, activities, or facts of interest to anyone not normally receiving that communication. Materials to be screened would include the monthly reports of research and development departments, marketing and marketing research departments, divisions, and so forth.

Networks

Once a system for managing the broad areas of published and internal information has been established, attention can be turned to areas of particular importance to one's industry and company. For specific needs one might consider establishing networks to cover (1) political and economic developments, (2) tariff rates and nontariff barriers, (3) currencies, and (4) studies of the future.

Literature, meetings, and seminars can provide most of the needed information about political and economic developments. As a supplement to these sources a network of on-the-scene observers can often provide interpretations and insights unobtainable through literature. For international companies the network could consist mostly or entirely of regular employees.

A number of research studies conducted by T. J. Allen of the Sloan School on how information flows in a small research laboratory has led to some interesting, even startling conclusions. The research revealed that there were two distinct classes of individuals within the laboratory. First the majority who had few information contacts outside the laboratory. Second the minority of six individuals who had extensive contact with technical people outside the laboratory and were also more exposed to the technical literature. This latter group was called "gatekeepers." Now the gatekeepers did not all tend the same gate. Some relied primarily on the literature, others on oral sources. What is significant is that two of the six gatekeepers were responsible for introducing all four of the "most interesting technical ideas" that had been introduced into the organization during the preceding year.

Some of the major conclusions of the research were that attempts to bring information to a project directly from outside the organization had usually been ineffective. And the best way to keep a project team abreast of outside developments was in understanding and making proper use of existing information systems, particularly the gatekeepers.

Whirlpool Corporation applied several of the concepts gained from Allen's research on the small laboratory in developing the Whirlpool Information Network (WIN). C. L. Tierney, manager of WIN, has described it as a system that transmits and stores documented technical information that has been analyzed or interpreted by Whirlpool employees on specific job assignments.

WIN works like this:

1   A WIN summary, a form that permits about 900 typed or handwritten words of results, observations, conclusions, recommendations, and drawings and sketches, is prepared by an employee when he feels he has technical information of interest to others in the corporation.

2   A hard copy file or a microfiche file of WIN summaries is duplicated and located at each division or subsidiary. The numerical sequencing of this file gives a chronological organization with broad subject categories that permits informal browsing of file data.

3   A computer-generated alert is issued monthly that cites all information entering the system during the month and arranges the citations in a scannable format by subject category.

4   A detailed computer-generated subject and author index to WIN summaries is developed annually with quarterly cumulated supplements.

In critiquing the WIN system, Tierney reached these conclusions:

1   Quality of decisions was improved when the range of relevant data was increased.

2   New concepts and techniques submitted by Whirlpool employees were more readily accepted than those submitted from outside sources.

3   Technical information tended to flow vertically rather than horizontally in the organization.

4   Oral channels (e.g., meetings, telephone conversations) were considered faster and more responsive than written channels.

5   Documented information structured by media or source rather than subject was a major barrier to effective communication of documented technical information.

Although, as reflected in the WIN illustration, employee networks are most effective, for emerging international companies, which do not yet have a worldwide organization, employees' observations must be augmented by those of outsiders such as bankers, government officials, business acquaintances, and hired intelligence services.

Since the reporting in newspapers and magazines is often inaccurate, networks such as we have been describing offer an obvious advantage. For the networks to be successful, however, the observers must be deeply interested in their work and willing to devote time and much effort to it. They must also be kept informed about what is of primary interest to executives. (A periodically updated watchlist, mentioned earlier, can help to alert the observer, and he in turn can provide some of the information from which the watchlist is developed.) Finally observers should be given copies of communications in which *their* inputs, as well as the inputs of other observers, have been used. One possibility is to send out a brief listing each month of those pieces of information that appear to be the most significant to a company's operations, for these listings help to keep observers vigilant.

For the development of international strategies and the conduct of business overseas, information on *tariff rates* and *nontariff barriers* is needed. There are, of course, problems and complications. Different countries use different standards and systems for classifying products, and changes in rates and the kind and number of regulations are common.

There are two basic types of tariff information systems—centralized and decentralized. Of the two, the decentralized system, which uses a tariff network, is perhaps the best for a worldwide organization, as a brief case history will illustrate:

One multinational company first acquired tariff information through a centralized system. Inquiries for tariff rates were channeled into one office, where extensive records were maintained on tariff rates and nontariff barriers throughout the world and on historical classifications of products in the various countries of the world. The staff of this office constantly faced three types of problems. They had to:

1   Keep up with changes in tariff rates.
2   Keep up with changes in classification of present products by tariff boards of foreign governments.
3   Obtain information on how new products might be classified.

The decentralized system that ultimately evolved consisted of a tariff coordinator in each major area of the world. When the central office received an inquiry for a foreign tariff rate, the staff sent a cable to the appropriate tariff coordinator for an answer. Inquiries for U.S. tariffs were sent to the company's Washington, D.C., office. This decentralized system eliminated elaborate record keeping and yet was accurate and up to date.

The fluctuation of the dollar in recent years, accompanied by the worldwide instability of other currencies, has placed greater importance on systems that maintain up-to-date information about the prospects for further devaluations and revaluations. Decisions on hedging, transfers of funds, debt structure, pricing, debt repayment, and inventory position should be based on this information. Hence, a network of currency experts is needed. They must answer three major questions: Is a currency change in prospect? When will it occur? What will be the direction and percentage of change?

Because knowledge of currency is so specialized, currency networks should probably be composed of bankers and other outsiders rather than members of one's own company. Even the executives of a company that does employ a currency expert would be wise to compare his opinions with those of a small network of outside experts—such as bankers, financial consultants, currency experts in government, and currency specialists in other companies—to obtain a consensus.

So much is written about what is likely to happen in the future that one should try to find individuals or groups who have already surveyed the field, or pieces of it, and screened out the bad from the good. Some of the groups who provide this service for a fee were mentioned in Chapter 2. An internal group can also, however, be useful; its members have the advantage of knowing the company and the events that will have a substantial impact on the company.

One company formed a group that consisted of about 20 members divided into four sections—technological, socioeconomic, business, and international—with a chairman heading each section. The individuals who made up this group were interested in the subject because they believed they would acquire information that would be useful in their jobs. Among the members were the corporate planning director, international planning director, research director, marketing managers, patent department director, business development managers, and management information service managers. Two members were outsiders, included because of their knowledge and experience in futuristic studies.

Monthly dinner meetings were held. The four section chairmen usually took turns as discussion leaders, but often an outside expert in a particular field was invited to be the discussion leader. Occasionally, the group presented its major conclusions in a special program before a large group of company executives and employees.

COMPUTERS AND COMPUTER MODELS

Computers and computer models are treated jointly as the second part of an information system because they are much like Siamese twins. Whenever a computer is programmed to do certain tasks, some kind of computer model— mathematical equations that represent a description of the tasks and constraints—must be developed.

For companies with large numbers of products and markets, computers and computer models offer great time savings and a wide range of capabilities.

Within the information center, computers can:

● Provide convenient storage for data used in planning.
● Facilitate the updating of data.
● Retrieve data with lightning speed.

They also enable processers within the information center, and planners, who are the end users of information, to:

● Emphasize the process of decision making rather than the decision itself.
● Test the reasonableness of many sets of assumptions and select the most plausible.
● Consolidate area forecasts from the field into a worldwide plan.
● Foresee the effects of alternative strategies and compare these effects to the relevant company goals and objectives.

● Assess sensitivity and risk by posing "what if?" questions (what would be the effect on the company if we have overestimated the rate of growth of a given business by x%? What if a particular project should fail?).

Let us look at how one company used its computer to reduce busywork drastically.

The company sold 100 product lines in six major areas of the world. Planners developing strategic and operating plans decided that they needed the following information:

● A simplified income statement by geographic area.
● A balance sheet for foreign subsidiaries.
● Capital expenditure forecasts for the current year and for the next 3 years by geographic area, broken down into three levels of certainty:
  ● Approved
  ● Planned but not yet approved
  ● Possible.

Forecasting beyond 3 years was considered too inaccurate for decision making. Long-term income projections exhibited a "hockey stick effect," the curves rising gradually for the first 3 years, like the handle!

Company planners felt that they needed at least some rough quantitative guidelines extending beyond 3 years. The business groups were therefore asked for 5- and 10-year projections of sales. Using these sales figures and the computer, the central planning group could then calculate all or any part of the income statement or balance sheet and estimate capital requirements on the basis of historical ratios for profit margins, turnover ratios, sales-to-inventory ratios, and so forth. Historical ratios were modified whenever the planners were contemplating strategies that would create basic changes in the character of the company's business. But the central planning group always compared their thoughts with those of the business group involved before making any changes.

Company planners in time learned to work effectively with the computer. For instance, they would sometimes plug in a new income figure and then calculate what profit margins and turnover ratios would be required for achievement of such an income. They would then consider the kinds of changes that would have to be made in strategies for these profit margins and turnover ratios to be realized.

The historical data in the computer program initially covered only 2 years but over time were supplemented until they spanned 5 years.

When the system had been fully programmed and all the historical data inserted, copies of the program and data were sent to all world areas. Each area then used the program to store its own forecast figures, as well as to help in the development of its own forecasts. The business and area directors began to realize, as the planners had before them, that the system was a time-saver and a powerful forecasting tool. For example. the directors might estimate that over the next three years sales would increase at a given rate (usually at a modified historical rate) and that profit margins, turnover ratios, inventory ratios, and days outstanding for accounts receivable would stay at about the levels of the past two years. Within minutes the computer could provide a printout of a projected income statement and investment figures for the business.

Company planners also used the computer to weigh financial needs against financial resources and thereby to develop corporate financial plans for the next three years. Cash flow was predicted from projections for new fixed capital requirements, and amounts of additional working capital needed were calculated from balance-sheet projections. These corporate plans were broken down into complete schedules for the acquisition of new long- and short-term funds required for each entity and area. Before long, forecasts of currency devaluations and revaluations were being programmed into the computer, and strategies on hedging against currency valuation losses were modified or changed.

The entire software program just discussed was developed in only nine months and cost about $8,000.

DISTRIBUTION MEDIA

Let us examine the final component of an information system—the part that is designed to ensure that the right people get the right information.

In a small company one person with a keen knowledge of employees' current interests and an excellent memory will serve. In a large company, where there are frequent changes in personnel and complex interrelationships of people, an administrator and staff are required. They can distribute information in several ways.

The first of these and perhaps the most common is the rifle approach.

Certain people receive memoranda containing information they need to know. At first glance the rifle approach seems refreshingly simple, but it suffers from the same fundamental problem as all other approaches—the sender must somehow learn who should receive what information.

Knowing a person's job title is not enough. Some companies have developed systems for keeping track of people and their interests. Computerized payroll systems often provide completely current information on job titles, job classifications, and physical locations. Some companies have developed systems to locate employees for filling job openings within the company by building up and maintaining information on individuals' skills, educational background, and experience in addition to present responsibilities. We believe that this is a reasonably good system for identifying peoples' interests, but it can be quite costly to maintain.

Whoever is to provide people with up-to-date information must know at all times where to locate them. Frequent organization changes complicate matters.

Systems which quickly regenerate organization charts every time that there are reassignments of personnel are available and can be very helpful. Few companies have such systems. More typical is a two-to-three month lag between the announcement of organizational changes and the issuance of new organization charts. A cheap and effective solution to problems created by the lag is for a secretary to write in the changes on old charts until the new ones are issued.

Sometimes, rather than search for people who should receive information, it is better to decide what job requires what kind of information. One technique is illustrated by the matrix in Exhibit 3.2. Major segments of the company organization are shown on the horizontal axis, and the urgency of each segment's "need to know" each type of information is indicated in the boxes.

A second approach for distributing information, especially abstracts from published information, is the use of newsletters. They are useful when many people in an organization need special kinds of information— for example, when there is a major reorganization within the company, and product divisions that formerly operated only domestically are suddenly given worldwide responsibility. Newsletters are also useful when an information staff group seeks to gain recognition. But newsletters by their nature are short lived or at least should be; otherwise, they quickly degenerate into just more pieces of paper duplicating much of what the receiver already knows or covering such a broad range of interests that he is interested in only a small fraction of the

Exhibit 3.2   Information Distribution Matrix, Showing Urgency of Need to Know

Legend: A = Urgent; a = Routine

Column groups and headings:

- **Top Management:** Board of Directors; Planning Committee; Operating Committee; Corporate Budget & Control; General Mgr.; Staff Dept.; Lower Echelon
- **International:** Area Directors; Area Directors' Staff; Lower Echelon
- **Areas:** Presidents; General Managers; Product Managers; Planning & Business Devel.
- **Operating Companies:** Public Relations; Personnel; Law; Patent; Engineering; Purchasing; Distribution; Systems; Central Research; Finance; Adv. & Mktg. Devel.

Row labels (Kinds of Information):

- **Financial**
  - Corporate and company
  - Total international
  - Area
  - Company by area
  - Product group by area
  - Entities
- **Plans/goals/guidelines**
  - Corporate
  - Company
  - Total
  - Product group
  - International
  - Total
  - Area
  - Feedback
- **Policy**
  - Corporate
  - Company
  - International
- **Organization (Structure and job functions)**
  - Corporate
  - Company
  - International
  - Staff depts.
- **Other**
  - New product/process
  - New services
  - Business environment
  - Political/economic
  - Long-term environment and technical forecasts

contents. We believe that, when newsletters have been used by a company for 3 years, they should be thoroughly reevaluated.

Most pertinent and valuable are communications on key issues or events (the resumption of trade with China, for example, or the entry of the United Kingdom into the European Economic Community). One should not assume that factual information alone will stimulate action. Interpretation is also called for. What new threats or opportunities are associated with the event? What are the implications for company strategies?

A centralized "intelligence" group is frequently not sufficiently broad in its exposure and experience to decide whether information is important. Hence, it is often worthwhile to solicit the opinions of key people in an organization about what they think is important. The central intelligence group might distribute a watchlist and ask recipients to suggest revisions and supply information on any of the items listed.

Two areas of information and communications that are particularly important to the outlying areas of a world organization are:

● New product developments within the company.
● Changes in management thinking, strategy, mood, or style.

To keep people in the field informed of new developments, there is no substitution for bringing them into headquarters at least once a year to have face-to-face discussions with the principals doing work in new areas that have reached or are approaching commercialization. In between visits, however, much can happen to change the picture, and it is important that field personnel receive the most up-to-date information so that they will recognize new opportunities or, conversely, refrain from spending time on developments that have had setbacks in timing or feasibility. A central intelligence group can fill this need by keeping a list of new developments and the people responsible for them, holding periodic consultations with these individuals, and communicating significant changes to the field.

Changes in top executive thinking and policy are tremendously important but at times are very difficult to identify and therefore to communicate. Managers in the field can easily operate under false assumptions unless kept aware of change. Few management groups have a formal approach to communicating such matters except for obvious and well-publicized changes. For subtle changes, which some managers do not see, we know of no easy, automatic solution. The best system is perhaps a very informal one, in which heads of operating units (recognizing the importance of communications as a major part of their job) hold frequent, informal, face-to-face meetings with the principal management teams in each area to advise them of the "climate at the summit."

CHALLENGES INHERENT IN INFORMATION SYSTEMS

Formidable challenges face those who set up and manage information systems. These challenges are posed by the nature of information itself and by the potential weaknesses in any information system.

Information Explosion

Although the amount of printed material in existence has been increasing ever since Johann Gutenberg invented the printing press about 1456, volume has skyrocketed in recent years. More books have been printed in the past 20 years than were printed during the four centuries following Gutenberg's invention. The mountain of information contained in books, newspapers, magazines, journals, and so forth, published in the past few months is so large that we shudder to think of the difficult task of those who prepare indexes of this information. Certainly no person or staff is capable of reading all the material pertinent to business operations. Moreover, some type of screening is needed for the elimination of information that is redundant, out of date, or in error.

Interdependence of Information

Because information on one element in the external environment can frequently provide insights into future conditions in another, companies search for ways of measuring the degree of interdependence. In the previous chapter we discussed two of the best methodologies now used— cross-impact analysis and input-output analysis. While both may help executives to discover patterns and formulate hypotheses, they are not complete; they still need to be refined and improved.

Computer Experts versus Managers

While the computer offers many valuable capabilities, its use adds new human problems and challenges. Top executives may not be acquainted with computers, computer languages, new mathematics, or operations research.

On the other hand, computer specialists and operations researchers are frequently too young to have the experience to understand business thoroughly. Whereas top executives are critical of possible decreasing marginal returns from extensive use of computers, computer specialists and operations researchers strive for thoroughness in their analyses. Top executives are often unable to define their problems precisely. Computer specialists and operations researchers tend to look at these problems as only symptoms of a larger problem; consequently, they may do more work than necessary.

Some computer devotees have gone so far as to assert that the extinction of executives, who rely principally on experience and intuition, is near at hand. More often than not these executives have shown a bronco-like ability to unseat their critics. The result of this disparity of viewpoints is, of course, that in many companies computer simulations or synthetic experiments that could be of value to top executives are never used. The situation is not, however, hopeless. The trend in recent years has been for top executives to become better acquainted with the efficient use of computers and quantitative methods. Still, those who set up and manage information systems face many difficulties in attempting to bring computer specialists and top executives to a common view.

Cost of Computer Operations

Today most medium-sized and large companies use computers. The initial cost of an IBM computer can range from $65,000 to more than $500,000. Additional peripheral equipment is required to make the computer system operational. Programming and training costs are incurred. In brief, computer operations are costly. Manual information systems may, however, be even more costly and, according to computer advocates, are less accurate, less nearly complete, and less flexible. The manager's task is, we believe, to obtain maximum value in information for the cost incurred—in brief, to approach the optimal point on the information cost-value curve.

IMPORTANCE OF JUDGMENT

Despite the advances that have occurred in recent years in computer technology, new mathematics, the behaviorial sciences, and information theory, no source or technique yields perfect information. The problem described by Karl von Clausewitz 150 years ago in *On War* still persists:

A great part of the information obtained in war is contradictory, a still greater part is false, and by far the greatest part is of a doubtful character. What is required of an officer is a certain power of discrimination, which only knowledge of men and things and good judgment can give. The law of probability must be his guide.[2]

Some modification is needed, of course, to fit von Clausewitz's statement to the internal and external environment of business. For example, it is probably but not conclusively true that information on the external environment of business is easier to obtain and generally more reliable than information on the deployment of an enemy's armed forces during war. It is broadly true that the information available on the external environment today, especially on the United States, is of reasonably good quality for the development of forecasts. But good judgment remains indispensable.

When World War ll was drawing to a close, many economists and statisticians predicted that the war's end would throw 10 million or more workers out of jobs. This dire forecast was supported by an impressive array of statistical data. Bernard Baruch and John M. Hancock, however, saw no large-scale unemployment. They foresaw at least 5 to 7 years of uninterrupted prosperity, no matter what anyone did. They made no additional statistical studies of purchasing power or "consumer attitudes" or any of the other indices of the future. Their judgment was based on the fact that war would leave large parts of the world in ruins and that "men and women, people and governments would beg, borrow, and if necessary steal," but they would find a way to restore their homes and meet the needs that had gone unsatisfied during the war.[3] Baruch and Hancock merely searched through the mass of existing information and selected the significant facts.

SHORT-CIRCUITING INFORMATION SYSTEMS

Sometimes the executive's judgment leads him to short-circuit his information system or bypass it altogether. Even in the best information systems sooner or later false information will appear and bump up against solid realities. Reports from the field—other than routine or statistical accounting reports, which can quickly be verfied—provide a subjective picture of the exter-

[2] Karl von Clauswitz, *On War,* edited by Anatol Rapoport, Penguin Books, Ltd., Harmondsworth, England, 1968, p. 162.
[3] Bernard M. Baruch, *My Own Story,* Henry Holt & Company, New York, 1957, p. 321.

nal environment. And many individuals in corporate headquarters are busily engaged in putting forward their "case," often with little regard for accuracy or fairness.

Wise executives and administrators recognize these human traits and seek ways to compensate for them.

From time to time the executive may personally evaluate key elements in the external environment. Alternatively he may use the observations of a trusted member of his staff or turn to a disinterested consultant.

When William S. Seawell became the chairman and chief executive officer (CEO) of Pan American World Airlines, executives could no longer remain in New York City and depend mainly on the company's formal information system in making decisions. All officers were required to make extensive inspection trips to share the perspective and experiences of people in the field. For many it was a new experience, "to discover there is a real airline out there," as one executive put it.[4]

Henry Kissinger sent his White House staff assistant, General Alexander Haig, to South Vietnam every 6 months between 1970 and 1972 to assess conditions there for President Nixon, who was keenly aware of the discrepancies between the reports of the joint chiefs of staff and the actual military situation in South Vietnam during the Johnson administration.

Even when executives and trusted staff members make visits to the field, objectivity is not easily attained. People in the field always seem ready to flatter an ego or conceal ugly facts. Consultants and professors can be helpful to management, since they are outside the superior-subordinate relationship. Their weakness, on the other hand, is often a lack of knowledge and experience about the particular company and industry.

We cannot leave the topic of short-circuiting information systems without mentioning industrial espionage. Although largely confined to industries characterized by intense competitive pressures, short product life, and high research and development (R & D) costs (e.g., the drug, automobile, toy, fashion, and chemical industries), industrial intelligence gathering has expanded to such an extent that it is currently estimated to cost the nation between $1 billion and $5 billion.[5] We are concerned, not about normal intelligence work such as the gathering of trade statistics and so forth, but about that part consisting of outright thefts of trade secrets, the use of inside spies and electronic or photographic equipment. Although Sun Tzu, the

---

[4] "Pan Am Fights to Revive Its Credibility," *Business Week,* February 3, 1973, p. 56.
[5] Frederick Harmon, "Business Spies are Still Busy," *International Management,* June 1969, p. 58.

great Chinese military strategist, felt that the best way to obtain information was through spies, we believe that excellent information can be obtained inductively, deductively, and from experience without recourse to illegal acts. In the long run and often in the short run, information strategies calling for illegal acts are extremely poor ones used by the cunning rather than the wise.

INFORMATION'S FUTURE IN CORPORATE ORGANIZATION

When its importance is more fully and widely understood, we believe that information handling will be treated more as a centrally coordinated function, headed perhaps by a vice president of information. He will be in charge of a system for collecting, interpreting, and disseminating information on anticipated external events, as well as internal information on costs and results of operations to assist line executives in making better decisions. A system much like we have discussed in this chapter headed by a vice president of information could limit the possibilities of outside events' taking management by surprise and could enhance internal control. In brief this route with alternatives previously suggested would represent one plausible information strategy.

CHAPTER 4

STRATEGIES AND THE HUMAN ELEMENT

Strategies and the human element are interwoven, for no strategy can be successful without the deep involvement of people. Indeed, some writers in management believe there are only two principal functions of management: planning goals and strategies and motivating others to assist in developing and implementing them. We have already discussed the importance of planning goals in Chapter 1, and planning strategies, and in some instances implementing them, has been and will continue to be discussed throughout this book, We focus our attention now on why people in an organization are not motivated to assist in developing strategies.

It is curious and significant that, whereas most top executives say that motivating line and staff to develop strategic plans is vitally important, line and staff frequently lack motivation. We believe there are four basic reasons for this inertia:

1   The chief executive officer's (CEO) lack of commitment.
2   Ineptness in planning.
3   Vagueness of roles.
4   Human weaknesses.

THE CHIEF EXECUTIVE OFFICER'S LACK OF COMMITMENT

Almost 200 years ago Warren Hastings, then the British Governor-General of India, considered commitment of superiors the first principle of all good government. In business today it would be mere self-deception to pretend that successful strategy development can be accomplished without top management's commitment. Line and staff executives look to top management, especially the CEO, for managerial leadership. When the CEO enthusiastically backs strategy development, they will usually do the same. When the CEO is not committed to strategy development, they will focus their attention on other activities that seem to count.

The words of CEOs are never enough. What they say merely reflects their political side; what they do reflects their executive side. How then does one know if CEOs are committed? Here are some questions about CEOs that will help:

1   Do CEOs spend little of their own time on strategic planning?
2   Do they cancel strategic planning meetings or reports because "something more important came up?"
3   Do they have their directors or vice presidents of corporate planning report to someone other than themselves?
4   Do they fail to relate the individual goals and plans of their managers to the goals and plans in the corporate long-range plan?
5   Do they have strategic planning conducted once a year with little or no activity or followup during other times?

Yes answers to all these questions should make it obvious that the CEO looks upon strategic planning as a minor part of the job.

No CEO can totally ignore the vast amount of literature and the numerous lectures, seminars, and college courses on strategic planning. Strategic planning is in vogue; it is the thing to do. Typically a CEO decides that there had better be strategic planning in the company. Then the CEO sets up a planning department and hires or appoints someone to head it, looking upon this department as an appendage that will periodically present interesting ideas upon which occasionally the CEO will be asked to make some decisions.

What the CEO frequently fails to consider is that a shift from intuitive decisions to systematic, quantitative ones requires a traumatic change in behavior, like "giving up smoking, cutting down on drinking, and giving up your mistress to boot."

What can be done then when the CEO is totally disinterested? There are only a few options. Those interested in strategic planning could try to have the CEO replaced, but such actions border on the frivolous and are generally not recommended.

Replacing a CEO is exceedingly difficult; odds of success are low. In most companies the board of directors must take action with the impetus coming from the outside board members. Such action does not usually occur unless the company has been doing poorly for several years. Moreover, a wise CEO will make it a point to enlist all the key board members.

Sometimes a corporate planning director or vice president in whom the CEO has much confidence can help by exposing the CEO to advocates of strategic planning who are knowledgeable and highly respected in the business community. This executive can encourage the CEO to hold long-range strategic planning meetings that can be interesting and meaningful—once every month or two.

Sometimes a consultant can be helpful. This must be an individual with stature who can be kept on a retainer fee for years and who must know the company well.

If all attempts to raise the CEO's interests have failed repeatedly, strategic planning still does not stop completely. To some extent it continues informally but inefficiently. For the most part those who are advocates of strategic planning will have to bide their time until the CEO leaves. This approach is, of course, apathetically passive but perhaps the only practical solution.

INEPTNESS IN PLANNING

Even if CEOs are committed to strategic planning, they must understand their role thoroughly. Otherwise their ineptness can result in frustration and inertia at lower organizational levels. The kinds of mistakes CEOs and their staffs most frequently make are:

- Failure to set corporate goals.
- Failure to set realistic goals.
- Failure to set the right time horizons for planning.
- Failure to provide policies or guidelines.
- Failure to schedule strategic planning at the right time.
- Failure to follow up.

● Failure to see the major issues.
● Failure to see that strategic planning is an intergrated process.

Failure to Set Corporate Goals

Setting corporate goals must be the first step in any strategic planning process. For it is self-evident that no strategic planners can determine how to get somewhere until they know where they want to go. Yet it is no exaggeration that many CEOs fail to set corporate goals, or more frequently state them so poorly that they are almost valueless. The difficulty of setting corporate goals that provide real direction without excessive detail is the rock on which the whole process founders. Assiduous skill and hard work are required. Corporate goals cannot be prepared adequately, as some CEOs think, in a morning or afternoon. Two full-day meetings a week of the CEO and the immediate staff over several weeks seems more realistic.

Failure to Set Realistic Goals

The failure of managers to set realistic goals is widespread. Sometimes goals are set too low, but typically they are set too high. In either case the motivation of those responsible for developing strategies dips quickly. When financial or activity goals are set too high, extreme frustration also occurs and action plans for accomplishing goals become meaningless.

Setting goals that are too high or too low is the result of human limitations and seldom intentional. (There is one principal exception: when CEOs set goals extremely high to stimulate maximum effort from all in their organization.) Let us look at some human limitations.

Most executives will agree that financial goals for the next year— usually referred to as "the budget"—are usually quite accurate unless unforeseen major economic changes take place during the budget year. Obviously the unforeseen changes, for example, the oil crisis in 1974, are the result of human limitations, the inability to grasp all events that can lead to major economic changes.

Many managers feel that, because long-term forecasts are less accurate than short-term forecasts, plans based upon the former are valueless. This viewpoint is in error for these reasons:

1   Short-term forecasts, such as the budget, in periods of rapid economic change are often no more accurate than long-range forecasts.

2   All forecasts, short and long term, are inaccurate to some degree. Long-term forecasts may be crude if they provide order of magnitude figures in the right direction. All forecasts should be looked at as fluid and subject to reevaluation when it becomes clear that they will err considerably.

3   All decisions, plans and actions taken by a corporation are based, consciously or unconsciously, upon the future. And who can say with certainty what the future will bring? An educated guess, a systematic approach is unquestionably better than ignoring the future entirely.

Planning activity programs for accomplishing goals are equally as difficult as making accurate long-term forecasts. Usually more is scheduled than can possibly be accomplished. And when the divergence is too great, motivation and morale decline precipitously.

To sum up, allowing for unexpected events is probably the important factor in realistic scheduling of activity goals. The tendency is to assume that unexpected events will not occur, but they almost always do. When achievement is tied into salary and bonus compensation programs, morale is seriously affected. The best approach to take is to allow deviations from goals when the unexpected, the unforeseen occurs.

Failure to Set the Right Time Horizons for Planning

"Fifteen years is so far out that it staggers my mind. It has no meaning for me. There is nothing that I shall or can start today that will take that long to accomplish. Either it will have been accomplished long before 15 years is up, or it shall have fallen by the wayside and been dumped. I won't be here anyway 15 years from now," said one manager whose corporate planning group decided that long-range plans would be extended to 15 years.

How far in the future to project long-range strategic plans cannot be determined with absolute certainty. It will vary for each industry and company. The answer depends primarily, therefore, on how far in the future line managers can see the effects of today's decisions. For instance, in high-technology industries 10 years may elapse from the time a new plant is proposed until it is operational. For the retail business, results of many decisions are fully realized within a year or less.

From our experience we think that time horizons for planning should not exceed 10 years and for many businesses should range from 4 to 7 years.

Failure to Provide Policies or Guidelines

"Sorry, but that is not the kind of business that we want to be in," was the final remark made by one CEO in response to a proposal to enter into a new line of products by a development group in the company.

The proposed new line was put forward for exploration in the long-range plan and closely related to other lines. Economic analyses indicated a high return on investment. Members of the development group felt that the chances for approval were excellent. After the proposal was rejected, the development group became apathetic. They felt that hundreds of man-hours of work had been wasted. Why hadn't they been informed at the outset of what kinds of business the company should be in? Why weren't guidelines or policies provided? The CEO failed to see that policies and guidelines were necessary to give direction to the development group and that policies and guidelines limit choice and thus prevent excessive muddling about.

Failure to Schedule Strategic Planning at the Right Time

A fairly large proportion of CEOs fail to see the importance of scheduling strategic planning at the right time.

One example will show the results of this mistake. Consider product managers who have just obtained approval for the next year's sales and expense budget. They probably started working on them 6 months earlier. During the month prior to approval, figures had to be changed, and meetings and presentations on the matter probably took 50% of their time. They are now anxious to give full attention to supervising the operation. At this time they should not be required to prepare updated formal long-range plans. They are not psychologically or even physically ready. Consequently CEOs should select a period when there is a seasonal lull, or when the product managers will be more relaxed to think about the past year and the future.

Failure to Follow Up

The general manager of Division A has a deadline date of July 1 to submit his written long-range strategies covering the next 8 years backed up by specific plans. He and the staff have been working on this plan since April 1. The final draft of the report was preceded by five earlier drafts, six full staff meetings, and numerous other meetings and consultations with individual product managers.

The general manager meets the deadline date and feels he has done a good job. Days, weeks, months go by. He receives no comments, no questions, no recommendations, no criticisms. He hears nothing. He senses that the CEO doesn't place much importance on these documents, or there would have been *some* reaction. He has learned a lesson. The next long-range strategies will get a perfunctory treatment.

This is, of course, a hypothetical example, but it is based on real situations. It makes vividly clear this point: if the CEO does not follow up on strategic planning, subordinates will not take the procedure seriously.

Failure to See the Major Issues

Most long-range strategic plans are too long and cover too much. Thus, at the outset, the top-management group is encouraged to scan rather than read them. Whether they scan or read them, one thing is certain. In most instances they will have a hard time finding the major issues, and the CEO is partly to blame. The CEO or the corporate planning staff must point out what is important, for example, major issues and actions to be taken. Furthermore they must *tell* those managers, who contribute to the long-range strategic plans, to be brief, to present in a few pages the situations, the strategy recommendations, and the decisions required in order to proceed. Supporting and background information can be shown in an appendix.

Failure to See That Strategic Planning Is an Integrated Process

Often CEOs fail to relate organizational plans, financial plans, personnel plans, social-responsibility plans, management by objectives, or management by results to the strategic planning process. We may ascribe this failure to their inability to see that strategic planning is highly integrative.

Managers feel it is unnecessarily time consuming because they do not understand that what they do today is directly related to the corporation's, division's, or department's strategic plan. Consequently, few companies have an integrated concept of the strategic planning process. Most corporate planning staffs are still involved with the narrow concept of once-a-year putting together a long-range plan dealing only with strategies and plans of product lines. The other facets of strategic planning—financial planning, organizational planning, and so forth—are carried out in other, separate groups and are usually not recognized as being a part of the same system.

VAGUENESS OF ROLES

In many corporations today too many people have only a vague notion of their role in the strategic planning process. It wasn't always that way. Before the establishment of a corporate long-range planning department the chief financial officer (CFO) typically played the major role in this planning. After a corporate department is established, his role becomes unclear. He may even feel that his authority is threatened.

Concurrent with the development of long-range planning departments has been the rise in importance in many corporations of management science or operations research departments. If a corporation has one of these departments, its head usually feels an obligation to play an important role in long-range planning but also looks at the planning department as a threat. After all, the head is a systems person who has powerful mathematical tools and the computer available. Still, he is never certain how important his role should be. His function is a new one in most organizations, and it frequently lacks the solid support given by top management to the traditional functions of business.

Let us then sum up the problem. The CFO and the head of management science or operations research feel they have important roles to play in long-range planning. These roles become vague, even threatened when a corporate long-range planning department is formed.

The result of this vagueness of roles and loss of authority is frequently internal conflicts, especially when the CFO or the head of management science or operations research attempts to usurp the major roles in long-range planning. And conflicts of this kind strangle the proper development of long-range plans.

Courses of action can be taken to prevent conflict. In some companies the CFO leaves this job to become the head of corporate planning. We question this approach for several reasons. First the CFO is frequently overly concerned with numbers. Second the seeds of conflict are still present. Finally the uncertainty of the relationship with management science or operations research still exists.

We believe a wiser solution is to make the CFO and the head of management science or operations research an integral part of the process; make them heavily accountable along with the corporate planning officer for long-range plans so that they will be committed to getting the best results. The head of corporate planning must assume the leadership role but must draw heavily on the efforts of the other two. To accomplish this task, the head of corporate planning must have certain qualifications that we shall cover in Chapter 10.

One more point remains to be made about vagueness of roles. The role of the corporate planning staffs is not to do the planning but to assist the line managers in planning. Only line managers have the necessary understanding and experience to plan for their corporations, product groups, divisions, or departments. Assuredly staff planners can provide expertise, techniques, schedules, formats, and so forth, but their role is only to assist the line. We shall discuss this important role in more detail in Chapter 10.

HUMAN WEAKNESSES

Certain human weaknesses stagnate the effective development of strategic planning. These include the following:

- Difficulty in thinking creatively and conceptually.
- Difficulty in thinking about and reacting to unpleasant events and ideas.
- Difficulty in broadening a point of view.
- Difficulty in overcoming personal interests.

Difficulty in Thinking Creatively and Conceptually

One weakness is that most people resist taking the initiative in thinking creatively and conceptually. Harold J. Leavitt, professor of organizational behavior and psychology at the Stanford Business School, calls this weakness the tendency of business managers to "respond to the programmed tasks facing them before responding to the unprogrammed ones."

With programmed tasks the individual simply needs to follow instructions. Most people prefer to perform these tasks rather than unprogrammed tasks, which require them to think and decide on how they should best spend their time. Strategic planning requires creative, conceptual thinking of the first order. It is the epitome of a highly complex unprogrammed task.

Difficulty in Thinking about and Reacting to Unpleasant Events and Ideas

Not only are unprogrammed tasks difficult, but so also are thinking about and reacting to unpleasant events and ideas. The possibility of an atomic attack upon the United States is real, but most people tend to block it out of their mind. Large segments of the population gave ample warning that they were opposed to industrial pollution. Yet few companies reacted soon enough to correct the problem and ward off stifling laws and regulations. The present shortage of liquid hydrocarbons was forecasted years ago. Yet most companies using liquid hydrocarbons made no effort to guarantee themselves sources of supply.

There are numerous other examples: the growing shortage of raw materials, more stringent regulation of multinational corporations, the growing gap between the rich and the poor, the menace of galloping inflation. For most businessmen all of these are unpleasant events. Yet, pleasant or unpleasant, these events must be considered in developing corporate strategies.

Difficulty in Broadening a Point of View

Most managers have a hard time broadening their point of view beyond the day-to-day problems of their business. To look at the problems of the economy, of society, or even of their industry is usually a detraction from their primary functions. Moreover, they do not like taking the broad view.

Such attitudes lead many managers and their businesses into trouble. Economic, social, and political changes affect businesses, and competent managers anticipate change and make corrections for it. The few companies, like Dow Chemical, that anticipated the higher interest rates of the seventies and the shortage of liquid hydrocarbons and took appropriate action have improved competitive position and performance.

Difficulty in Overcoming Personal Interests

In most companies, if managers' sales are 10% over forecast, they are praised. If sales are 10% under, they are reprimanded. If sales are on target, they receive no comment. The ambitious manager has a strong motivation to project sales results as low as will be allowed by superiors. When short-term forecasts are tied into an incentive compensation system, the bias toward low-side projections is even greater.

Short-term forecasts, such as for the first few years of a long-range strategic plan, are involved in this behavioral phenomenon of projecting on the low side. In the longer range projections the manager is motivated to produce forecasts that are overoptimistic. It is in one's self-interest to make it appear that one is a dynamic individual, full of enthusiasm, charged with the ambition to do the impossible in putting the business for which one is responsible on a new plateau of growth and profitability.

Managers are gambling that their projections will not be checked, and they are usually right.

Donald H. Woods saw the conflict of personal interest and reliable forecasting. He wrote: "Control systems are for the purpose of influencing managerial behavior whereas the purpose of projecting the future is to provide objective information based upon best judgments for decision-making."

We think top management has two choices for handling this conflict. They can decide which result is most important and give it emphasis, or they can maintain two sets of figures—one for influencing behavior and one for decision making.

In this brief chapter we have tried to make one major point—line and staff frequently lack motivation to develop strategies and there are four basic reasons for this inertia. Top executives, especially the CEO, can motivate line and staff to develop effective strategic plans by understanding and overcoming these four basic causes of inertia. And when inertia cannot be overcome, attempts should be made to limit the effects.

CHAPTER 5

PRODUCT STRATEGIES

What flour and eggs are to bakery products, what hydrocarbons are to petro-chemicals, so product strategies are to total corporate strategies. For these are the building blocks on which total corporate strategies are based. Until the former are defined, one cannot talk sensibly about the latter.

Take one simple test. Try to prepare a total corporate strategy without having some idea of a company's future sales of major products or services and the impact of these sales on needs for new plant and equipment, working capital, research and development (R&D), new marketing approaches, and human resources. It can't be done. Corporate strategies are not, however, merely a total of individual product strategies. When product strategies are first submitted to top management for approval, they may or may not be correlated with corporate goals. If not, a "planning gap" exists and some adjustment must be made to either the corporate goals or the product strat-egies.

Product strategies must apply to a specific profit center. A profit center may consist of a single product like an electric drill, but usually it comprises a line of products like a complete set of power tools.

One person must be accountable for the planning of the product line and for its performance and may have the title of president, vice president, gener-al manager, project manager, and so forth. We shall refer to him or her as the product administrator.

We observed in Chapter 3 that reliable and timely information is crucially needed before strategies can be developed. Product strategies are no exception. The product administrator must gather oral and written information from line and staff people in sales, market research, production, engineering, research and development, finance, corporate planning, and when applicable, the international division before he or she can prepare a product strategy.

Information from the field sales force is particularly valuable. Being closest to the market, salespersons are in the best position to evaluate competition, and first to sense new trends developing. Reporting systems are often established by product administrators to enable sales people to know what kind of information should be reported and how and when to submit it. Information from all parts of the country and, in some cases, the world are pieced together to identify new price trends, new products introduced on the market, new marketing strategies by competitors, changes in customer needs, and significant technological change.

After reviewing all the pertinent information on hand, the product administrator can begin writing the product strategy, preferably working from an outline and including the following sections:

1   *An Executive Summary.* This section of one to three pages should clearly identify the major issues involved and include the recommendations of the product administrator.

2   *Background.* This section should contain a historical background of the product or product line, present situation, and future prospects. It should include the time of introduction, past sales trends, selling prices, profits, competition, where the product or product line currently is on the life cycle, present major customers, size of end-use markets, and market share for each. Finally the section should identify future sociological, technological, and economic trends.

3   *Strategies.* This section should cover alternatives open to the company and specify the product or product-line strategies preferred. In this section the overall strategy is divided into substrategies, such as R&D, geographic, raw material, organizational, licensing, pricing, customer, and manpower.

4   *Goals.* This section should include longrun results, shortrun goals, and the major assumptions.

A discussion of these four steps inevitably raises this question—how accurate and detailed should the product strategy be? The judgments of people who have devoted a great deal of time and attention to the matter are good enough. For example, if a modified Delphi approach implies the odds of success for a new process are about 60%, that probability would suffice. Attempts to seek greater precision are usually not worthwhile. Keep in mind that the product strategy is merely the "top of the iceberg," the part highly visible to top management. Substrategies could be written, but greater detail is not required at this time. Once the product strategy has been written and approved, particulars will be needed for the development of a detailed plan, which will be discussed in Chapter 10.

To provide the reader with a more concrete understanding, a case history of one product strategy of the Rundel Corporation follows. Like most case histories, names have been disguised and only the most relevant facts included. We make no claims that the case is the perfect model for written product strategies, but we think it is a good one. It illustrates and quantifies when possible the major factors that should be taken into consideration for one line of products.

Now let us turn to The Rundel Corporation's product strategy.

THE RUNDEL CORPORATION'S WORLDWIDE STRATEGY FOR MOLDING
AND EXTRUSION PLASTICS: EXECUTIVE SUMMARY

Major Issues

New intense competition and ecological restrictions on POLYMEXES require a reexamination of product model and world area strategies for this family of molding and extrusion plastics.

For the past several years Rundel Corporation has had two goals. First to be a low-cost producer of commodity-grade POLYMEXES in all world areas where the company sells the products. Second to depend on the introduction of new specialty grades of POLYMEXES for sales growth. Rundel has been the lowest cost producer in North America only. The company has been successful, however, in maintaining worldwide the highest market share for specialty grades.

The ecology movement, the most important external factor, must be considered. The movement primarily threatens current packaging products, but also appliances, automotive, toys, furniture, and building materials. These threats to current products can be viewed as opportunities for new ones that will meet ecological standards.

Recommendations

The following are recommended:

1 Increase research expenditures by $350,000 a year for the next 2 years on the new process for commodity grades in an effort to improve the process. Expenditures on R & D next year will increase from $420,000 to $800,000:

	This Year	Next Year
New models for specialty plastics	$300,000	$330,000
New process for commodity grades	$120,000	$470,000
	$420,000	$800,000

2 Hire a manager of environmental control for POLYMEX along with a qualified research scientist to devote full time on developing new specialty-grade plastics that will be disposable, fire resistant, and nontoxic.
3 Phase out commodity grades in Europe, subject to approval of a detailed ·phase out plan to be presented within 3 months.
4 Determine the feasibility of building an economic-size raw-material (monomer) plant in Europe.
5 Phase out the building and construction end-use market.
6 Do not attempt to produce crude oil. Instead select one oil company that will provide the best long-term deal for raw-material feedstock.
7 Initiate a personnel hiring and training program that will add 150 additional professionals over the next 10 years.
8 Schedule new fixed capital expenditures for POLYMEXES as follows:

Year	Millions of Dollars
1977	17
1978	12
1979	23
1980	21
1981	13
	$186

BACKGROUND

The POLYMEXES are a family of molding and extrusion plastics, widely used throughout the world. Rundel Corporation was one of the pioneers in their development. Research was started in the early 1940s. By 1947 the company had made substantial advances in technology and had in operation a 25,000-ton-per-year plant. Today, Rundel has a worldwide capacity of about 450,000 tons with 25 plants in 12 countries.

In the early 1960s, research was initiated on a new line of POLYMEX-ES— high-heat-resistant plastics—which now provide the principal potential growth for POLYMEXES.

By the 1960s the original POLYMEX product line had become a low-priced, high-volume, commodity plastic, whose profitability was principally dependent on being a low-cost producer. The goal has been to be a low-cost producer on commodity-grade POLYMEXES in all world areas where we sold the products.

Two external developments in the late 1960s and early 1970s are having a major impact on POLYMEXES. The first is the ecology movement, which is imposing new requirements on disposability, reprocessing, inflammability, and testing for approval by the Environmental Protection Agency (EPA) of the U.S. government. The second is the growing liquid hydrocarbon shortage with an accompanying increase in raw-material costs that makes being a low-cost producer of commodity-grade lines difficult.

The world market of commodity-grade POLYMEXES is about 2.5 million metric tons valued at $1.3 billion and with real growth about 10% per year. The specialty-grades world market today is about 45,000 metric tons valued at $60 million and with real growth about 20% per year. The life cycle status of these two major product groups is shown in Exhibit 5.1.

Exhibit 5.1   Life Cycle Status of POLYMEXES

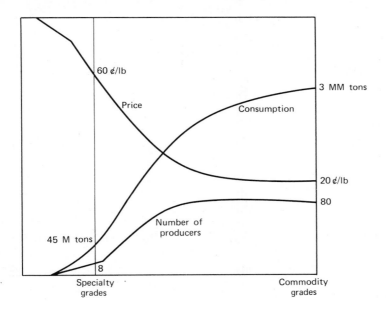

The POLYMEXES are an important product line to the company; they represent 10% of total sales and 15% of total gross investment. Competition has forced prices down, particularly in the past 3 years; hence, the product line contributes only 8% of total operating income.

For many years Rundel, one of the original POLYMEX producers, held more than 40% of the market. Today more than 80 separate companies produce and sell POLYMEXES throughout the free world. Twenty of these are in the United States, 35 in Europe, and 10 in Japan. Two United States competitors, the Thayer Corporation and Archer Corporation, have made serious inroads during the past 10 years.

In high-heat-resistant POLYMEXES, Rundel currently has a technological lead that has enabled the company to capture and hold a large share of this market—about 50%.

The largest single market for POLYMEXES is packaging, which accounts for approximately 25% of world demand. The detailed breakdown is as follows:

Market	% of Total Company Sales	% of Total Industry Sales	Projected Compounded Growth Rate Next 5 Years
Packaging	30	25	8
Appliances	15	20	30
Automotive	15	13	25
Toys	12	9	15
Furniture	10	8	20
Building and Construction	8	5	10
Others	10	20	5
	100	100	

High-temperature-resistant grades have special use principally in the appliance, automotive, toy, and industrial fields, where toughness and tolerance to high temperatures are important.

Competition

Rundel, Thayer, and Archer rank far above all other producers. Each has a dozen manufacturing locations and about 500,000 tons of worldwide capacity. Thayer appears to have about 25,000 tons more capacity than Rundel. The Hirsch Corporation, a West German Company, is fourth in worldwide capacity with more than 150,000 tons at one location in Germany.

Rundel's raw material costs in the United States are lower than Archer's and about equal to Thayer's. In Europe, however, Rundel's raw-material costs are higher; there, Thayer, Archer, and Hirsch manufacture their raw materials, while Rundel purchases its by a long-term contract.

In technical services and marketing Rundel has an advantage over competition since it has a broader line of polymers to offer. Still, the company has not used this broader line to full advantage; competitors have been more aggressive in working closely with customers and more imaginative in setting pricing policies.

Rundel pioneered high-temperature-resistant technology, and Archer and Thayer began research a year or two later. At present Rundel has maintained its technological lead. It has been issued several patents, but none are "origin of matter" patents; hence, Rundel's patent position is not judged to be strong. Its greatest technological strength lies in the buildup of unpatented, internal know-how.

Thayer and Archer seem to be emphasizing overseas expansion. During the past 7 years both companies have been aggressive in Europe. They have increased their market share in a growing market, while Rundel experienced declines. Hirsch still has, however, the largest share of the European market because of location and reputation in the area.

In Latin America Rundel had maintained a leading position for several years, but once again Thayer has been active there during the past few years, along with Japanese companies, and they have cut Rundel's market share.

For industrial-type products, a 35% or more market share almost always provides highly satisfactory profitability, whereas 15% or less market share is almost always unsatisfactory. (Conclusion based on PIMS research covered in an earlier chapter.) A recent profitability analysis of POLYMEX market by market indicates that this empirical conclusion is also quite applicable to POLYMEX; hence, market share is an important factor in developing strategy.

The recap of commodity-grade market share by world areas is as follows: Market share for POLYMEXES is shown in the next two tables:

	Commodity-Grade Share of Market (%)					
	North America	Western Europe	Latin America	Asia Pacific	Row[1]	World Wide
Archer	21	10	7	8	10	14
Hirsch	2	28	10	3	15	13
Rundel	30	8	11	5	7	16
Thayer	25	13	25	22	20	20
Others	22	41	47	62	48	37
	100	100	100	100	100	100
Size of market ($MM)	490	465	75	170	60	1,260
Projected compounded growth rate next 5 years	8%	9%	12%	15%	10%	10%

[1]Rest of world

High-Heat-Resistant Specialty-Grades
Share of Market (%)

	North America	Western Europe	Japan	Row[1]	World Wide
Archer	10	15	15	10	12
Hirsch	0	15	0	5	6
Rundel	60	40	50	50	50
Thayer	25	20	30	30	25
Others	5	10	5	5	7
Size of	100	100	100	100	100
market ($MM)	24	21	6	9	60
Projected compounded growth rate next 5 years	20	18	25	15	19

[1]Rest of world

These tables point out that:

- In high-heat-resistant specialty-grade POLYMEX, Rundel is strong in all markets.
- In commodity grade, Rundel has major strength in North America but weakness in other world areas where projected growth rates are higher.
- Thayer has achieved excellent geographic diversification.
- North America and Western Europe are by far the most important markets; together they constitute 75% of the total free world market.
- In all areas the smaller, local producers have captured a significant share of the commodity-grade market.

Strengths and Weaknesses

A summary of major strengths and weaknesses is as follows:

Strengths	Weaknesses
Broad, well-known product line.	Low share of market in world
A strong, worldwide sales	areas outside of North America.
organization, seasoned and	Low share of market in building
in place.	and construction end-uses and
A network of strategically	relatively low in toys and
located plants to serve major	furniture.
world markets.	Poor knowledge of end-use
Strong position in North	markets outside of North
America; low cost producer	America.
in the area.	Poor coordination between
A technical lead over	domestic and foreign product
competition in the high-heat-	groups.
resistant field; largest	Higher monomer costs outside of
market share in all world	North America.
areas.	
A well coordinated program for	
large international accounts.	

STRATEGIES

Research and Development

Three principal alternatives are open to Rundel:

1 Maintain the forward program on specialty plastics as now conceived, but increase R & D expenditures on commodity grades to achieve break-through on the new process.
2 To the R & D effort add the development of new product models that will help solve problems of disposability, fire resistance, and toxicity.
3 Substantially reduce the R & D effort on specialty plastics since most of the technological breakthroughs have already been achieved; Rundel holds a technological lead and now can afford to deemphasize R & D effort and concentrate on marketing.

Ballpark price tags on these alternatives are as follows:

• The total R & D budget now is $420,000 per year broken down as follows:

New models for
specialty plastics $300,000
Commodity-grade new-
process research   120,000
                                                                                      $420,000

- Debugging the new process for commodity-grade POLYMEX would require approximately 2 years and cost about $700,000. The potential rewards are a reduction in cost of goods sold of 1¢ per pound, which under the present price and competitive conditions would provide $10 million in new gross profit per year. The odds of success are about 60:40.
- The cost of continuing research on new models of high-heat-resistant plastics will be $300,000 increased 10% for the next 5 years. This program is viewed as necessary to hold a technological lead. If this lead were lost, share of market would drop to perhaps one-half of what it is today. Hence, by not spending this R & D money, Rundel would stand to lose $1 million per year at an increasing rate of 10% per year over the next 5 years. Hence, total loss over a 5-year period would be in the neighborhood of $6¼ million.
- The cost of initiating an R & D program to provide greater attack on the ecology problems would initially be about $100,000 per year but escalate to $200,000 per year by the third year. To put a return value on such an expenditure is difficult. If Rundel did nothing, ultimate loss in market share would result, and 1% loss of market share is a net income loss before taxes of about $600,000. Conversely, if Rundel did better than competitors, the company would conceivably increase market share, and every percentage point increase is worth about $600,000 in increased net income.

Recommendation

- Continue research on the new commodity-grade process. Budget an additional $350,000 for the next year and schedule a formal review of progress every 6 months to decide each time whether to continue this research program.
- For development of specialty plastic models, budget $330,000 for the next year and plan to increase this amount 10% each year for the next 4 years subject to reevaluation of the program every year.
- Hire a manager of environmental control for POLYMEX along with an ecological research scientist, both members of the new-models research group, to enable POLYMEXES to meet ecological standards.
- Provide an R & D research budget for the next 3 years as follows:

	Thousands of Dollars			
	This Year	Next Year	Second Year	Third Year
Comodity-grade new- process research	$120	$470	$470	$100
New models for specialty plastics	$300	$330	$360	$390
Additional cost for ecological research	0	$100	$150	$200
	$420	$900	$980	$690

Geographic Emphasis

In Europe Rundel's current position is poor in commodity-grade POLY-MEXES. Overcapacity exists in the industry. The company has high-price raw-material contracts with suppliers. Hirsch, the major competitor in this market, has the lowest raw-material costs. The raw-material costs of Archer and Thayer nearly approximate Hirsch's. Since they have more modern plants than Hirsch, they probably have nearly equal production costs. Rundel's production costs are probably highest of the four major suppliers.

To achieve satisfactory profitability in this market with general-purpose POLYMEX would require obtaining a lower raw-material cost and an increase in market share from 8% to 25%. Costs of a new plant would be about $200 million. Additional sales, administration, R & D, and engineering costs would be about $10 million. The odds for success would probably be less than 50:50.

In Latin America Rundel has a strong position in Brazil but not in other Latin American countries. In Brazil Rundel holds 50% of a 25,000-ton market. Prices, protected by high tariffs and import restrictions, are substantially above world levels. The major competitor is Thayer; Mitsubishi of Japan is rapidly becoming a competitive threat.

In Mexico, the second largest Latin American market, Rundel holds 10% of a 20,000-ton market. The major competitors are Archer and a local producer, IPSA (Industrias Plasticos, S.A.).

Rundel's major competitors have had joint ventures with large Japanese companies for several years. Rundel has not yet made an entry into the Japanese market—the largest in Asia.

In Australia Rundel has 55% of a 10,000-ton market. Future growth will be about 10% per year. Rundel has a strong raw-material base and the largest sales volume and plant capacity and is the lowest cost producer. Because of tariff barriers, market prices are above free-world prices. The government policy to reduce tariffs gradually each year, combined with constantly increasing labor rates and other inflationary factors, puts a constant squeeze on profits. Surviving and holding market share depend, therefore, on maintaining the lowest cost producer status.

In Africa and the Middle East Rundel has no investment, and its export marketing capacity is weak. In some countries no sales agents represent Rundel's products; in others some agents are weak and need to be replaced.

In North America Rundel has 30% of the current 1-million-ton commodity-grades market, which is expanding at about 8% per year. Raw-material cost and polymer technology are equal to or better than competitors'. Price attrition from foreign competition in commodity-grade POLYMEX has been severe and is forcing some small producers out of business.

The alternatives concerning geographic emphasis are as follows:

● Maintain the status quo on market share in all areas. This is hardly a satisfactory alternative since only in the North American market does Rundel have an adequate market share on commodity grades.
● In Latin America and Asia select certain countries where a high market share is already in hand or attainable at reasonable cost. Stay out of the other countries.
● In Western Europe the choice is either to get out of the market on general purpose or increase market share from the present 8% to 20%–25%. A key question is whether or not this is a practical possibility in the light of the formidable competition in the area. The roughly estimated cost to do this is about $200 million in new plant and about $10 million per year of additional sales, administration, R & D, and engineering expenses.
● Another alternative in Western Europe is to drop out of commodity-grade POLYMEX and concentrate in that area solely on specialty polymers.

Recommendations

In North America.
● Rundel's strategy will be to maintain its leading market position in both commodity-grade and specialty-grade POLYMEXES. The key factor for preserving this leadership role in commodity grade will be to stay a low-cost producer. A breakthrough in a new process for the commodity grade is a key factor in this strategy. If this breakthrough is not achieved, the

alternative will be to put increased emphasis on cost reduction programs and to consider dropping out of the toy and furniture markets.

- With specialty POLYMEX markets growing at 20% per year and the prospects for profit margins remaining high for at least the next 3 years, strategy will be to place emphasis on research and development as previously outlined combined with aggressive marketing and market development programs.

In Europe.

- Phase out commodity grades in Europe and concentrate on specialty polymers. A detailed plan for phaseout will be presented within 3 months.
- The decision to withdraw from the commodity-grades market in Europe precludes consideration for a raw-material plant based solely on captive need. Long term, however, as specialty polymers volume builds up, captive raw-material demand will again approach a volume that will support an economic-size plant. A study will therefore be made to define future captive need for POLYMEX raw material in Europe under the assumption of commodity-grade phaseout, along with a study to define the long-term supply-demand outlook for monomer raw material in Europe so as to determine the feasibility of building an economic-size plant in Europe in the near future that would supply the needs of other users, as well as Rundel's own future captive needs.

In Latin America.

- Strategy for Latin America will be to hold a dominant position in Brazil and gradually increase market share in Mexico, Argentina, Colombia, and Venezuela, in that order of priority, by capturing a major proportion of market growth in these countries. The other countries of Latin America will be handled opportunistically; that is, investment opportunities will be considered only when they come to Rundel's attention as an unusual opportunity; no attempt will be made to seek out opportunities in these countries.

In Asia.

- In Japan it is too late to enter the market with commodity-grade POLYMEX; instead a partnership with Sumitomo for production and sale of specialty polymers will be pursued. Negotiations are now in progress.

- In Australia Rundel will concentrate on remaining a lowest cost producer by holding or increasing share of market, decreasing production costs, and continuously introducing the company's most advanced technology.
- Of the remaining countries in the area Indonesia would appear to have the brightest future. A depth study will be initiated to pinpoint opportunities and to develop a detailed strategy and plan for that country.
- The Philippines, Malaysia, Thailand, South Korea, Hong Kong, Singapore, and Taiwan will be candidates for investment only if an unusual opportunity comes to Rundel's attention.
- The remaining countries of the area are not candidates for investment at this time under any circumstances.

In Africa and the Middle East.

The only country that will be considered for investment is South Africa and then only opportunistically. Rundel will not make any effort to seek out investment opportunities in this area and will not consider an investment in the area, except in South Africa.

- With respect to export marketing in countries where Rundel does not have its own sales office the general strategy will be to have sales agents to handle POLYMEX sales but to replace these agents with the company's own sales force as soon as sales volume can economically justify such action.

Pricing

Pricing of commodity-grade POLYMEX is based on competitive conditions existing in each market. Prices vary from country to country. Dumping on the part of the Japanese and Italians has resulted in continuing price attrition. Examination of the experience curves in Exhibit 5.2 suggests that this attrition has gone further than would normally be expected. Hence some improvement can be expected. Rundel's policy will be constantly to test the possibilities to raise prices of commodity grades to bring about this improvement.

Price levels of specialty grades will be established at U.S. price levels plus ocean freight to destination. In areas where competitive conditions make this policy unworkable, minimum price levels will be established by the product administrator, below which price quotations may be made without approval.

Exhibit 5.2   Commodity Grade Polymex

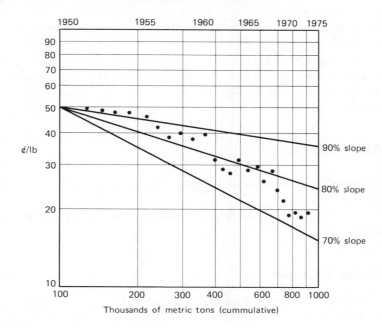

Licensing

Some of the company's commodity-grade POLYMEX know-how will be aggressively marketed to increase "other income," significantly. The policy will be to sell only that know-how that can be obtained from others and where Rundel has technology equal to or better than that of competitors. In some world areas Rundel will work through engineering firms where such firms have special strengths in the local market place and where the economics favor working through them; Eastern Europe and the Far East are in this category. In the latter half of the decade the company will begin to sell or license both selected kinds of specialty-grades know-how.

Raw Material

The three basic alternatives concerning raw materials are: (1) try to own and control mineral and oil resources, (2) rely on long-term arrangements with a major oil company, and (3) do some of both.

Most competitors are attempting to own basic resources but lack expertness. Rundel would be at a disadvantage in trying to follow their example. The oil companies are experts in this business. Hence, some tie-in with one of them by an imaginative, long-term contract would seem to be the best strategy to explore at this time.

Long term, oil resources of the world will become depleted. The most important energy and technical feedstock resource that will gradually move in to fill the gap will undoubtedly be coal. Hence, some interest in coal should be considered.

Recommendation.

- Negotiate a deal with one oil company for long-term hydrocarbon requirements.
- As a hedge against oil consider investing in strip mining coal field operations.

Customer Strategies

The company has 21 major customers, as indicated in the following customer distribution table. Typically, more than 30% of total sales are to these customers.

Size of Annual Purchase	Number of Customers	Dollar Volume (Million)	% of Total Sales
More than $20 million	6	200	15
$10-$19.9 million	15	225	17
$5-$9.9 million	35	200	20
$2-$4.9 million	50	175	13
$1-$1.9 million	200	265	20
Less than $1 million	600	195	15
	906	1,260	100

Of these 21 companies, 6 are particularly important to the continued growth and profitability of POLYMEX. They will therefore be given special attention as follows:

- Detailed strategies and plans will be written for each one. These will contain everything that can be found out about the firm and will be accompa-

nied by detailed action plans indicating who is to do what and when over the next 2 years.
- The product administrator will assume full responsibility for these firms and for developing and implementing the strategies and plans for each firm. He will use the full resources of Rundel in the process, including involvement of the vice president of marketing.

Manpower

Manpower planning is currently out of phase with growth planning for POLYMEX. Availability of trained personnel is limiting present growth plans. At present Rundel has about 300 professional personnel engaged in POLYMEX worldwide. A recent personnel survey indicates that up to 150 additional trained people will be required over the next 10 years.

Organization

As mentioned under "weaknesses" Rundel has some internal, organizational weaknesses in communications and planning between international and home-office-based management. The root of the problem is lack of an adequate system to take into account the knowledge and expertise of the international management group. As the company becomes more international, the problem will be solved, but this approach would take too long and in the meantime Rundel would undoubtedly lose market share.

The alternatives have been researched through discussions with several companies who have had the same problem. From this, the major alternatives would appear to be as follows:

- Incorporate in the formal planning process of the company that the head of international, or his designee, participate as a full voting member of the POLYMEX strategic planning board.
- As the initial step in devising or revising strategy for POLYMEX, require that each world area develop an initial draft of strategy for its area that then through negotiation and discussion is agreed upon by both the area group and the home office group and ultimately incorporated in the total worldwide strategy for POLYMEX.
- An alternative to this would be for the home office group to develop an initial draft of strategy for each world area that would then be submitted to each world area for comment or approval.

- Require in the budgeting and planning process that accountability and responsibility for achieving sales and income goals be geographic rather than worldwide; for example, the POLYMEX product administrator would be held responsible for achieving sales and income goals in Europe, North America, Japan, and so forth as individual areas and also worldwide.

Recommendations

- Invite the international division general manager, or his designee, to become a full voting member of the POLYMEX Strategic Planning Board.
- For each foreign area, assign responsibility to the POLYMEX manager in charge of that area for writing the initial draft of strategy for that area, followed up by a visit to the home office for discussion and ultimate agreement on the strategy to be incorporated in the worldwide strategy for POLYMEX.
- Require that budgets and long-range quantitative goals be broken down by geographic area; fulfillment of responsibility will be judged on the accomplishment of these goals area by area.

Exhibit 5.3 Summary of Capital Programs Required to Carry Out These Strategies as now Conceived:*

	Fixed Capital Expenditures					Millions of Dollars
	1977	1978	1979	1980	1981	Total
North America						
Approved projects						
C.G. plant expansion, Pittsburgh	10	1				11
C.G. plant expansion, Toronto	4					4
Planned projects						
S.G. plant, West Coast U.S.A		5	2			7
S.G. plant expansion, Pittsburgh					2	2
Europe						
Planned projects						
Monomer plant, France			5	7	2	14
S.G. plant expansion, Antwerp					2	2

Latin America						
Approved projects						
C.G. plant expansion, Brazil	3					3
Planned projects						
C.G. plant, Mexico		1	2	2		5
S.G. plant, Argentina			2	2		4
S.G. plant, Colombia				2	2	4
S.G. plant, Venezuela					2	2
Asia/Pacific						
Approved projects						
S.G. joint venture, Japan		5	10	5		20
Planned projects						
S.G. plant-site, location to be decided			2	3		5
	17	12	23	21	10	83

*C.G. = commodity grade;
S.G. = specialty grade.

Exhibit 5.4 Financial Goals over the Next 10 Years

	Millions of Dollars				
	1977	1978	1979	1980	1985
Commodity-Grade POLYMEX					
Sales	150	140	150	190	240
Cost of goods sold (COGS)	119	112	120	152	192
RESA (Res., eng. sales and admin.)	20	18	17	21	27
Other income	3	3	4	5	7
Operating profit	14	13	17	22	28
Income tax	7	6	8	11	14
Net income	7	7	9	11	14
Gross investment	215	217	220	240	300
ROI (%)	3.3	3.2	4.1	4.6	4.7
Share of market (%)	13	11	11	13	13
Specialty-Grade POLYMEX					
Sales	50	65	85	140	260
COGS	31	42	55	94	198
RESA	8	10	15	21	31
Other income	1	1	1	3	5
Operating profit	12	14	16	28	36
Income tax	6	7	8	14	18
Net income	6	7	8	14	18
Gross investment	35	42	60	125	200
ROI (%)	17	17	13	11	9
Share of market (%)	50	50	50	49	30

Exhibit 5.4

Total POLYMEX					
Sales	200	205	235	330	500
COGS	150	154	175	246	390
RESA	28	28	32	42	58
Other income	4	4	5	8	12
Operating profit	26	27	33	50	64
Income tax	13	13	16	25	32
Net income	13	14	17	25	32
Gross investment	250	259	280	365	500
ROI (%)	5.2	5.4	6.1	6.8	6.4
Share of market (%)	15	15	16	19	18

These goals are based on the following assumptions:

● The new process for commodity-grade POLYMEX will be successful and will become commercial in 1980. This will permit holding gross profit margin at about 20%.

● For high-temperature-resistant specialty polymers, gross profit margins will gradually erode, as competition becomes more intense, from the present level of 38% to 24% by 1985.

● Research, engineering, sales, and administration expense (RESA) for commodity grade will go from 13% of sales in 1977 to 11% after 1978. This can be accomplished by elimination of some duplication in R & D effort and by phaseout of commodity grades in Europe in 1978.

● RESA expense of specialty polymers will reach a peak of 18% of sales in 1977 and then gradually come down to 12% of sales by 1985.

● A successful program for increasing licensing income from sale of commodity-grade know-how and specialty-grade POLYMEX know-how (in the latter half of the decade).

● Reasonably good success in developing products that help to answer the ecological problems of POLYMEXES.

● Approval and implementation for hiring and training 150 professional people over the next 10 years.

Putting the Rundel Corporation Product Strategy in Perspective

To deal with the Rundel Corporation's case effectively, one must recognize the three most important principles of product strategies. The first two are market share and market segmentation, and they are closely allied.

Market share is essential for profitability. But the term *market* itself is not clear and must be restricted by definition. The concept of market segmentation provides that restriction.

It is quite possible for a company to have a low market share in an industry but still have high profitability. What really counts is a high share of one segment or a few segments of the total industry. For example, Heublein, a highly profitable company in the liquor industry, ranks fifth in the industry in market share but first in the vodka segment of the market.

Segmentation applies to geographic markets, as well as to end-use markets. In the Rundel Corporation case, for instance, the company was strong in packaging, appliances, and automotive but relatively weak in toys, furniture, and building and construction. The company decided to retreat from the building and construction market so as to concentrate better on those end uses where it has greater strengths and better opportunity to improve its position.

Geographically the company was strong in North America and Latin America but relatively weak in other world areas. Retreat from one segment of the European market was again a decision designed to permit the company to concentrate better on other segments where it had greater strengths.

Some successful companies know well the importance of high market shares in a small market segment because this idea of a niche in the industry is the grail of small and medium-sized companies.

A third principle—the importance of defining a business broadly to offset marketing myopia—seems contradictory to the first two. Yet, when applied to the Rundel Corporation, it would prevent fixation on POLYMEXES and would lead to further analysis of other materials and possibly services.

Notice the Rundel Corporation's product strategy excludes production or manufacturing strategies, and this is a mistake. To point out the importance of production strategies, we are inclined to paraphrase W. Wickam Skinner's article, *Manufacturing—Missing Link in Corporate Strategy.*

Skinner states that what is not always realized is that different product strategies and approaches to gaining a competitive advantage place different demands on the manufacturing arm of the company. Too often an assumption is made that low costs and high efficiencies are the objectives of all manufacturing policies. Actually, different product strategies may require different manufacturing strategies, policies, personnel, and operations. Product managers should be aware of the constraints or limitations on manufacturing operations imposed by the economics and technology of the industry. They should also be aware of the trade-offs in designing and operating a production system to meet different product strategies (see Exhibit 5.5).

**Exhibit 5.5 Some Important Trade-Off Decisions in Manufacturing—
or "You Can't Have It Both Ways"**

Decision Area	Decision	Alternatives
Plant and Equipment	Span of process	Make or buy
	Plant size	One big plant or several smaller ones
	Plant location	Locate near markets or locate near materials
	Investment decisions	Invest mainly in buildings or equipment or inventories or research
	Choice of equipment	General-purpose or special-purpose equipment
	Kind of tooling	Temporary, minimum tooling or "production tooling"
Production planning and control	Frequency of inventory taking	Few or many breaks in production for buffer stocks
	Inventory size	High inventory or a lower inventory
	Degree of inventory control	Control in great detail or in lesser detail
	What to control	Controls designed to minimize machine downtime or labor cost or time in process, or to maximize output of particular products or material usage
	Quality control	High reliability and quality or low costs
	Use of standards	Formal or informal or none at all
Labor and staffing	Job specialization	Highly specialized or not highly specialized
	Supervision	Technically trained first-line supervisors or nontechnically trained supervisors
	Wage system	Many job grades or few job grades; incentive wages or hourly wages
	Supervision	Close supervision or loose supervision
	Industrial engineers	Many or few such persons

Exhibit 5.5 continued

Decision Area	Decision	Alternatives
Product design/ engineering	Size of product line	Many customer specials or few specials or none at all
	Design stability	Frozen design or many engineering change orders
	Technological risk	Use of new processes unproved by competitors or follow-the-leader policy
	Engineering	Complete packaged design or design-as-you-go approach
	Use of manufacturing engineering	Few or many manufacturing engineers
Organization and management	Kind of organization	Functional or product focus or geographical or other
	Executive use of time	High involvement in investment or production planning or cost control or quality control or other activities
	Degree of risk assumed	Decisions based on much or little information
	Use of staff	Large or small staff group
	Executive style	Much or little involvement in detail; authoritarian or nondirective style; much or little contact with organization

Source: Harvard Business Review: May-June 1969, p. 141.

CHAPTER 6

CUSTOMER STRATEGIES

In this chapter we cover an indispensable part of product strategies—customer strategies. Because these strategies are so critically important in increasing sales and market share, they merit special attention.

When most people hear the term *customer strategies* they think of those used continuously to entice ultimate consumers to buy everything from automobiles to toothpaste. Behind such customer strategies are attempts to put consumers on a couch to find out what they are thinking and what their physical and psychological needs are. So much has been written on these strategies—from Vance Packard's *The Hidden Persuaders* to scholarly treatises written by behaviorial scientists —that we pass them by quickly.

We give our full attention to customer strategies for industrial buyers, wholesalers, and retailers—customers who occupy a place in channels of distribution that precede the ultimate consumer. With the exception of retail stores the bulk of the income of most companies is earned through sales to a few large industrial buyers, wholesalers, and retailers. In fact this phenomenon of a few customers' accounting for a major portion of total sales dollars has occurred so frequently that, when represented by a graph, it has a characteristic shape called Pareto's curve.

If big customers are to be satisfied, their needs must be clearly identified and fulfilled. Nothing should be left to chance. Suppliers should think of customer strategies then as ways to focus on their largest potential sales.

Multinationalism has made customer strategies important. Multinational corporations want worldwide uniform quality of products and services and turn to their suppliers to meet these needs. Suppliers should first, therefore, evaluate their customer's total corporate strategy and then develop strategies. Suppliers often feel that their strategies should be confidential and should not be made known to customers. We strongly disagree. Although sensitive parts should be withheld, about 90% of a customer strategy can and should be revealed to the customer. Invariably reaction will be positive; customers are flattered to be given so much attention. Sometimes a customer will even make suggestions on how to improve the strategy.

COMPONENTS OF CUSTOMER STRATEGIES

All customer strategies should include the following:

- Background information on the customer.
- Appraisal of the competitive situation.
- Identification of customer's needs.

Background Information on the Customer

Background information on customers should be comparable to that developed on competition in Chapter 2. It should include a thorough financial analysis of the company, its competitive position in major product lines, the character and personality profiles of key decision makers, most recent actions on new projects, plant expansions, divestments, contractions, a list of plants and what they produce, domestic and foreign marketing methods, apparent strategies, and the company's strengths and weaknesses.

Because it has a different purpose, customer strategy information differs in some ways from analyses for evaluating competition. One difference in particular is the importance of identifying the key decision makers in purchasing and of documenting their backgrounds, likes, dislikes, and idiosyncrasies. Titles usually provide no clues. The actual decision maker is sometimes a technician in a research laboratory, an engineer in a plant, or a middle manager. Regardless of title the actual decision makers must be identified and their relationship with the rest of the organization understood.

In developing a customer strategy, the customer's sales history of major products in standard units or in dollars, production capacities, production rates, and future plans for expansion and new plants must be learned if sales potentials are to be assessed. The sources of this information are the various functional and operational groups in the customer's organization, for example, purchasing, marketing, manufacturing, research, planning, product administrators, and other sources, such as the customer catalogues and annual reports, periodicals, trade associations, salespersons' reports, and "gossip" in the trade from industry contacts.

Information on sales history and plans for increased capacity is needed for cross-checking the customer's statements on future requirements. Cross-checking is necessary because: (1) customers tend to be too optimistic in good times and too pessimistic in poor times; (2) customers want an adequate supply at all times, and hence, they give "liberal" estimates of future requirements. To use customers' estimates without cross-checking is a serious mistake.

Appraisal of the Competitive Situation

Competition keeps a supplier from getting a customer's business. Hence, an accurate appraisal of competition is critical and should include at least order-of-magnitude answers to the following: identification of the low-cost producer; the competitor's share of the customer's total requirements; its relative strengths and weaknesses in product quality, technical service, and research and development (R & D) capabilities; and its amount of influence with key purchasing decision makers.

Insight on competition's behavior patterns must also be considered. As Bruce D. Henderson, president of the Boston Consulting Group, said in one of his monographs:

> It seems unreasonable for high cost competitors to sell at lower prices, grow faster, and use more debt than low cost competition, but they often do. . . . Successful business strategy requires that the low cost competitor be persuaded indirectly to give up his market share and with it his cost leadership and profitability. . . . Since all strategy depends on competitors' behavior, all strategy choices are based on forecasts of competitors' plans and reactions to your initiatives.

Some customers become competitors since all companies are constantly involved with make-or-buy decisions. Relative costs determine how the decision will be made, and there are many ways to consider costs. Policy influences a decision, but again policy merely considers cost in the long run rather than the short run. Some companies have, for instance, adopted a policy against integrating vertically to raw materials unless absolutely necessary to ensure supply. The rationale is that raw-material and intermediates producers usually have the lowest costs in the long run. Most companies get a better return on equity over time by investing funds in end products rather than in raw materials or intermediates. The price at which customers can obtain requirements figures in their calculations. The supplier's pricing strategy is, therefore, all-important in keeping key customers buying rather than making.

Once customers produce a previously purchased product, they seldom return to buying it. Suppliers must, therefore, ward off a buyer's threat to make before any action is taken.

Several things set former customers apart from other competitors: Their risks are lower because they have an assured market; product lines are limited because they produce only what they themselves need, and hence production costs on these lines may well be quite competitive; they seldom switch to improved raw materials and intermediates because they are committed to what they are using until their production facilities are fully depreciated; and their production capacities are typically geared to "normal" demand, requirements beyond production capacity in peak periods often requiring supplementation from outside suppliers. All things considered, they tend to subject their industry to larger variations in operating capacities and profits during the peaks and the troughs of business cycles.

Identification of Customer's Needs

Customers have needs that must be identified. In addition to product needs, they have economic, information, ego, and service needs.

Economic needs can take several forms. One common to all customers is the need to obtain the lowest possible cost of all the products and services purchased. This does not necessarily mean the lowest price, because numerous other things must be taken into account, such as product quality and consistency in quality, assurance of continuity of supply, technical service, and ingenuity of the supplier in developing new product models.

Most customers will have special economic needs from time to time because of unusual circumstances. For instance, a customer may be in a temporary liquidity bind because of heavy cash outlays for expansion programs or because of some financial losses. An interim need may exist for special credit arrangements that requires up-to-date information on the customer's financial statements and plans. If the company is publicly owned, much information will be available in annual reports, IOK[1] Reports required by the Securities and Exchange Commission, quarterly statements, and the press. But if the company is privately owned, ability to develop this information will depend mostly on the integrity of the customer and the closeness of the relationship with the supplier.

Customers have *information needs*. They need information on where products are being made, the volume, the quality and performance, and the price. With this information they can evaluate the cost of using a supplier's products and the risks involved.

Customers often need a steady stream of new products and new designs for old products to remain competitive in their industry. They therefore want to know about future products and new designs of old products of their suppliers.

Customers also want news on developments or happenings that would affect the company or industry, education on new management techniques and services and new technology, and even information on changes in the supplier's organization.

Customers also like to get information on competitors. But the astute supplier gives only information that is of public knowledge. If the supplier gives sensitive or confidential information, a feeling of distrust will be created. The customer wonders: will the supplier give confidential information on my company to my competitors?

Key purchasing decision makers are human; they have *ego needs*. Many like to be entertained, receive favors, and be recognized for achievement. How to treat them requires, however, the utmost finesse. Many companies have policies against the receipt of gifts and entertainment from suppliers. Moreover, individual purchasing decision makers have their own personal ethical standards.

Service needs extend from routine to special. Routine servies include order handling, delivery of merchandise, and technical service. Special services include technical seminars in areas related to a customer's products, advice, and sometimes financial support for their advertising and sales promotion campaigns, assistance on expanding or improving their distribution network,

---

[1] IOK reports, required by the Securities and Exchange Commission within 90 days after the end of a fiscal year, are available to the public. Copies are most easily obtained by writing to the company or to Disclosure, Inc., Bethesda, Maryland.

assistance in planning, and a whole host of other possibilities in almost any phase of business.

Once a customer's total requirements are evaluated; competitive position and estimates of their share of business analyzed; and their economic, information, ego, and service needs identified, the supplier is able to develop a customer strategy.

STEPS IN DEVELOPING A CUSTOMER STRATEGY

The first step in developing a customer strategy is to establish goals by share of business for each product. The usual goal is an increased share, but many times the same share or a minimum decline is an acceptable goal.

Next, a customer strategy must identify ways the goals can be accomplished. The third step requires a deep understanding of how the customer views the priorities and a realistic appraisal of the supplier's ability to beat competition. Finally the strategy should include the possible actions of competitors, alternatives open to the customer, and several alternative strategies.

We think a detailed guide or checklist for developing a customer strategy is helpful and have, therefore, included one (see Exhibit 6.1). This checklist is not intended as a complete inventory of all points that should be raised. In fact we have limited it to only 19, but these are what we consider the most important questions.

FOLLOWUP

After the customer strategy has been written and approved, followup is necessary. Shortly after customer strategy and detailed implementation plans have been written, they will probably be out of date. New information and new developments occur and nullify or modify some previous concepts and conclusions. Constant attention must, therefore, be given to making changes in the strategy.

When the decision is made to change the strategy and action plans or both, downward communications should be made promptly. If there is too much delay between the decision to change and the communication of the decision, wrong actions are inevitably taken. In addition, prompt, thorough downward communications signal executives and employees in the organization that the strategy and accompanying program guide management's actions.

Exhibit 6.1   Customer Strategy Checklist

1. Do you have sufficient background on the customer — approximate size, products, and markets — to provide a "feel" of the account?

2. Do you know the account's corporate and divisional objectives (whichever are pertinent) and their forward plans either announced or implied?

3. What are the company's international interests? Does it manufacture overseas as well as export? If so, about what is the split in sales between export and local foreign manufacture?

4. Where are the customer's plants? What products are manufactured in each plant in what quantities?

5. Are your company's long-range objectives in relation to the customer clearly defined? Do you have different levels of goals for different alternative strategies?

6. Have you checked the reasonableness of your objectives with past historical growth of the customer and with the customer's own estimates of future growth?

7. Do any other departments or subsidiaries of your company sell the customer? If so, what products are sold and in what quantities? What are the goals of these other departments or subsidiaries?

8. Are the customer's key needs defined? (A long list is not necessary or desirable; list only the *key* needs.)

9. Have you defined the possible alternative strategies that might be used to satisfy the customer's needs?

10. Is satisfaction of the customer's needs important enough from his point of view to permit your achieving the sales goals established?

11. Are the strategies realistic? Are they practical for your own company as well as acceptable to your customer?

12. What competitive countermoves might take place in response to your strategies?

13. Have competitive trends been adequately considered in forecasting the share of total customer's business that you can achieve and maintain?

14. Have you estimated competitive position in relation to yours and your competitor's unit manufacturing costs?

15. Have you adequately taken into consideration your competitive position in relation to external forces such as prospective changes in tariff rates, freight costs, and taxes?

16. Have you adequately assessed technological developments that may affect your products, your manufacturing cost position, or your marketing costs?

17. Do you have the necessary manpower requirements to carry out the strategy built into the plans for implementation of the strategy?

18. Have you clearly identified your customer's key purchasing decision makers?

19. Do you have a mechanism for checking on the progress in implementing action programs and for taking corrective measures when implementation lags?

We are now ready to review the Corcoran Company, a case history of a customer strategy. The supplier who developed the strategy is, of course, anonymous. Observe closely the steps that the supplier took in preparing a customer strategy for the Corcoran Company. When evaluated according to the standards that have been stated, the strategy seems quite good. Notice also that the framework for the strategy is not limited to resin supplies; it has wide application.

THE CORCORAN COMPANY

Background

The Corcoran Company manufactures a broad line of plastic flooring materials in plants located at Newark, New Jersey; Racine, Wisconsin; Dallas, Texas; and Los Angeles, California. Our sales of resin and plasticizers to Corcoran are now about $4 million per year.

Four years ago, Corcoran initiated a major reorganization and expansion. The marketing and commercial development organization was restructured and $30 million was spent expanding and modernizing its manufacturing facilities.

The stated purpose of this program was "to provide Corcoran with maximum flexibility in quickly reacting to changes in consumer preferences for style and color and to improve the capability for development and introduction of new products." Today Corcoran is the leader in the plastic flooring materials industry.

Corcoran has executive and purchasing offices and a research center in Stamford, Connecticut. Each plant has its own purchasing agent who reports functionally to the central purchasing department but administratively to the plant manager. Central purchasing recommends preferred sources of supply to plant purchasing. The plant purchasing agent has some freedom of selection from an approved list, but the trend is toward more central purchasing control. All formulations must be approved at the research center in Stamford.

By contract Corcoran purchases 50% of its resin requirements from the Horner Company. Formerly Corcoran had an equity interest in Horner. The purchase contract was part of the divestiture agreement and expires this year.

Corcoran's sales last year were $390 million. A few months ago Corcoran announced its intention to purchase the Westfall Corporation, a company in the plastic film and sheeting business. Final stockholder approval is expected in a couple of months. This acquisition would add a complementary line to

Corcoran's floor tile business and additional sales of about $125 million. It has been announced that the present management of Westfall would be retained but that an unnamed person from Corcoran would be assigned to Westfall's management to coordinate the gradual integration.

Key personnel in Corcoran are as follows;

Clifford P. Boulch		President and CEO
Charles E. Waggoner		V.P.—manufacturing
James P. Kelley		V.P.—marketing
Henry W. Meng		Director of purchasing
Charles C. Abel		Assistant purchasing director
William J. DeGeal		Director of research
Newark plant:	Ralph E. Plummer	Manager
	Ronald E. Scheid	Purchasing agent
Racine plant:	Robert B. Gudder	Manager
	William C. Allen	Technical manager
Dallas plant:	James L. Kister	Manager
	Robert I. Mayer	Plant chemist
Los Angeles plant:	Donald G. Ehrle	Manager
	John P. Williams	Purchasing agent

At executive headquarters the two most important purchasing decision makers are Henry Meng, director of purchasing, and William J. DeGeal, director of research.

Meng is about 50 years old. He has been with Corcoran for more than 20 years. He and his wife Alice have four children—the oldest being 19 and the youngest, 12. His hobbies are hunting, skiing, and boating. He has strong rapport with Mr. Boulch, who also likes upland game hunting, and during the hunting season they frequently hunt together. Meng is a "rough diamond" sort, egotistical, bombastic, but a shrewd negotiator. He has trained his staff well in estimating suppliers' costs when bargaining on price.

DeGeal's personality is entirely different. He is quietly gruff and extremely hard to get to know. He is about 45 years old, married, and has one son, 12 years old. He has been with the company about 13 years. His principal hobbies are mountain climbing and working in his yard. He is an excellent R & D man. In his work he has Boulch's full confidence. He has strong opinions on which suppliers have the best quality products and plays a key role in selection of suppliers.

Corcoran's major strengths are its high quality of products and innovation of designs and formulations. Its major weakness is an inability to cope with new ventures out of its immediate field of expertise. Seven years ago the company tried to diversify into upstream production of resins, since much was used captively. The venture failed and was ultimately divested. Since that time the company's principal strategy has been to maintain its leading position in floor tile with diversification into film and sheeting—fields closely related technically and commercially.

Objectives

Corcoran's total purchases today of products that we could sell to them come to about $15 million. On the basis of their known expansion plans and purchase of the Westfall Corporation, this will likely increase suddenly to about $20 million and then grow at the rate of 9—10% per year for the next 5 years.

Our objective is to increase our share of Corcoran's business from 27% to 40% over a 3-year period and then to maintain that position. We believe that it is not reasonable to try to do better than 40%, because of the company's general policy of dividing up their business between three or four suppliers.

Our present share of business and our goals, product by product, are as follows:

		Millions of Pounds				
Plant	Products	Corcoran's Total Use 1977	Our Sales 1977	1978	1979	1980
Newark	X-100	2	1	1	2	2
	L-520	5	2	2	2	3
	PC-10	3	0	1	1	1
	PS-240	6	1	1	2	3
	SL-215	4	1	1	1	1
		20	5	6	6	10
Racine	X-100	1	1	1	1	1
	PC-10	2	0	0	0	1
	SL-215	2	1	1	1	1
		5	2	2	2	3
Dallas	X-100	2	1	1	1	1
	L-520	5	1	2	2	3
	PS-240	1	0	0	1	1
		8	2	3	4	5

Los Angeles	X-100	2	1	1	1	1
	L-520	5	2	2	2	3
	PC-10	3	0	1	1	1
	SL-215	2	0	0	1	1
		12	3	4	5	6
Westfall	AB-31	9	0	2	3	4
Plants	X-100	1	0	0	1	1
	LN-24	2	0	1	1	1
	PC-10	3	0	1	1	2
		15	0	4	6	8

The following is a record of Corcoran's total purchases of products that we can supply along with our record of our sales and goals:

	Corcoran's Total Purchases ($ millions)	Our Sales ($ millions)	Participation (%)
1972	9	2.3	25
1973	10	2.3	23
1974	10	2.0	20
1975	12	3.0	25
1976	13	3.4	26
1977	15	4.1	27
1978	20 (f)*	7.0 (f)	35 (f)
1979	22 (f)	7.9 (f)	36 (f)
1980	25 (f)	10.0 (f)	40 (f)

*f =forecast.

Competition

Our major competitors are The Horner Company for resins and the Plastex Corporation for plasticizers. By contract the Horner Company has had for several years 50% of Corcoran's resins business. When the contract expires this year, Horner will probably lose part of its share; we understand that Meng has been displeased with Horner's service and feels that having a long-term contract has made them "lazy." We should be able to gain a larger share of Corcoran's resins business.

Other competitors will also be seeking a larger share of this business. Since our products are no better (or no worse) than those of our competitors, relationships and service will tell.

With plasticizers, Plastex has aggressively been trying to gain market share. They have cut prices; this approach has failed because we remain price competitive. They have tried to supplant our products with substitute products, and this approach has failed because the substitute products have been inferior.

An important advantage that we hold over competition is our close relationship with Bill DeGeal. He is an exceedingly difficult person with whom to establish a close relationship. We have done it; our competitors have not.

A recap of our major strengths and weaknesses is as follows:

Strengths

1   We have a broad line of resins and plasticizers that gives us an advantage over some competitors. We can work with Corcoran on a wider range of their raw-material problems, provide combined shipments, and thereby reduce delivery costs. (Pricing in the industry is f.o.b. plant.)

2   We have three producing plants, well located to service the widely scattered plants of Corcoran from the standpoint of delivery costs and continuity of supply in the event of strikes, fire, floods, and so forth.

3   We have strong technical capability. This has led Corcoran to work with us on evaluations of some of their new formulations and to let us use them for cooperative programs on the development of new resins and plasticizers.

4   We have an excellent relationship with DeGeal, who must approve the use of all resins and plasticizers.

5   We have excellent sales and technical service coverage at all of Corcoran's plants.

Weaknesses

1   We lack the raw-material feedstocks of some of our competitors. Until now, when assured of continuous supply, we have maintained a policy of buying raw materials rather than making them. This policy has paid off and has given us overall a higher return on our investment than competition. But now we are threatened with a hydrocarbon shortage, and we may have to reverse this policy and face a difficult catchup period.

2   We have not been as willing as our competitors to custom blend for Corcoran on small-volume items.

3   We have not had as aggressive or as imaginative a pricing policy as our competitors.

Corcoran's Needs

Clifford Boulch has publicly declared the basic objectives of the Corcoran company:

1 Maximize flexibility to changing consumer preferences in style and color.
2 Develop new flooring concepts.
3 Minimize time required to develop and market new products.
4 Improve effectiveness of distribution network in terms of numbers and types of outlets and their penetration.
5 Maintain reputation of top quality products.
6 Improve service to customers while reducing their costs.
7 Improve image with the investing public and institutional groups so as to improve average price/earnings ratio from around 8–10 to 15. Along with other factors, this will require a steady growth rate of earnings per share of about 10% per year.

Most of these objectives (all except the last one) are for marketing and R & D. Discussions with Waggoner, Meng, and DeGeal have provided additional objectives in the production, purchasing, and R & D areas.

Production

1 A better understanding of the limitations and capabilities of equipment that can lead to alterations in the equipment needed for new flooring concepts.
2 A pilot plant for use in developing new product ideas.
3 Better process control to reduce rejects.
4 A better definition and determination of how various operating conditions (temperature, speed, humidity, pressure, etc.) affect quality (blistering, dimensional stability, luster, etc.)

Purchasing

1 Reliable sources of supply for raw materials that will avoid production delays.
2 More accurate estimates of the production costs by various suppliers of raw materials to endure lowest cost purchases overall.
3 Close liaison with R & D in determining: (a) the opportunities for raw-

material substitution, (b) what new raw materials will be needed for new products that are in prospect, and (c) raw materials from which suppliers adversely affect quality.

4   Sources of supply that offer the best combination of quality, price, and service.

Research and Development

1   Information on new raw materials and assistance in their use for new formulations.

2   Rapid evaluation of new products introduced by Corcoran's competition.

3   Ideas for new products.

4   Evaluation of opportunities for raw-material substitution.

Strategy Definition

Our overall strategy will be directed at protecting our plasticizer position and substantially increasing our resins position with termination of the Horner Company contract.

At the top management level, we shall propose to Clifford Boulch a semi-nartype meeting at our Stamford Headquarters for presentation of how we carry out management functions in which they would be particularly interested. Mr. Boulch will be invited to bring with him as many of his associates as he would care to. We shall propose subjects such as R & D with particular emphasis on our system for fostering creativity; our system of quality control and use of computers in controlling operating conditions, our "software" computer program for inventory control; our product-marketing system with emphasis on technical service; and our production-planning system and telex network for handling orders, forecasting, budgeting, and long-range planning.

At the plant manager and plant purchasing level, we shall propose a plant visit to Newark to show our production methods directed at ensuring quality at the lowest possible cost. To Henry Meng we shall present economic evaluations using various plasticizers/resin combinations based on price and performance.

A major target is to maintain our strong position with Corcoran's research department. Short term, we shall furnish data to DeGeal that demonstrate the high performance of L-520 and PC-10 vinyl composites for use in floor tiles. This will include data on migration resistance, dimensional stability, scuff resistance, toughness, nonstaining characteristics, and economics. We shall demonstrate how changes in some of their present blends may give them a better price and performance ratio.

Longer range, we shall propose a cooperative program to develop new tile concepts and the testing of new products. This program will include a schedule of meetings between appropriate members of Corcoran's research department and our own, sample preparations and testing, production of plant trial quantities, and so on.

We shall study how the Westfall operations will be integrated with Corcoran and, after we reach conclusions, how this strategy needs to be expanded and changed.

We shall also determine Corcoran's and Westfall's international involvements and work with our foreign department in developing a strategy and plan for selling resin and plasticizer to their foreign affiliates and licensees.

Possible Actions by Competitors

Entrance of two additional manufacturers of X-100 is a real possibility. This could affect our 50% split of this business. If they do make a bid for the business, it will likely be on a price basis. Because of the price-sensitive nature of Corcoran's markets and the relatively narrow profit margins on floor tiles, Corcoran would be interested. In the event of such a development, four alternatives would be open to us:

1   Take action now on lowering the price in an effort to ward off either or both of the two manufacturers. The consequences of such action would be loss of about $50,000 in gross profit but no loss of sales volume (pounds).

2   Take no price action now. Wait and see if these two manufacturers offer a lower price and if they do then meet it. If no price cutting develops, losing $50,000 of gross profit would be avoided. But if it does develop, $50,000 gross profit would be lost, and maybe more if either or both competitors made market share inroads.

3   Take no price action, even if either or both manufacturers make a bid for the business on the basis of a lower price. Try to ward off any reduction in our share of the business by emphasizing the role we have played technically and stress the cooperative research programs with Corcoran that are underway and in prospect. Then suggest that, if either or both of these manufacturers are wanted as a source of supply, their share come from Corcoran's other suppliers. If this strategy were successful, the conse-

quences would be to maintain our share at no price reduction, and hence, no loss in gross profit or sales volume.

4 A fourth alternative is a combination of (2) whereby we meet price part way or completely (if necessary) to retain our share of the business and (3). The consequences would be no loss in share of business but some loss in gross profit up to $50,000.

The strategy that we shall adopt initially is (4), on the basis that it provides a high probability of success at a low-level loss in gross profit margin.

Action Programs

The following are specific actions that will be performed over the next several months, along with assignments of responsibility for implementing these actions and timing for when the actions should take place.

Who	What	When	Date Accomplished
J. A. Smith and E. W. Parker	Calls at plant locations to determine problem areas, needs, and competitive activity.	Monthly	
J. A. Smith and W. L. Schultz	Call on Boulch to explore corporate needs. Discuss visit to Connecticut headquarters.	Second quarter	
J. A. Smith and P. S. Kalk	Coordinate visit to Connecticut headquarters.	Fourth quarter	
J. A. Smith	Present to Meng and DeGeal an economic study of various resins/plasticizer blends.	Quarterly	
J. A. Smith and W. L. Schultz	Discuss and arrange trip to our Hudson, New York, plant with Meng and Plummer.	Fourth quarter	

Who	What	When	Date Accomplished
I. U. Peters, J. A. Smith, W. L. Schultz, and O. P. Lang	Discuss research programs and arrange series of meetings between DeGeal and our research director, Powell.	First quarter	
R. B. Burke	Develop an in-depth report on the Westfall Corporation using both internal and external sources. Suggest a strategy and plan for participating in this new acquisition's business.	Second quarter	
J. A. Smith, R. B. Burke, and C. B. Charles	Develop information and report on Corcoran's and Westfall's overseas activities. Develop a strategy and plan for maximizing our participation in this business and recommend a program for coordinating the domestic and international marketing effort.	Second quarter	
J. A. Smith, R. P. Burke, and C. B. Charles	Develop information on profitability/sales/ cash flow (whatever can be made available) on Corcoran's major product lines.	Try to have a first-attempt evaluation by yearend.	

The Corcoran Company Case in Perspective

The Corcoran Company Case demonstrates two of the more important prerequisites for developing a customer strategy: (1) deep understanding of the company and its needs; (2) deep understanding of the key executives that influence purchasing decisions. The two factors synergistically complement each other: historical background helps to understand the motivations and behavior of its executives and so does, of course, understanding their psyche.

The Horner Company's relationship to Corcoran demonstrates the importance of historical background. Understanding this relationship provided the basis for a strategy to substantially increase share of Corcoran's resin requirements. Similarly, knowing Corcoran's historical emphasis on maintaining quality of its present line of products indicated clearly to the supplier the need for stressing its technical competence as one of the keys to salesmanship strategy.

Equally important in development of strategy was knowing the likes, dislikes, personality traits, and character of the key executives . . . to the point where their behavior could be predicted with some accuracy. Note, for instance, how the case brought out the research director's strong technical capability accompanied by a gruff, introvertish personality and how this was taken into account in developing plans for a no-nonsense economic study and a series of to-the-point technical meetings.

Better information on Corcoran's own competitive position is one area where the supplier could improve his understanding of Corcoran. The amount of cash flow for each product line, along with the product lines' growth rate, and Corcoran's relative competitive position in the line could be of major help in identifying for which product lines Corcoran must obtain the lowest price possible from its suppliers and those product lines where price may not be as important as other factors. But this kind of information is very difficult to obtain. Usually the company itself has not made this kind of an analysis. Information for such an analysis is typically non-public, held in strict confidence; hence, it can be pieced together, if at all, over a period of time and then only approximately—not with precision.

CHAPTER 7

ORGANIZATIONAL STRATEGIES

What strategies should be used to structure, or more frequently, restructure a business organization? What theories and hypotheses should guide? Repeatedly business people and scholars have raised these questions; there are no quick and ready answers. We believe, however, that we have something helpful to add that we have learned through experience.

WHY ORGANIZATIONAL STRATEGIES?

"Why organizational strategies?" is a question seldom raised by people in business. Yet it is critical and must be answered, or answers to the much-raised questions we have just asked will be askew. This paradox requires some comment. Most people in business don't ask the reason for organizational strategies, because for them the answer is intuitively obvious. They know that these strategies are routes necessary to provide focus on systems of communication and coordination and emphasis on business strategies—from product strategies, the most important, to strategies for the motivation of employees and development of tomorrow's top managers.

BENEFITS OF THEORIES AND HYPOTHESES

Many theories and hypotheses on organization have been solidly established on a foundation of experimental evidence and practical experience. For the businessman looking for help a review of the literature provides both broad directions and clear-cut constraints. For instance, Alfred D. Chandler, Jr.'s thesis that structure follows strategy; Mason Haire's view that the best organization plan requires a clear idea of the objectives of an organization; and Joseph A. Letterer's view that organizations are shaped by their goals provide broad direction. All of these authorities are saying, "you have to know where you want to go before you can construct a vehicle to take you there."

That strategies, and particularly product strategies, shape organizational strategy is shown by the example of Boise Cascade:

> The traditional strategy for Boise Cascade and other land developers had been speculative. Land was bought, cut up, developed, and sold before complaints could mount. Ecologists, however, mobilized public opinion against Boise Cascade's recreational communities being planned for a Puget Sound shorefront and a Hawaiian beach.
>
> After careful analysis, company executives decided that their product strategy had to change from selling land for speculation to selling it for use. The financial strategies, therefore, had to change. Heavy front-end investments would now be needed for swimming pools, golf courses, and sewerage systems. To carry out new product and financial strategies a reorganizational strategy was required. A five-man management council was set up, and under this council finance, strategy, and human resources committees were formed.

Here are two theories on span of control that provide clear-cut constraints. V. A. Graicunas's theory—no one person should supervise the activity of more than five or at the most six other individuals whose work is interrelated—applies to executives at the top of the organization and is based on a theoretical, mathematical formula.

Edward C. Schleh's theory—if work is simple, routine, and repetitive, a supervisor might handle 25 or 30 people—applies to executives at the first decision-making level of the organization and is based on practical experience with organizations.

Even though both theories provide clear-cut constraints, it does not follow that the numbers prescribed for span of control are absolute, that they have universal application.

DRAWBACKS OF THEORIES AND HYPOTHESES

The drawbacks of most theories and hypotheses are the following: (1) What they provide is not always true, (2) their broad directions can be too broad to be a suitable guide, and (3) their constraints need extensive qualifications.

Probably more nonsense has been talked and written about span of control than any other topic on organization. Top management has limited supervision to five, six, seven, and eight executives only to find this span of control unsatisfactory. Consider the case of H. A. Pope and Sons, restaurateurs. The company comprised 24 units of cafeterias, restaurants, and caterers in the St. Louis area, each headed by a unit manager. Reporting to the president, Harry Pope, were three general managers, each supervising eight unit managers. Harry Pope was not pleased with the organizational structure (the executive span of control was close to what Graicunas might have recommended) and so sought change.

He describes a series of events that occurred:

One day the youngest and most junior general manager presented a suggestion that we should have a vice-president of operations who would have the responsibility of coordinating the work of the general managers. He reasoned that this new position would make it possible for employees to move to each of the company divisions, and they would develop and make easier the exchange of ideas between divisions. The general manager pointed out that he would be best qualified to handle the new position.

Because the idea seemed reasonably sound, I made the appointment, and for a while the new plan appeared to work. Then, the vice-president of operations suggested that a third general manager was needed to relieve him of responsibility for supervising units, so that he could concentrate on his ever increasing duties and responsibilities.

It was at this point that I reviewed the entire organizational structure; it seemed illogical to substantially increase our overhead costs. An investigation showed that the two other general managers were working half heartedly, their morale having suffered when the junior general manager was promoted over them.

Also, the general managers and the vice-president were spending much of their time driving from unit to unit. The rest was spent supporting and supervising a few weak managers. The stronger managers neither required nor desired the help and supervision of the general managers. Then, I had a flash of insight. It would be more economical and effective to eliminate the general managers and all unit managers who needed supervision and adopt this policy: "people who need supervision are not qualified to be managers." The vice-president, alone, could supervise all of the units.

The loss of status was more than the vice-president could bear; he found backers and went into business for himself.

Then I decided to apply the new policy and operated with no levels of supervision between unit managers and the central office. There would still be a need for someone to visit the units, not for the purpose of supervising, but to coach, communicate, and evaluate. I solved this problem by hiring a chauffeur and acquiring cars which could be used as moving offices. I stopped spending most of my time in the office and, instead, began to do my office work in the back seat of one of the cars while being driven from unit to unit by a chauffeur. At each unit, only a few minutes were required to quickly evaluate whether the manager was capable of maintaining our standards without supervision.

Frequently, a manager needed coaching, and this could be provided during the visit. If the manager had questions or needed information, I could tell him directly and thus, eliminate costly, time consuming, and expensive written communication.

The chauffeur was available to drive other members of the central office staff when it was necessary for me to be in the office.

The new system of management made us more flexible, more adaptable to changing conditions, more economical than the old system.

We did find one serious flaw. By eliminating the intermediate levels of supervision and the vice-president, we eliminated the logical successor to myself and other key positions in the company.

We recognized this problem and solved it through the development of our "Executive Council." The executive council consists of the top fifteen people in our company; central office department heads and the managers of our largest units. We have a dinner meeting once each month at which all operation problems, policies, and decisions are screened.

In the discussions and deliberations of the executive council we are developing people and learning through the group inter-action, which individuals have leadership qualifications.

We select from the executive council, those people best qualified to serve on the Board of Directors which directs the company and selects a chief executive.

In this short glance at H. A. Pope and Sons restaurateurs organization we see that Graicunas's principle did not apply. The executive span of control that seemed to work best was 24. Clearly the determination of the right executive span of control depends on the personality, innate ability, and stamina of the executive doing the supervising; the effectiveness of his staff; the nature of the tasks to be performed; the abilities of those supervised; and the adequacy of span of control at the first decision-making level.

Schleh's span of control of 25 to 30 for the first decision-making level also needs qualification. He says emphatically that adjustments must be made to these figures for the newness, variability, and complexity of work, staff, and outside relationships and abilities and location of those supervised.

Most executives will readily agree with Chandler's theory that structure follows strategy. Scholars like E. Raymond Corey and Steven Star have added the corollary that organization shapes strategy; the way a business is organized influences its choices of strategies. Most executives will agree with them, too. Disagreement, frequently violent disagreement, occurs over concrete situations. For example, what particular objectives, goals, and strategies should shape structure, and to what extent should units, departments, or divisions be added, enlarged, or deleted from the organization?

ORGANIZATIONAL STRATEGIES SHOULD BE BASED ON COMPROMISES AND TRADE-OFFS

Surely it is plain that no ready-made and ready-working apparatus exists for structuring or restructuring an organization. Principles and hypotheses must be tested for the condition under which they may hold; strengths and weaknesses of key people in the organization must be understood, and intuition and judgment must be applied. For instance, all segments of product and product group strategies must be balanced with financial strategies. For an organizational structure must permit product managers to work with production and financial managers to develop plans and implement them. And so each segment of the structure must be arranged to provide a unity of action toward achieving corporate strategies.

To make our point clearer, let us cite two illustrations. Look at a bureaucratic organizational structure; typically the chain of command is also the promotion ladder. Most changes in organizational structure require a trade-off between the number of levels in the chain of command and the number of levels in the promotion ladder. Most practitioners and theorists accept the principle that levels of authority (chain of command) should be as few as possible because each additional level distorts communication. Most also accept the principle that a promotion ladder is necessary to give employees incentive to remain in an organization. In practice, however, reorganization must represent some kind of trade-off or compromise between these two principles.

Look at an organizational structure tested in Texas by the General Motors Acceptance Corporation (GMAC). An executive in charge of the credit collection function, for example, field collections, office collections, accounting, and customer service, and an executive in charge of sales, for example, promotion, examination of retail customer credit, audits, and purchasing of wholesale and retail automobile paper, reported to a regional manager. The collection function was highly centralized so that GMAC sales representatives could work closer with automobile dealers. One weakness in this organizational structure became obvious— communications were slower and often less accurate. Under the old organizational structure a collection manager could talk directly with the credit manager about a bad retail account, since both were in the same office. Under the new organizational structure the two managers would be located in different buildings in different cities or towns and would have to depend on telephone calls and memos.

The new organizational structure provided a unity of action for reducing collection costs and increasing sales penetration but not without a trade-off—the loss of face-to-face communications.

We could add numerous illustrations. All would show in different ways that organizational strategies depend on the situation (current research attempts to determine what organizational forms have proved most effective under different situations). All would show that organizational strategies should be based on compromises and trade-offs.

ORGANIZATIONAL STRATEGIES SHOULD BE ADAPTED TO CHANGING CONDITIONS

We said in Chapter 1 that the internal and external environments are changing and will continue to change vastly and swiftly. The most successful companies visualize the impact of change and develop strategies to take advantage of it.

Organizational strategies should always be alive, dynamic. The best organizational structure for a company today may be unsuitable in 5 years. To be current, organizational strategies should be reviewed continually, probably once a year. In general we prefer changes step by step over several years because this method is less disruptive and more readily accepted by members of the organization. Sometimes major organizational changes are made irregularly and quickly, and there are usually two basic causes. First a new chief executive officer (CEO) has instigated a reorganization to make a dramatic impact. Second, organizational changes have been neglected for so long that only sudden, major changes can help the organization.

Changes are delayed in many organizations because responsibility for reorganization is not easily placed. In the next section we discuss what individuals and groups are the most likely candidates.

ORGANIZATIONAL STRATEGIES ARE THE CEO's RESPONSIBILITY

All things considered, the CEO must be responsible for organizational strategies. Other individuals and groups who could assist the CEO in the task are:

- Chairman of the board.
- Assistant to the CEO.
- A top-level committee.
- A committee of outside board members.
- Consultants reporting directly to the CEO.

A chairman of the board is usually a good choice. This executive has probably been the CEO and has the knowledge and time to carry out the task.

A staff assistant to the CEO may also be acceptable, provided this person is the CEO's confidant. This assistant thoroughly knows the present organization, its history, and idiosyncrasies; is well acquainted with organizational theory and practice; and is not a contender for the CEO's position or another key position in the organization.

A permanent but more often an *ad-hoc* top-level committee is used when an abrupt major reorganization is contemplated. These top-level committees should be chaired by someone acceptable to the CEO. The chairman, being the key person in any committee, should know about and be concerned with reorganization and should also know the functions of a chairman: how to conduct meetings, how to listen correctly, how to stimulate members to contribute, and how to evaluate these contributions. The committee members must know about and be concerned with reorganization.

A committee of outside board members has the advantage of being objective since its members are not part of the operating organization. Its disadvantage is that its members are usually not acquainted with lower levels of management.

Consultants are often used. They may report directly to the individuals or committees just cited. They provide objectivity and can often persuade people in the company to talk confidentially about their views and problems. Their weakness is they do not and cannot know the inner workings of the organization and individual personalities.

For the rest of this chapter we concentrate on organizational strategies for the multinational corporation because all the problems of the purely domestic corporations are covered and international problems are added. We discuss briefly some of the major issues in multinational organizational design and then present a case history on how one multinational company planned a reorganization.

MAJOR ISSUES IN MULTINATIONAL ORGANIZATIONAL DESIGN

Multinationals organize for worldwide operations either by (1) product or (2) world area, or (3) a combination of the two.

In organization by product the manager of each product group has worldwide responsibility not only for the products but also for all functions connected with that group, for example, marketing, manufacturing, research and development, and licensing. Such an organization fosters worldwide coordination of operations. Its principal disadvantage is that it may result in neglect of some areas, either because of some biases on the part of the product administrator, or more likely because of higher priorities on major market areas with not enough resources to spend time on others. It can also create a morale problem for the expatriate, who sees promotion potential lying back at home base and is anxious to return as soon as possible. It can also frustrate the ambitious national, who often feels that, if rapid promotion is to be gained, a move to world headquarters is necessary, although staying in the home country or region would be preferable.

In organization by world area, divisions or companies are established for the United States, Canada, Europe, Latin America, Asia, Africa, the Middle East, and so forth. The vice president or general manager of each of these geographic divisions reports directly to the CEO or a group vice president and is fully responsible for growth and profits in the area. A major advantage of this kind of organization is that it tends to promote more balanced growth of areas and conversely tends to avoid neglect of some areas because of disproportionate allocation of resources to the larger market areas. Moreover, since the divisions or companies operate independently and autonomously, the expatriate-national personnel problem is somewhat alleviated; both groups can accept more easily the possibility of satisfying a long-term career with the area company or division.

Finally world area orientation improves the chances for a more favorable image with the host country. With a properly designed public-affairs program, the multinational company can appear to be a part of the local community. As nationalism intensifies and pressures mount against the multinational company, the image becomes highly important.

The major disadvantage of world area organization is that it can hinder worldwide product coordination. It provides no mechanism for motivating area management groups to transfer up-to-date know-how promptly to all other world areas. To compensate for this weakness, corporations have placed product coordinators at the corporate level or in an international division with only moderate success.

A mixture of worldwide product and world areas is an attempt to obtain the advantages of both. Occasionally world area organization will be used for some lines of products and worldwide product responsibility for others. More frequently the mixture consists of worldwide product responsibility and area management organizations administered and serviced by an international division. The basic issue in the latter approach is: what should the balance of power be between the product groups and the area groups? With one company that had the major part of its business and investment in Europe the balance of power in Europe tilted toward the product groups, but in other geographical areas it tilted toward the area management groups. Too often decisions on these basic issues are not stated and thus are subjected to different interpretations. The result is friction, confusion, and erratic behavior.

Regardless of how multinationals organize for worldwide operations the final design depends on compromises or trade-offs among these key issues:

- How to motivate domestically oriented managers to do business in foreign countries.
- How to achieve a proper balance between product expertise and world area-country expertise.
- How to achieve balance between decentralized responsibility and authority and centralized overall coordination and control.
- How to coordinate sales and production activities worldwide.
- How to coordinate operations worldwide and maintain a strong national image in each world area-country.
- How to make sure that the expatriates will be willing to maintain foreign residence for a long time and that the nationals will feel that, to advance in the corporation, a move to worldwide headquarters is unnecessary.

WORLDWIDE ELECTRIC COMPANY—A CASE HISTORY IN REORGANIZATION

Whereas Worldwide Electric Company is a disguised name for a multinational corporation that prefers to remain anonymous, all the steps taken in the development of a reorganization strategy are real. We make no claims that what took place should serve as a model. We have no cookbook answers to offer. We merely want to show how one *ad-hoc* committee carried out a reorganization while working against the clock.

Worldwide Electric Company, ranked among the largest electric companies in the United States, manufactured a variety of products, including electrical appliances, military electronic equipment, transformers, and turbines, not only in the United States, but also in 18 foreign countries. Its products were sold through either company salespersons or distributors in almost every country of the free world. Foreign operations accounted for approximately 35% of operating profits, foreign sales, including exports, rising faster than sales in the United States. Total sales were more than $1 billion a year. After World War ll the company made a major policy change. The international division would be responsible for foreign sales and investment. This responsibility was administered through area management groups covering Europe (including Africa and the Middle East), Latin America, and Asia-Pacific. In the late 1960s operating divisions were given worldwide responsibility for the sales and profitability of their products. This created a dual concept of responsibility and organization that required close cooperation between the international division and the operating divisions. The international division provided expertise on areas; the operating divisions, on products. The area management groups under the international division were the experts on cultures, political trends, economic conditions, competition, and marketing needs and provided this information to the operating divisions. The international division was responsible for supplying and allocating the manpower and physical resources required to maintain efficient operations. The operating divisions planned, and the area directors provided the resources to carry out the plans.

In the early 1970s the president's office developed and issued a strategic plan for the corporation that had many implications for the international operations and organization of the company. The interpretation of this corporate plan by the vice president of the international division resulted in a new strategic plan for international operations. He believed that with the new plan a close appraisal and reevaluation of the international organizational structure was needed. He appointed an *ad-hoc* committee to carry out this appraisal. The international marketing director was appointed chairman.

At the outset the *ad-hoc* committee hired a consultant. He would not carry out interviewing within the corporation. Rather than tell the committee what to do, he would be asked to react to ideas presented to him. Presumably he would add greater creativity, objectivity, and breadth to discussions and final recommendations.

A senior partner of a large consulting firm was selected over a renowned scholar. Both had extensive consulting experience, but the senior partner had helped reorganize other groups in the company, and this tilted the selection in his favor. As one executive put it, "The only consultants who can really help us are those who know our executives, our policies, and our ways of doing things."

Next the committee developed a list of minimum organizational requirements that had to be met regardless of any changes that might be made in organization. The finished copy looked as follows:

1 Allow for the provision of coordinated, worldwide marketing services to international customers.
2 Present the image of a top-ranking local supplier within single areas and countries.
3 Permit production facility locations to be selected according to worldwide advantage.
4 Allow for worldwide access to raw materials.
5 Provide for centralization of strategic planning but decentralization of implementation.
6 Promote Worldwide Electric Company's image in foreign areas as an integral part and good influential citizen of the local economy and society.
7 Provide the motivating forces that will satisfy career ambitions with physical location in the area rather than in Buffalo.
8 Give the area director the necessary stature and power to "run" the area rather than be run by the various operating divisions.
9 Provide major strength in financial management.
10 Provide major strength in growth, particularly in new, area-oriented businesses.
11 Provide flexibility for the shifting of resources as required by changes in environment, corporate guidelines, and so forth.

The next step was to examine the most important external factors. The chairman prepared an initial list and in the committee meeting some factors were added, others deleted.

The final outcome was this list of external factors:

1 Nationalism is increasing.
2 In Latin America groups of countries, such as the Andean Bloc, will become effective common markets before all of LAFTA becomes effective.

3 Over a period of 25 years Africa will gradually emerge as an important industrial and agricultural area of the world, principally orientated toward Europe.

4 All the countries of Western Europe will ultimately become a part of the European common market.

5 In the Asia Pacific area an effective get-together of economic blocs will likely lag behind that in other world areas.

6 Arab–Israeli confrontations will continue for many years. A hotter war is likely in the Middle East.

7 There will be a tremendous growth in the electronics field where Worldwide Electric's greatest profit potential lies.

8 Governments will continue to exert greater control over business and economics; the need for businesses to try to influence governments' actions will grow.

9 A body of laws dealing with international companies will ultimately emerge.

10 Countries, including the United States, will continue to extend their "company control laws" outside the borders of their own country.

11 There will be an intensification of competition, particularly from Europe and Japan.

12 World trade will become freer, and the gradual breakdown of trade barriers will continue.

13 The trend toward a "smaller world" through major improvements in communications and supersonic air travel will accelerate.

14 Rapid change will require ever-increasing amounts of continued education.

15 Management manpower will be in short supply in the late 1970s because of the current population age distribution.

16 It will become necessary for the company to react faster to new trends.

17 People will change their attitudes toward leisure, their loyalties, and their preferences for place of work, uses for their money, and so forth.

All agreed that the major internal factors having major significance for future organizational plans were:

- Operating divisions were becoming more experienced in international operations.

- Some top-level executives were questioning the soundness of organizing by worldwide products instead of by world areas.
- A corporate objective has stated that the company will be one of the 25 largest multinational companies.
- The trend among the operating divisions was to appoint an "international director."
- There was an ever-increasing need for information and for more effective ways to communicate and evaluate it.
- Product groups were increasing, success for each depending on a particular, often widely different, marketing mix.
- International business was growing faster and becoming more profitable than domestic business.
- Attitudes toward the international division varied among operating divisions. Some divisions looked upon it as an encroacher, others as a valuable partner.

Next the committee reviewed alternative organizational models prepared by the chairman after discussion with several members of the committee. Six models were presented (see Exhibits 7.1 and 7.2).

Model 1 was similar to the present organizational structure except the head of the international division would report to a senior vice president, who would be one step in rank above group vice presidents. The committee reasoned that this structure would expand the influence of the international division on operating divisions, would avoid most political problems, and would least upset the present structure and operations. Group vice presidents would probably oppose the position of senior vice president.

Model 2 placed international operations completely under each operating division. Thus each product line division would have its own international group. This model eliminated any conflict between international and domestic divisions, but it would be expensive because more people would be needed. It would also create serious problems in coordinating total corporate activities in the geographic areas.

Model 3 added a third group vice president to whom area directors, raised to general manager status, reported. The international division was eliminated; certain staff functions would be transferred to the staff of the new group vice president. Operating divisions would retain worldwide responsibility. This model elevated the role of area directors and would make international influence felt. It would not, however, solve the problem of keeping sales efforts in line with sales potential or the problems created by nationals and

Exhibit 7.1 Organization Models

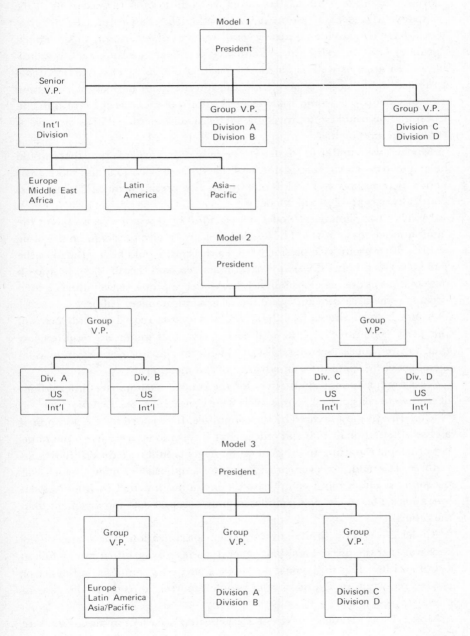

expatriates in overseas companies, who had strong feelings that they must move to corporate headquarters to realize ambition for advancement in the company. Moreover, if the model were adopted, changes in area directors would have to be made because several were not of general manager caliber.

Model 4 would create three group vice president positions, each responsible for an area, as well as for some operating divisions. This organizational structure would perhaps accelerate the international outlook of the group vice presidents but would make coordination between areas more difficult. Coordination could be improved by having the international division serve as staff to the president.

Model 5 was similar to Model 4. The only difference was that there would be only two group vice presidents, both having more divisions and more areas under their authority. The loss of a group vice president made Model 5 less politically acceptable than Model 4.

Model 6 was similar to Model 1. Instead of by a senior vice president the international division would be headed by a group vice president on the same level as other group vice presidents. Area directors would be upgraded to the same level as product division general managers and thereby help to smooth out conflicts of dual responsibility. Like Model 3, problems would be created because some area directors were not of general manager caliber.

A matrix form, shown in Exhibit 7.3, was used to record the judgments of the *ad-hoc* committee on how well each model met minimum requirements that had previously been established. The form was filled out by individual members of the committee in advance of the meeting.

Next organizational alternatives for the central headquarters international staff were considered. Four models were considered (see Exhibit 7.4).

Model 1 was most favored by the committee. It provided for the addition of a chief international financial officer. But if this model were used, the number of people reporting to the general manager would be reduced from eight to three. It would, however, provide greater emphasis to finance, which was becoming a much more complicated, demanding function in international operations. This model was considered more acceptable to management than the others.

Model 2 was most similar to the present organization. The major difference was that the present assistant general manager was shifted from a line to a staff position. This shift would not provide adequate emphasis on finance or needed reduction in the number of people reporting directly to the general manager.

Model 3 was identical to Model 2 except that area liaison managers were

Exhibit 7.2   Organization Models

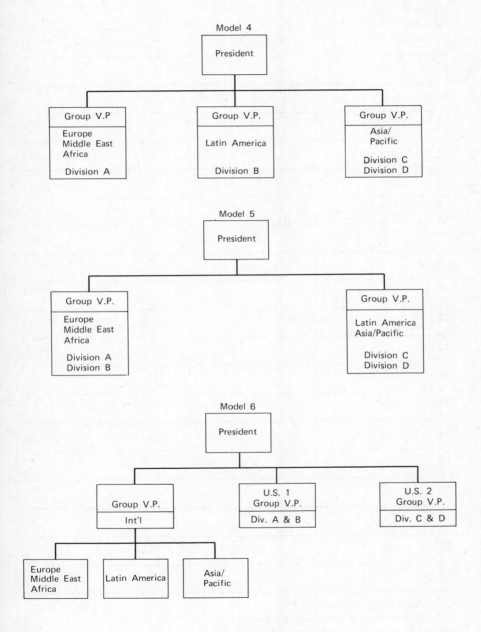

Model 4

President

Group V.P
Europe
Middle East
Africa

Division A

Group V.P.
Latin America

Division B

Group V.P.
Asia/
Pacific

Division C
Division D

Model 5

President

Group V.P.
Europe
Middle East
Africa

Division A
Division B

Group V.P.
Latin America
Asia/Pacific

Division C
Division D

Model 6

President

Group V.P.
Int'l

U.S. 1
Group V.P.
Div. A & B

U.S. 2
Group V.P.
Div. C & D

Europe
Middle East
Africa

Latin America

Asia/
Pacific

Exhibit 7.3*

Minimum Require-ments	Models					
	1	2	3	4	5	6
1						
2						
3						
4						
5						
6						
7						
8						
9						
10						
11						
12						
13						
14						
15						
16						
17						
18						
19						

*—Meets requirements well;
**—Meets requirements only somewhat;
***—Meets requirements poorly or not at all.*

Exhibit 7.4 Organization Models

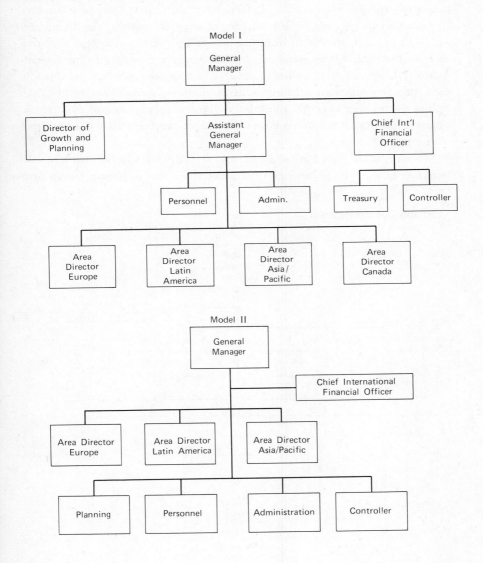

added to the international headquarters staff. These managers would serve as counterpart deputies at the headquarters for each area. They would be responsible for looking out for the interests of the area, assisting the area director in liaison activities with headquarters groups between visits of the area director to headquarters, monitoring results of the area, and informing headquarters on important activities in the area. This model had been tried before with only limited success. Moreover, this model would increase rather than reduce the number of people reporting to the general manager of the international division, who was often out of the country and needed a reduced span of control.

Model 4 would transform the international division into a corporate staff department that would provide international services to the operating divi-

Exhibit 7.4 continued

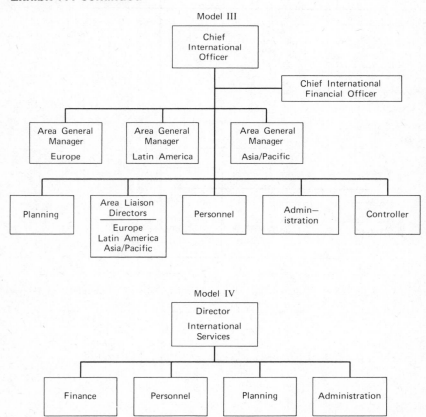

sions and to the finance and personnel corporate staff departments. It was decided that, although the international division might ultimately evolve into a purely staff position, such an evolution was several years away. It was felt that such a scheme would not work until the total corporation and particularly the operating divisions knew more about international operations. In the long run the committee concluded that the international headquarters staff might ultimately be stripped down to just three functions:

- Finance.
- Planning and diversification.
- Administration (would consist mostly of handling paper from the general manager's desk).

Personnel, order and billing, controllership, and other administrative functions would then be carried out by central staff departments, areas, and divisions.

From the standpoint of the committee, the key issues in reorganization were power and politics. How to manage the balance of power skillfully between operating divisions and the areas, clearer definitions of authority, "charter," and agreed-upon working relationships were needed. As a start two formats were developed: one dealt with degrees of responsibility between areas and the operating divisions (ODs), and the other with degrees of responsibility for the area general manager (see Exhibits 7.5 and 7.6).

To clarify the international division's authority, the committee also developed a new international division charter, as shown in Exhibit 7.8

Before preparing a final report, the *ad-hoc* committee requested a separate report from the consultant, one that would give the consultant's independent appraisal and recommendations. The consultant reached two major conclusions:

- The need for some additions to the international charter.
- The need for an "organizational capability," a way to deal with the balance of power between the areas and operating divisions.

Two additions recommended were that the international division should be given full responsibility and authority in those instances when:

- Businesses in the areas had little or no relationship to the business of the operating divisions.

Exhibit 7.5 Degrees of Responsibility: Areas versus Operating Divisions (ODs)

	Degree of Responsibility*	
	Area	OD
General Administration		
Organizational plans	1	5
Selection, appointment, or change in common products personnel	3	3
Selection, appointment, or change in other personnel	1	5
Civic affairs	1	5
Governmental relations	1	5
Marketing		
Pricing	4	2
Channels of distribution	2	4
Field sales management	1	5
Strategic product plan	4	2
Implementation of product plan	2	4
Advertising	3	3
Technical service	2	4
Commercial research	1	5
Finished goods inventory management	2	4
Manufacturing		
Product selection	5	1
Technical process and backup	5	1
Capability and monthly production schedules	5	1
Plant operation	1	5
Maintenance	1	5
Meeting standard costs	1	5
Setting standard costs	3	3
Meeting quality standards	5	1
Plant location	3	3
Setting quality standards	4	2

*1—Independent authority for action; 2—independent authority for action but after consultation; 3—shared authority for action; 4—prior consultation. No authority; 5—no authority.

Exhibit 7.6 Degrees of Responsibility: General Manager of Area

	Degree of Responsibility*
General Administration	
Organizational plans	2
Selection, appointment, or change in personnel	1
Civic affairs	1
Government relations	1
Marketing	
Pricing	2
Channels of distribution	1
Field sales management	1
Strategic product plans	2
Implementation of product plans	1
Advertising	2
Technical service	1
Commercial research	1
Finished-goods inventory management	1
Manufacturing	
Product selection	1
Technical process and backup	3
Capacity and monthly production schedules.	2
Plant operation	
Maintenance	1
Standard costs (set and meet)	1
Quality standards	2
Plant location	2
Research and Development	
Selection of research projects	3
Selection and screening of development projects	1
Location of research laboratories	2
Staffing for R & D	1
Organization structure	1

*1—Independent authority for action; 2—independent authority for action but after consultation; 3—shared authority for action; 4—prior consultation. No authority; 5—no authority.

Exhibit 7.7 Worldwide Electric Company International Division Charter

The international division provided expertise on areas, whereas the operating divisions provided expertise on products. With the dual concept the international division had overall area and overseas entity profit responsibility, whereas operating divisions had profit responsibility for their products in all parts of the world.

In any given location the operating divisions are responsible for profitability of individual products, but the international division is responsible for the composite whole and for supplying and allocating the manpower and physical resources required to maintain efficient operations and maximize earnings. (Financial resources are the responsibility of the financial department through the international financial officer.)

This requires close cooperation, constant interface, and spelled-out relationships between the international division and operating divisions; since the nature of products and local area circumstances differ markedly, this spelling out of relationships and respective responsibilities is required on a product-by-product basis for each area.

The international division has, therefore, the following special roles:

1. Initiates with the operating divisions the documentation of area product policies and plans, including agreed-to respective responsibilities.

2. Develops and maintains an image of Worldwide Electric in the area compatible with corporate, long-range goals.

3. In each major area, maintains those government relations required to influence local government actions and attitudes beneficial to Worldwide Electric Company.

4. Identifies and initiates programs to exploit opportunities for new businesses that are unique to foreign countries.

5. With the operating divisions, identifies foreign personnel needs and develops the career planning, training, and administrative practices programs that will maintain an environment of equal treatment for Worldwide employees, wherever they may be located throughout the world, and that will provide Worldwide foreign manpower resources needs compatible with corporate international goals and plans.

6. Provides the corporation's principal source for foreign "intelligence," sociological and technical trends and developments, leaving to the operating divisions, however, the commercial intelligence requirements for their products.

● Operating divisions decided with good reason that they did not care to act and delegated authority and responsibility to the international division.

To meet the need for "organizational capability," it was recommended that an International Management Committee, chaired by a senior vice president of the corporation, be formed. Other members of the committee would be the group vice presidents (to whom the operating divisions' general managers reported) and the international division general manager. The major function of the committee would be to judge the total impact on the company of proposed actions by either the operating divisions or the international division. The committee would decide on the best use of facilities, personnel, and resources. Exhibit 7.8 shows the proposed organization.

Exhibit 7.8   Proposed Organization

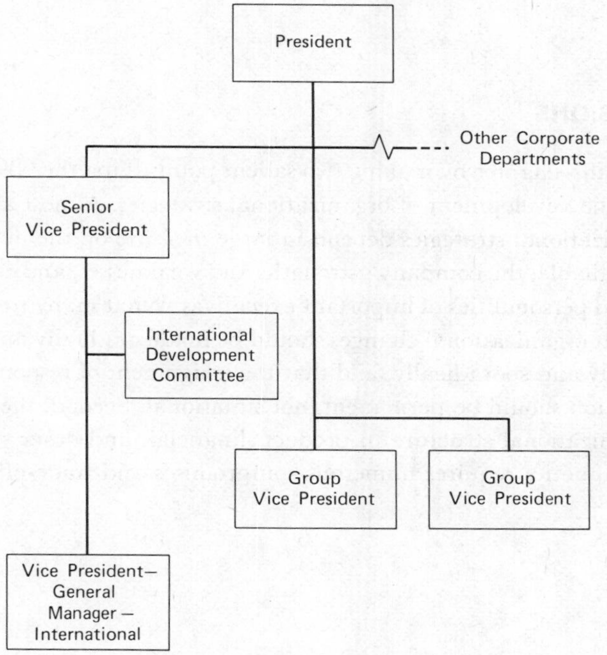

The *ad-hoc* committee accepted the proposals of the consultant. The International Management Committee idea was particularly well received. It was felt that such a committee would provide the relief valve needed to keep in proper balance the dual-responsibility role between the operating divisions and the international division.

Finally, recognizing the need for a continuing effort, the committee recommended assignment of responsibility to one individual to:

- Ensure that the decisions reached were implemented.
- Periodically reappraise organizational needs so that new strategies and plans could be developed and old ones modified.

The conclusions and recommendations of the *ad-hoc* committee were given orally and later presented in writing to the general manager of the international division.

He would make the decision: what to propose to the CEO. He would develop the strategy for acceptance, how to gain support from the product divisions, and, if they were uncooperative, how to gain support from the CEO.

CONCLUSIONS

Let us end this chapter by making two salient points. First the CEO is the key person in the development of organizational strategies. Almost all are aware that organizational strategies depend in large measure on the market opportunities available, the company's strengths and weaknesses, and especially the abilities and personalities of important executives. What many frequently fail to see is that organizational changes should be made gradually and regularly, not suddenly and sporadically, and that the assignment of responsibilities for reorganization should be permanent, not situational. Second, the adaptation of an organizational structure to product, financial, and other strategies, to power and politics requires numerous compromises and trade-offs.

CHAPTER 8

FINANCIAL STRATEGIES

Chief financial officers (CFOs) define financial strategies as the ways to minimize the cost of capital, or more simply as ways to provide the necessary funds when they are needed and where they are needed at the lowest cost. Definitions of financial strategies may go further and also include ways to obtain maximum return on liquid assets for a given level of risk.

Strategic planning begins with setting goals, and financial goals are critical. It ends with deciding the financial strategies needed to carry out all other strategies. This last point may seem too obvious to dwell on, but every strategy requires money for accomplishment. For instance, it would be sheer folly to develop a product strategy when a company has not and cannot obtain the funds necessary to implement it. Even with a public-image strategy, funds are required to produce pamphlets, articles, and books, to use other media, to support a public relations staff, and so forth.

Better financial strategies are more pressingly needed now than in the past. In domestic business, interest rates are higher and fluctuate more frequently. For many companies, shrinking profit margins have decreased the internal sources of financing and have required more borrowing. In international business different rates of inflation in each country have resulted in a continual revaluation of national currencies; heavy purchases of stable currencies, like the Swiss franc, and government controls have led to some unrealistic exchange rates. And advances in technology and lifting of controls have made short-term funds highly interdependent. All of these causes and effects (and many others) have introduced in recent years more complexities and risks.

What are the necessary factors that shape financial strategies? We list the following:

1   The need for financial resources.
2   The ability and image of the CFO.
3   A company's past actions and performance.
4   Financial policies on debt leverage, capital spending, hurdle rates, dividends, cost reduction programs, spinoffs and writeoffs, liquidity, and lead time for acquiring longterm capital.

THE NEED FOR FINANCIAL RESOURCES

What financial resources will be needed, when they will be needed, and even what financial resources are available depend on expected results. In manufacturing businesses financial resources are needed mostly for capital expenditures on new plants and expansions and increased working capital. In service industries financial resources are needed mostly for working capital.

What internal resources will be available depends on cash flow. Two major positive elements of cash flow are net income and depreciation and obsolescence. Depreciation and obsolescence are easy to set and are fairly accurate. (The U.S. Internal Revenue Service provides guidelines.) Net income forecasts require, however, considerable research and effort. Yet they are frequently inaccurate, since they depend on economic forecasts and a correct interpretation of how those forecasts will affect company sales.

THE ABILITY AND IMAGE OF THE CFO

The CFO and the chief executive officer (CEO) are the two most important people involved in financial strategies. Often, they are one person. When this is not so, an image of competence and trustworthiness for the CFO, both inside and outside the organization, becomes crucial for two reasons. First his image will play a major part in his ability to borrow and bargain effectively with the financial community. Second his image will play a major part in winning the CEO's confidence, a key element in management's attitude toward risk.

A COMPANY'S PAST ACTIONS AND PERFORMANCE

The past actions and performance of a company are constraints to financial strategies. If a company has recently obtained funds from capital markets, financial executives will not return for more funds soon lest they be accused of being poor planners. And take the case of a company whose top management's integrity was questioned because of an unfortunate timing coincidence. Top management felt that it was necessary to announce prematurely the introduction of a new product because of a security leak. The household consumer market reacted enthusiastically and the product was widely publicized. During this time the company was also floating a major common stock issue. The product subsequently turned out to be an utter failure. Investment bankers surmised the publicity was timed to create interest in the stock issue, and the company's image tumbled. It would be impossible for the company to float any new stock issues until enough time had passed to make the incident grow dim.

Cost-cutting programs play a role in the development of financial strategies. Such programs can eliminate inefficiencies or "fat" and make it possible to set realistically the amount of funds needed to achieve results.

Past financial performance is perhaps the most important constraint to financial strategies. It fixes the rating that a company will receive in its bond issues—the cost of capital through long-term debt. It fixes the price earnings ratio—the cost of capital through the issue of common stock. The image of a company that strong management, technical competence, innovativeness, and social responsibility bring are also important, but what really matter are the results—rapidly or even steadily rising earnings per share of common stock.

FINANCIAL POLICIES

Financial policies affect financial strategies since they provide guidelines and limitations. Unlike economic conditions, management has complete control of financial policies that simply reflect a "style" and attitude toward risk.

Debt Leverage

Long-term capital needs of a company can be obtained through debt, sale of capital stock, retained earnings, or some combination of the three. Company financial policies with adjustments to meet local country practices in international operations dictate what financial strategies will be used. Within a given industry in the United States, debt-to-equity ratios will vary from almost no debt to high debt to equity. For example, in 1972 DuPont had a ratio of long-term debt to total capitalization of 7%, while Dow Chemical had

46%. Dow's nearly 1:1 debt-to-equity ratio is considered high in the chemical industry in the United States but extremely low in the chemical industry in Japan, where a ratio of 2:1 debt to equity would be typical.

The right debt-to-equity ratio for a company varies with (1) the capacity of the company to cover debt-carrying charges and show a steady growth of common stock earnings per share after interest charges and (2) the investing public's and financial community's evaluation of a proper debt-to-equity ratio for the industry and a specific company.

The investing public and financial community's evaluation depend not only on the historical growth in earnings per share of common stock but also on the competitive position of the company and the opportunity this position provides to use debt leverage as a competitive weapon. For debt leverage can be used to provide a higher rate of return on stockholders' equity and to gain or hold market share through lowering prices without a loss of income for the common stock shareowner. High debt leverage is particuarly applicable to companies that are low-cost producers because it permits more debt with less risk than competition.

Although Dow had a lower return on gross investment than DuPont in 1972, Dow was able to show a higher return on stockholders' equity than DuPont. Dow's relatively good performance during the 1974–1975 recession further demonstrated that its strong competitive position permitted it to carry a high debt load without undue risk. Dow's use of a debt-to-equity strategy was undoubtedly one of the reasons why the company enjoyed a higher price earnings ratio than DuPont during the early 1970s.

Capital Spending

Capital spending requires the greatest use of financial resources. In fact the demand for funds for new projects often exceeds practical levels of availability. Capital spending policy must, therefore, be formulated to provide a balance between fixed capital needs and financial resources available.

For capital-intensive companies, capital expenditures are usually subject to wide fluctuations that are the result of cyclical economic changes combined with the need for large amounts of capital to build plants of sufficient size to be competitive worldwide.

Wide fluctuations in capital expenditures for a company that shall be nameless (Exhibit 8.1) resulted from delayed expansion programs during recession periods when there was much idle plant capacity. When economic conditions begin to improve, capital investment programs are revised and implemented but usually too late to have the new plants or additions on stream when needed. Other companies in the same industry react in much the same way. Thus many new plants and additions come on stream at about the same time and create overcapacity. Overcapacity continues until demand finally catches up with capacity. Then a recession occurs and the cycle just described begins again.

To avoid fluctuations in capital expenditures, some companies have adopted a policy of leveling out capital expenditures, as illustrated by a 5-year moving average shown in Exhibit 8.1. Thus, even in a recession a company will be maintaining a relatively high level of capital expenditures. New plant capacity is then available when needed in next periods of high demand when most competitors will be short of capacity. Yet the strategy helps to limit a large excess capacity during recession.

Notice in Exhibit 8.1 that the curve 1968–1973 was relatively flat, even though the industry sharply reduced capital expenditures in 1972.

A strategy of leveled-out capital expenditures seems logical and simple. Still, most top managers feel uncomfortable maintaining a high level of fixed capital spending when demand for their products is low. To do so requires confidence in staff research on the timing of economic cycles and its effect on demand for specific products for which plant expansions or new plants will be needed.

Exhibit 8.1   Five-Year Moving Averages for Capital Investments (1945–1975)

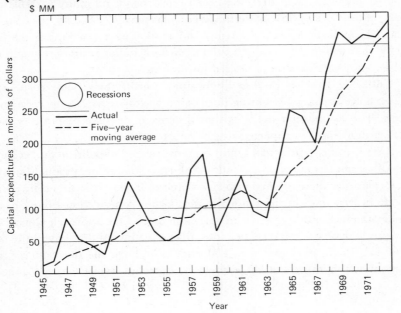

Hurdle Rates

Hurdle rates on capital expenditure projects (standards for evaluating profitability) limit financial strategies. Long-range profitability goals and the present level of profitability, combined with the company's estimated cost of capital, determine a hurdle rate. Once set, every major capital expenditure submitted for approval to the CEO or a top-management committee is expected to meet or exceed this standard.

The rationale for using cost of capital in determining a hurdle rate is that an investment must at least earn what it costs to raise the capital for the investment. Measuring the cost of capital is, however, a difficult, inexact procedure. Determining the cost of debt is easy. Determining the cost of equity is difficult because in large measure it involves subjective judgment on what stockholders expect in future earnings from the company. Thus, measuring the cost of capital is highly complex, inexact, and controversial. All figures are based on assumptions that can easily be challenged.

Determining a hurdle rate, too, is difficult. For most companies the number of approved projects that do achieve projected profitability is low. Research studies indicate that variances from forecasted earnings result primarily from errors in predicting a product's selling price. Overestimating sales volume is next. In most instances estimated plant and construction costs are closer in line with actual costs.

Selling price is least accurate because it depends on many variables, like competitors' prices, raw-material prices, elasticity of demand, economics of scale, technological breakthroughs, and marketing costs. Project managers know that selling prices are, therefore, hard to challenge and use manipulated selling prices to achieve desired hurdle rates.

Until now we have discussed only single hurdle rates. Some corporations have, however, variable hurdle rates based on differences in the risks of projects. The assumption made is that differences in risks of projects should reflect differences in expected rate of return.

Risks are of two principal types: (1) those related to political and economic conditions in a country or area and (2) those related to the product line itself. It is clear that there are higher political and economic risks for an investment made in Iraq than in the United States, for an American company has less understanding and experience in operating there. One approach places countries in four broad-risk classifications, that is, countries that have little or no risk, small risk, moderate risk, and high risk. Then the question is raised: How much more profitability should be expected from each risk category?

This profitability can be expressed in relative terms called risk factors to provide for changes in the hurdle rate. For example, risk factors of 1.0, 1.2, 1.5, and 2.0 might be calculated for the four broad risk classifications just mentioned whether the profitability standard is return on gross investment, return on net investment, net profit percent of sales, or discounted cash flow rate of return (see the tabulation).

Country Classification	Risk Factor
Little or no risk	1.0
Small risk	1.2
Moderate risk	1.5
High risk	2.0

The profitability rate of a project divided by the risk factor gives an adjusted profitability rate that can be compared with the current hurdle rate for the type of project in question. From the example cited, a country with high risk is expected to have twice the profitability of a country with little or no risk.

About risks related to the product line itself, it is not hard to conclude that investments for new developments are much riskier than investments for a well-established product line. Thus they should earn (and often do) a higher rate of return than normal.

Among a company's well-established product lines wide differences exist, of course, in rates of return on investment (ROI). For product lines in the late maturity or decline stages of product life cycle may have an average rate of return of 6%. Another product line having a high technology and a strong proprietary position may earn a rate of return from 12% to 18%.

When companies have such highly diversified product lines, a single hurdle rate does not apply. For example, a hurdle rate of 10% would be too high for the first product line and, if rigidly enforced, would lead to the end of the product line. The probability that new projects for the line would reach the 10% hurdle rate is small. Without new projects, new products, the product line merely continues along the declining stage of the life cycle and dies. For product lines having high technology and a strong proprietary position a hurdle rate of 10% provides no incentive for managers to maintain or upgrade the present level of profitability. After all, projects could be approved that earned below normal.

The point of our illustration is that a strong case can be made for using several rather than one hurdle rate. If several are used, one is still faced with the question: How should they be used? Should they be used throughout the company, or should they be used solely as a guide for top management? We think a blend of these extremes is best. If hurdle rates are used too openly or too rigidly, we suspect the product administrator will "make his figures come out right" when projects he proposes are really below the hurdle rate. If top management withholds information on desired hurdle rates, product administrators can waste much effort in preparing project plans for approval that are below hurdle rates.

All things considered, hurdle rates should serve only as a guide, not as an absolute standard. To apply hurdle rates to all capital outlays is impossible; at times options do not exist. Projects must be approved, even though projected ROI is substantially below normal or even negative. Projects to provide service facilities, or to prevent or eliminate ecological problems illustrate this point. Sometimes a facility with a low projected ROI is needed to complement an existing profitable operation, as in producing intermediates for plastics, fibers, and high-value-added organic chemicals. The profitability of the entire system must be considered, not just one project.

Dividends

Investors in common stock have three objectives: capital gains, income, or a little of both. Now when a company is growing rapidly, much of its cash flow is needed for reinvestment, and a financial policy of low or no dividends will probably be maintained. An assumption is made (usually correctly) that, if operations are profitable, enough investors will be interested in capital gains to support a respectable price earnings ratio. When a company has reached a stage of moderate growth, it will probably adopt a dividend policy of a certain percentage payout of earnings that the company feels can be sustained in future years.

Dividend policies, debt-to-equity policies, and capital expenditures policies are all interrelated. For instance, consider a decision to have a dividend policy that makes it necessary that additional funds be raised in the capital markets. This dividend policy may limit the amount of funds that will then be available for capital investment. Suppose the company decides that it will maintain a dividend policy at "real" dollar levels per share of stock and increases dividends to compensate for inflation. To provide resources also for growth, the financial strategy may require periodically raising additional funds through issues of stock or funded debt. There are, however, limits on debt because of traditional debt-to-equity ratios. When a company begins to approach this limit, it must reduce dividends, expenses, or capital investment or all three or raise additional funds through equity issues.

Cost Reduction Programs

As we said earlier, before new funds are acquired in capital markets, every effort should be made to see if cost reduction programs can eliminate or reduce the need for additional funds. Many companies achieve cost reduction through methods analysis and value engineering programs that seek to reduce costs without impairing any product functions.

After the effects of these programs are appraised, companies can then decide the amount of new equipment still needed to increase productivity. This point is exemplified by these comments by William A. Marquand, President of American Standard, Inc., in his 1976 letter to stockholders:

> Our objective is to exceed a 4 per cent return on sales after taxes. To this end we have accelerated our programs to improve productivity. In addition, capital spending will be increased by nearly 20 per cent in 1976 and the main portion will be utilized to provide new equipment and processes to renovate our facilities and thereby reduce our manufacturing cost.

Most companies, oddly enough, do not have continuous cost reduction programs in administration, marketing, and research and development (R & D). Like capital expenditures, these programs occur in waves coincident with downturns in the business cycle. The policy followed to reduce costs is to fire or lay off employees, and most companies let people go at about the same time. Conversely they will be actively rehiring at about the same time, and this forces up starting salaries, and the selection of high-quality candidates is cut.

Spinoffs and Writeoffs

In theory, assets of a company will be retained throughout their economic life. Moreover, when liquidated, they will have little or no book value. Naturally the theory works only part of the time. In practice, assets are frequently disposed of or written off before they have reached zero book value for these reasons: technological breakthroughs have made the assets obsolete; the assets are more valuable to someone else; or a project did not turn out to be as profitable as anticipated, and assets are divested through writeoffs, spinoffs, or a combination of both.

The effects of spinoffs and writeoffs on financial strategies are both psychological and real. Spinoffs can involve an increase in cash resources if a buyer with cash can be found for the assets. Psychologically such actions can have positive or negative effects on the investing public, but typically they are negative. The spinoff happens when a company stops being competitive or when a new project fails. In brief, spinoffs usually hint of failure and lower a company's image in capital markets.

Depending on the time and circumstances, spinoffs can hint of success. For instance, on March 19, 1976, Darwin E. Smith, chairman and CEO of Kimberly-Clark, announced the corporation's plans to sell its Kimberly Wisconsin mill, the last of its U.S. mills producing coated papers.

The corporation began its withdrawal from the coated-paper business in 1971 and 1972 when it sold four mills that had losses or marginal results. The Kimberly Wisconsin mill had a $7 million operating loss in 1975.

The market viewed these spinoffs as a necessary part of a master plan for greater future earnings.

Writeoffs do not hurt cash resources. They do bear on earnings, which, in turn, affect capital markets. Whether to write off assets requires judgment. Thus much latitude exists when the writeoff takes place. When earnings are unusually high, as they were for many companies in 1973, the tendency is to write off as much as possible; in such years the writeoffs are not noticed very much by stockholders, and, in addition, they help to set the stage for showing better return on assets in later years when earnings may not be as good.

When it occurs in a year of poor earnings, a large writeoff creates the impression that the company made a big mistake sometime in the past; this can be damaging to price earnings ratio and borrowing capacity.

Liquidity

Although no one financial ratio serves as a true criterion for liquidity, the most widely used is the current ratio, the ratio of current assets to current liabilities. Corporate management and the financial community have traditionally set the bottom level at 2:1. The assumption has been that companies that go below the 2:1 ratio were heading for difficulty if the unexpected should occur.

The case of a large manufacturer of electronic equipment illustrates at least a partial truth in this assumption. With a surge in sales and profits in 1967–1969, electronic equipment inventories were doubled and short-and long-term debt more than doubled. With a slowing down of the economy in 1970–1971, combined with an influx of new competition, sales ebbed and profits dwindled. The company survived; it had a current ratio greater than 2 : 1. It also had a strong cash and short-term securities position that could best be determined not by the current ratio but by the liquidity ratio, the ratio of total cash, U.S. government securities, and other securities divided by total current liabilities. What is interesting about the late 1960s and early 1970s is that current ratio for most manufacturing companies remained reasonably stable; the liquidity ratio (normally about .27) varied widely as accounts receivable and inventories skyrocketed for some companies and created cash binds.

Astute liquidity management, the right use of accounts receivable, inventories, accounts payable, and cash reduces the funds needed from outside sources.

In managing inventories, one must always keep in mind that the marginal costs of carrying each unit of inventory should be equal to or less than the marginal cost of being out of one unit of inventory. In other words it mustn't cost more to carry additional inventory than to be out of stock. Inventory managers must also weigh longrun and shortrun results. For instance, in the short run a company might decide that it will make more money by not selling to some customers during periods of peak demand, but the question that must be raised is: how will this action affect sales and profits during periods of slack demand?

In managing accounts receivable, a credit policy is also needed that ensures that losses from bad debts are compensated for by greater sales and profits.

In managing accounts payable, companies can gain working capital by slowing up on payments when discounts are not offered and paying on the last day of a discount period. Many companies take advantage of "float," the time it takes for a check to clear the bank on which it is drawn. For instance, to increase float, a company will pay a bill to a supplier in Chicago with a check on a New York bank. The Post Office Department's sectional-center concept has increased float time for checks drawn on rural banks, since all mail is now directed to sectional centers, although it may first pass through the town for which it is destined. We have been told that, when promoting new business, executives of a bank in a small town in North Carolina make it known that it takes longer to clear a check from their bank than any other bank in the United States.

One result of the excessive use of float has been the attempt to reduce it by use of electronic transfers. Moreover, when money is tight, supply is usually tight. If a company is slow to pay accounts payable, its relationship with suppliers must be good lest it be cut off from suppliers or have its credit rating damaged.

Cash Management

A sound cash management policy is necessary to combat liquidity problems. Clearly, cash flow projections are needed for estimations of inflows and outflows of cash. Companies would like to operate with just enough cash to meet normal expenses and have a cushion for the unexpected. Besides the use of "float," companies can improve their cash position through good loan negotiations with banks. Generally banks have similar interest rates, but some permit a smaller balance of deposits than competitors and thus make more cash available. Companies obtain maximum return on their cash by holding checking accounts to a minimum or sometimes by moving cash from banks to short-term government securities with higher interest rates.

In international business, cash management is knotty and complicated. Devaluations and other actions of governments and of pressure groups must be given close attention. With the instability of many world currencies companies must hedge against devaluations. Forecast must pinpoint not only the amount of devaluation but also when it will occur to minimize devaluation losses. Governments can and do restrict the flow of funds across their borders. For example, the U.S. Office of Foreign Direct Investment (OFDI) (now terminated) set restrictions and requirements on transfer of certain funds from and into the United States. In many companies, public opinion, the threat of criticism, and investigation limit the extent to which currencies can be shifted from one country to another.

Lead Time for Acquiring Long-Term Capital

"Seek long-term capital only when you need it" seems like a wise policy. Yet this policy may prevent a company from minimizing its cost of capital, its fundamental financial strategy. Too many companies have waited for a need to arise before seeking long-term capital only to experience great difficulty in trying to float a stock issue during a downturn in the stock market or a bond issue when interest rates are soaring.

Timing is essential if the lowest cost of capital is to be attained. For example, with the upturn in business in 1976 many companies began to float bond issues. The result was, of course, an increase in the cost of capital to those who entered the bond market late. During the mid-1960s and early 1970s rates of ROI were declining for many industries (see Exhibit 8.2). In some instances the cost of capital was higher than the rate of ROI. Yet some firms had the insight to borrow funds at the lowest cost of capital during that period and

Exhibit 8.2   Return on Stockholders' Investment of Selected Manufacturing Industries

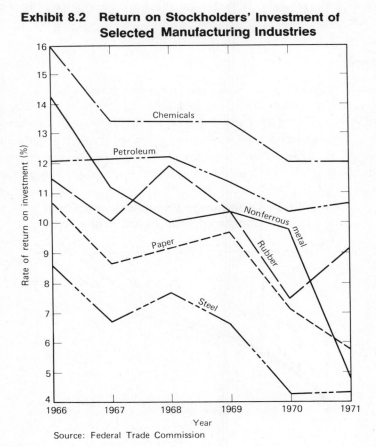

Source: Federal Trade Commission

use the funds to add new plants and equipment. The result was greater productivity and a higher rate of ROI.

INCOME STATEMENT AND BALANCE SHEET FORECASTS

That a critical relationship between income statement and balance sheet forecasts and financial strategies exists is an unalterable fact. What financial resources will be needed and when they will be needed depend principally on income statement and balance sheet forecasts. Poor forecasts undermine financial strategies. If forecasts are wrong, financial strategies will be wrong. Therefore, a sense of realism, proper interpretations of economic forecasts, and contingency plans for crucial events that have a low probability of occurrence are called for.

Realism

Corporate long-range projections of income, when graphed for a succession of years, create a configuration that looks like the characteristic shape of a tornado (see Exhibit 8.3). The heavy solid line in the graph represents actual income. The lighter lines are a record of projected income. Typical income projections for the first 2 or 3 years are near actual, but beyond 3 years they rise far above actual. The optimism suggested by the graph is in part under-

**Exhibit 8.3   Long-Range Projections of Income
Compared with Actual Projections**

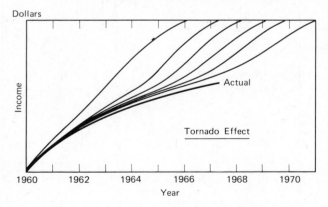

standable. Businessmen and businesswomen, as a group, tend to be optimistic, or they would not be in business. Moreover, why not be optimistic about the long run when in most instances one will not be held accountable for errors? In answer to excess optimism, we make our plea for realism. Controls, such as past financial ratios, can be used to test projections and keep them in line.

Proper Interpretation of Economic Forecasts

Everyone agrees that forecasts of economic conditions are of primary importance in the development of financial strategies. But there is a major complication to economic forecasts—they must be further interpreted to provide quantifiable estimates of sales and income for each company. Proper interpretation requires (1) a logical model that reflects how sales and income vary with different economic conditions and (2) forecasts of the different economic variables used in the model.

Now it is frequently asserted that a model for a company should be determined by the nature of the company's business. And this general statement cannot be challenged. One can challenge a model, however, on how well it correlates sales and income with different economic conditions and on the accuracy of its predictions.

In recent years improved computers, software, and quantitative economic forecasting services have made model building easier. Still many difficulties exist. One problem every model builder faces is the unavailability or uncollectability of required data.

Contingency Plans

Until now we have assumed that certain events will take place both within the internal and external environment. We have failed to mention what is done to account for crucial events that have a low probability of occurrence.

The term *contingency planning* is typically applied to detailed schemes that take these events into account. Contingency planning, incidentally, is highly relevant to the finance function.

There are many illustrations of contingency planning. Hedging against devaluation is one. Devaluation often occurs without warning. Yet it is significant, and once it occurs, little can be done to negate its effects. Disaster planning is another. It may deal with race riots, plant explosions, and the kidnapping of key executives. They also often occur without warning. In 1970 a Conference Board Survey indicated that many companies also broadly use contingency planning for economic downturns. Most, however, lacked detail and failed to tie in with the corporate budget or long-range plan.

WAYS TO IMPROVE INCOME STATEMENT AND BALANCE SHEET FORECASTS

Accuracy of income statement and balance sheet forecasts can be improved by:

1   Using a multiple technique.
2   Placing products into categories by reliability of forecasts.
3   Using financial-planning models.

Using Multiple Technique

Bottom-up and top-down forecasting are two basic approaches that provide a cross-check. With the bottom-up approach, forecasts of product-line groups that are added together constitute the corporate forecast. With the top-down approach, top management with the aid of staff directly makes the corporate forecast.

When for greater accuracy both are used, a "management discount" is applied. Usually, top management applies the discount. And as one might expect, the discount invariably reduces the bottom-up forecast.

Top-down approaches vary in the use of techniques from a seat-of-the-pants "feel" for the situation to a computerized model based on correlations with economic conditions, trend analyses, or the use of input-output tables. The bottom-up approach is also diverse since heads of product-line groups use different methods.

Placing Products into Categories by Reliability of Forecasts

Mature products that have been sold in domestic markets for years are the easiest to forecast. The total market and the company's market share are usually known. Even how sales vary with economic conditions is known or can be determined. Sales forecast accuracy for these products is typically within ±10% of actual.

If products have already been manufactured and sold in some foreign countries, predicting sales and growth rate in others is not difficult. Especially if these products have already been exported to these other countries, even though amounts may have been small.

Comparative marketing techniques can often be used to estimate sales and sales growth once plants have been built and marketing networks established. These techniques usually consist of tracing past sales growth patterns in other countries and making "guesstimates" of sales growth patterns for the new country or countries.

Sometimes known dollar sales, as a percent of total industry sales for different countries, is plotted against time (the number of years a company has had a successful agent, sales force, or plant in each country). If industry sales are not available, gross domestic product is sometimes used. Points are then plotted and a line is fitted that can be used for predicting sales and growth rates for a new country (see Exhibit 8.4).

Exhibit 8.4   Fitting a Line for Predicting Sales and Growth Rates

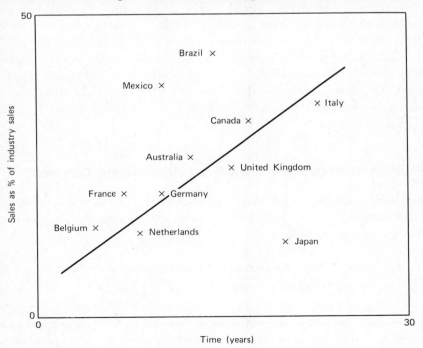

Keep in mind that this technique is more applicable to free economies than for controlled ones.

Completely new products are without question the most difficult to forecast since they provide no historical data. They vary from mere "gleams in a product manager's eye" to products being sold in test markets.

Categorizing products by degree of uncertainty makes forecasting decisions easier. Furthermore the product administrator and top management can feel more confident and comfortable in being able to identify products whose forecasts are accurate and those whose forecasts are almost a guess.

Using Financial-Planning Models

Because they can be used to answer "what if" questions, financial-planning models make it possible to grasp the impact of a forecast, especially of unusual events. They are, therefore, the source for strategies when unusual events do occur.

A financial model that also includes detailed planning in marketing, production, and purchasing provides the clearest picture of the impact of events. For example, a financial planning model would permit a company to pinpoint products that would be affected by crude oil shortages and high prices. It would show to what extent these products could be affected. The model would make it possible to identify new strategies needed for pricing, product allocations, production schedules, product substitutions, and capital expenditures. The model could also show how new strategies would affect income statements, balance sheets, and cash flow. Finally it would show the capital resources needed.

Financial Strategies for the Small and Medium-Sized Company

Financial strategies for small and medium-sized companies are much like large companies—they must minimize the cost of capital. There are, of course, some major differences:

1 The investor's basis for credit ratings and evaluation of risks.
2 The availability of sources of funds.

For smaller companies, and especially recently formed ones, quality of management and soundness of objectives and strategies are weighed more heavily than past company records. Take Cray Research, Incorporated, formed in the mid 1970s. Seymour Cray, the founder, with some brilliant new ideas for a scientific computer and an outstanding track record at Control Data Corporation, easily floated a 600,000-share stock issue in early 1976. The stock was oversubscribed at $16.50 a share and immediately opened with a bid of $24.00 a share after issue. Investors were assuming that Seymour Cray would be successful. The man was more important than the company.

Even for established small and medium-sized companies the quality of management is more important to lenders and investors than in the large corporations. For smaller businesses risks are higher than they are for larger business. There are, therefore, fewer sources available, and the cost of capital is higher. Most small businesses are not listed on a stock exchange. They are seldom nationally well known, if they have no past record of performance. For the most part public issues of stock or bonds are not possible. Private loans and private sale of stock are the chief methods of getting outside financial resources.

Other than the two major differences we have cited, everything we have said about managing financial strategies applies to small and medium-sized companies. They do not, of course, have the specialized staffs found in big companies. One might argue that they don't need them, but it is more realistic to assume that they need them but can't afford them.

We are not so foolish as to think that this chapter can do much more than point out the key factors that shape financial strategies. We have stated that accurate forecasts and projections are necessary but have said little about the kind that should be used. Let it suffice for the moment to say that there are many books and articles on the subject. One book we like is "Forecasting Methods for Management" by Steven C. Wheelwright and Spyros G. Makridakes. It covers economic and business forecasting thoroughly. An article we highly recommend appeared in the July–August 1971 *Harvard Business Review* and was titled "How to Choose the Right Forecasting Technique." Don't forget that many techniques have proved unreliable, and all of them must be supplemented with flexibility and quickness of action when unexpected events occur.

CHAPTER 9

PUBLIC-AFFAIRS STRATEGIES

William Vanderbilt, the railroad tycoon, once said, "the public be damned." But the world has changed since William Vanderbilt's days. Corporations must now either serve the public interest through sound public-affairs strategies or risk the wrath of the public and government.

Public-affairs strategies are, of course, offsprings of corporate image strategies that have been around since the 1930s. Corporate-image strategies should have been designed for customers, financiers, Wall Street, suppliers, employees, stockholders, governments, competitors, dealers, distributors, retailers, the press, the public, and other companies. But they weren't. A study by A. Sandgren and Murtha, Inc., showed that they typically concentrated on customers, financiers, and Wall Street. Public-affairs strategies correct this imbalance in part by concentrating on the broad public interest, the objectives of society.

Research studies make it clear that the need for sound public-affairs strategies has been long overdue. This conclusion of one study is typical.

Twenty years ago, American industry was riding the crest of a wave of popularity. Over 60% of the general public supported American industry, felt that corporations were good, and that bigger corporations were better corporations. Today, the public has made an about face. Over 60% of the general public considered industry self-serving and not interested in the public. And they seek more government intervention and control.[1]

The Research Corporation Surveys of 1951 and 1973 make a point that is particularly alarming—the youth in the United States are losing confidence in a private-enterprise system and want more government control.

In answer to criticisms Xerox launched an offensive. It appears to have got results. A survey of 300 graduate business school students interested in the relations of business and society showed that they rated Xerox first in social performance among 50 giant corporations.

Other companies have followed Xerox's path and have:

● Created corporate-responsibility offices and in some cases appointed a vice president of public affairs or of social responsibility.
● Created a corporate-responsibility committee at board level.
● Increased charitable contributions as a percent of pretax earnings.
● Increased the number of minorities employed and the number holding upper level positions.
● Placed blacks on the board of directors.
● Placed women on the board of directors.
● Maintained deposits in minority-owned banks.
● Participated in fund raising for black schools.
● Expanded purchases from minority suppliers.
● Developed "career progression" programs to advance minorities into more responsible positions.
● Established plants in ghetto areas.
● Made a training seminar on minority affairs mandatory for all management trainees.
● Conducted educational programs on drug abuse.
● Required executives to take part in community affairs.
● Adopted social-service leave programs that permit employees to take up to 2 years' leave at full pay to pursue a self-elected volunteer project.
● Run a day-care center for the children of employees.
● Advertised in prominent newspapers and on TV and radio:

To present progress reports on environmental protection and civic affairs. To explain company's role in the economic and social fabric of modern life. To explain how company stands on the "hot issues."

[1] "How Business Faces a Hostile Climate." *Business Week*, May 20, 1972, p. 70.

- Landscaped areas scarred by company's operations.
- Publicized pollution-control programs.
- Included specific social-responsibility goals in plans.

If the private-enterprise system is widely questioned in the United States, even where many companies like Xerox have given high priorities to public affairs, it is easy to surmise what has happened elsewhere— private enterprise is under constant attack. A survey of 196 businessmen in 65 free-world countries by the Conference Board in 1971 revealed a growing negative attitude toward business. These businessmen agreed that something must be done but disagreed over *what*. Naturally, antibusiness feelings are rare in the Communist-dominated countries because, as Will Rogers put it, there "your complaint is your epitaph."

Now the chief targets are the multinational corporations—those giant enterprises, like General Motors, Unilever, and Matsushita, that operate in different countries under a common ownership and corporate strategy. For them, the fierceness of the attack grows daily, and there is no sign of a letup. Aligned against them are implacable enemies who fear that the multinationals are too powerful and are dangerous threats to societies and nations. These enemies point to the prediction by futurists that, after 1980, multinationals will account for 15–20% of the world's gross product; by the year 2000 about 300 multinationals will dominate world production and trade and will allegedly achieve power by controlling the allocation of world resources.

The list of complaints cited against multinationals is long (see Exhibit 9.1). Some complaints are true, others are false, and most are half-truths.

The methods of attack are often subtle and varied. The results sought are always the same—to control and restrict the multinationals' power and activities. Professor F. T. Haner, reporting that national states first make mild attacks and gradually make them tougher, lists four phases:

1 Loss of remittance flexibility.
2 Loss of operating profits.
3 Loss of assets.
4 Loss of opportunity.

Exhibit 9.1   List of Complaints against Multinational Companies

1. They do not adequately take into account the host country's "culture"; they simply transplant their own.
2. Multinationals borrow too much locally and repatriate too much of their earnings or use them to buy local companies.
3. They have increased the gap between the poor and rich countries.
4. They have enticed people to change dietary habits or purchase goods they shouldn't buy through TV, movies, comic books, commercials, and advertisements.
5. They have a decided competitive edge over local businesses.
6. They do not exercise the same levels of product quality and standards of protection to the consumer that are exercised in their home country.
7. They interfere in host countries' political activities.
8. They often dominate key industries of host countries.
9. They suppress competition through takeovers, patents, licenses, know-how and trademarks, tie-in purchase clauses, and market allocation.
10. They contribute to price inflation.
11. They exploit low-cost labor.
12. They alienate employees.
13. They exploit natural resources.
14. They hire away the most talented personnel; concurrently they restrict the learning-by-doing process by staffing key technical and managerial positions with expatriates.
15. They have influenced their base countries to set terms of trade that favor them at the expense of companies in poorer nations.
16. Their often unsuited technology is too costly and creates unemployment in the host country. Frequently, the transferred technology is prohibited from being used for exports.
17. They tend to do nearly all their research in their home country and prevent host countries from improving their own research capability.
18. They have transfer pricing policies that do not reflect fair market value but serve instead as an indirect way of allocating markets and evading taxes.
19. They encourage host countries to compete against each other in granting tax concessions and evade taxation through the use of tax havens.
20. They are able to borrow from local banks and other financial institutions on better terms than local businesses and therefore divert local savings from productive investment by nationals.
21. They have developed techniques in banking to expand their control over non-banking sectors which often is against the public interest.

Exhibit 9.1   List of Complaints against Multinational Companies

22. They do not provide enough information on their operations and results and also conceal or distort information that is vital to the economic planners of host countries and home countries alike.

23. They have aggravated the world's hunger problems by (a) contributing to the concentration of income, (b) by complicating the problems of food distribution through gaining control over available land.

24. They pollute the environment and upset the ecology by encouraging waste.

Here are a few examples among hundreds of restrictive measures initiated:

Phase 1. Restrictions on repatriation of profits and capital through new laws, policies, or different exchange rates.

Phase 2. Tax discrimination; laws requiring training of nationals; lowering of elimination of patent protection.

Phase 3. Equity phaseout laws; expropriation.

Phase 4. Certain industries declared out of bounds for foreigners.

To meet some of these attacks, multinationals have taken the following actions:

● Placed nationals in charge of local companies wherever possible.

● Made available some percent of equity ownership to nationals in overseas subsidiaries in advance of laws and regulations making local ownership mandatory.

● Placed nationals on board of directors.

● Developed charitable contribution programs compatible with the local environment and similar to programs used at world headquarters.

● Made executives participate in community affairs.

● Adopted policies to prevent involvement in local political issues.

● Developed public relations programs directed at improving the image of the company in the community.

Now that the social-responsibility problems facing all companies and especially the multinationals have been discussed and attempts at solving them noted, let us focus in depth on an approach for developing public-affairs strategies and including them in corporate planning. Our vehicle is a case that is a composite picture of several company's public-affairs strategies and activities. Our aim is to show step by step the approach an astute Vice President of Public Affairs might take.

MONTAGE PHARMACEUTICAL COMPANY

Our composite case begins with the appointment of an executive to the newly created job of vice president of public affairs—we'll call him Dan Wilson. The president and chief executive officer (CEO) of Montage Pharmaceutical Company, a multinational company, has made the following announcement:

> Our company has played a significant role in the pharmaceutical industry throughout the world and will play an even greater role in the future. In the past many companies existed only to make a profit. Now, none can ignore social responsibility. Because your management feels social responsibility is vitally important to the company, Dan Wilson has been appointed Vice President of Public Affairs and will report to me. I expect everyone to give Dan Wilson their fullest cooperation.

Wilson's Actions

Dan Wilson strived first to assess his situation, to judge what was needed for success in his new job. He decided that the full support and understanding the CEO gave him was crucial. He also knew that he would have to accomplish results through others, and line managers would, therefore, need to understand the role of public affairs and be interested in it. They would support public-affairs programs if the CEO did.

Wilson saw that key social-responsibility and public-affairs issues had to be identified quickly. He recognized that some problems were industry wide, such as trends toward price controls and tougher government requirements on the sale of certain drugs. Others were unique to the company, such as the poor image of the company in the area where one of its plants emitted air pollutants. Wilson decided that company problems should be broken down into two categories—those in the United States and those in foreign countries. Having worked overseas, he knew that problems in foreign countries were often totally different from those in the United States.

He believed he should know what the company was doing in public affairs, and specifically, what was considered public affairs and what was not.

Finally he decided to learn the attitudes of key personnel in the company on public affairs and to gather their views on present problems and possible solutions.

Dan Wilson was pleased with the apparent support of the president suggested by the announcement. He also knew, however, that the president had decided to establish the social-responsibility and public-affairs office after having attended an industry meeting where the president learned that two of his competitors had recently established a similar office in their organizations. Wilson wondered whether his function would have a permanent, important place in the company's organization. He needed a strategy that would keep the president interested and involved.

He wrote a letter in the president's name addressed to all division managers, overseas area general managers, and department directors explaining the major purposes and goals of the social-responsibility group. The letter mentioned that Dan Wilson would be coming to talk to them to find out what they were currently doing, what problems they saw, and what their ideas were on possible new activities.

Wilson spent the first 2 months of his new assignment interviewing these people and some of their subordinates. From these interviews he learned of the following activities:

Charitable Trust   The company had a charitable trust fund that over the past 5 years had given away about 0.8% of net income after taxes. The contributions were all for causes inside the United States and largely oriented to the community where the world headquarters was located. The divisions or plants could also make contributions to local communities. The policies and practices of charitable donations varied widely, depending on the attitudes of headquarters executives and local managers. The individual who managed the charitable trust fund was a member of the public relations department.

Educational Fund   The company had a trust fund that provided a few college scholarships per year to children of employees. The trust had been set up 3 years ago by the founder of the company. The funds available from the trust had not, however, kept up with the large increases that had occurred in the cost of education; the sum available to any one student could cover only a small part of the amount needed.

Washington Office   Many years ago the company had opened a Washington, D.C., office to provide constant and direct contact with the government on a variety of activities, such as sales to the government, product clearances, taxes, government policies and regulations, tariffs, passports, and legislation. One of the principal responsibilities of the head of the Washington office was to get to know key members of legislature, particularly those who represent districts where the company has plants. He wanted to keep legislators informed of corporate views on pending legislation and to provide them with pertinent information. Reporting to the head of the Washington office were a few people whose responsibilities were to keep the company informed and to make it influential on regional, political, and governmental matters.

Corporate Advertising   The company had a director of advertising who had sole responsibility for corporate advertising. Product advertising was the responsibility of advertising managers in divisional product groups. These managers had a staff relationship with the corporate advertising director. Some of the corporate advertisements had at times been directed at explaining the company's position and activities on public-affairs issues such as pollution control and drug addiction.

Multinational Corporation Issues Committee   In 1972 the corporate vice president to whom the Washington office manager reported formed an *ad-hoc* committee to deal with the Burke–Hartke bills in congress that were attacking direct overseas investment. Later the committee's interests were expanded to include many other issues, including those involving foreign countries. Members of the committee were representatives from the Washington office, law department, public relations, tax department, and the international division.

The committee was to keep informed of developments affecting multinationals and to decide on actions the corporation might take. Usually, they turned to the public relations department, which provided literature on issues to people within and outside the company.

Participation—Community Affairs   The company encouraged participation in community affairs and once conducted a course in practical politics. Occasionally the company permitted an employee to run for political office with the understanding that he or she would be given the necessary time off with pay to perform his or her duties.

Minority Groups   About 5 years ago the company had adopted a policy of hiring a much larger number of blacks. In 1972 the percentage of blacks to total employees at the company's headquarters was 3%. A goal of 10% had been established for attainment within 10 to 15 years.

Problems

From his interviews, several problems came into view:

- A wide gap existed between individuals on the extent to which they were informed on social-responsibility and public-affairs issues both with respect to external developments and trends and to what the company was doing. Whereas the company had been active in public affairs people in the company were not informed.
- Most public-affairs activities had been directed at short-range issues. For instance, when the Burke–Hartke bills became prominent, the company joined the industry in developing information to refute the contention of the bills, wrote a "white paper" on the company's position on the bills, and called on Congressmen and Congresswomen to explain its position. The company seldom, if ever, tried to identify major issues before they became prominent so that programs could be developed to defuse them before they became serious. Some interviewees felt that the company should take this longer range approach. Several questioned, however, if such activity would be worthwhile on the basis that, if the company assumed this role, it would probably waste a substantial amount of its manpower and money on issues that would die out anyway on their own accord; they suggested that an inbetween better strategy might be to wait until it was certain that the issues would become prominently important and then take action.
- Internal information about social-responsibility issues was neither regularly made available to its managers nor uniformly interpreted for them. For instance, among the 36 people interviewed, only the personnel director knew what percentage of blacks made up the total employment of the company. Similarly, only two people had general knowledge of the level of the company's total corporate giving program and the ground rules by which the program was administered.
- More attention needed to be focused on the problems outside the United States. At present nearly all activity was directed at domestic problems, and yet the problems outside the United States' had a greater long-range impact.
- Nationalism was becoming a particularly serious problem. New rules and regulations directed at controlling or phasing out foreign investment were a constant threat. The position of being a guest, particularly a multinational guest, instead of a host, was a real challenge in maintaining a favorable image in the local foreign communities where the company had operations.

There was evidence that the company needed more clearly defined policies on minority group hiring; charitable contributions—world headquarters versus domestic and foreign locations; and involvement by the company's employees in community affairs—is it an across-the-board policy or an agreement between the individual and the company?

New Programs Suggested

Several new programs were suggested:

- Develop a manual on social-responsibility issues for managers and supervisors. Sections of the manual could then be used by managers and supervisors for talks with new and regular workers and speeches to outside groups. Film slides could be used to present the material. Special sections of the manual could focus on specific interests and problems of individual communities.
- Prepare "white papers" stating the company's position on important social-responsibility and public-affairs issues.
- Maintain a list of possible developments that might become important issues to the company. Review the list at least quarterly. When some developments emerge as threats or opportunities, then develop strategies and programs to meet them.
- Form a permanent social-responsibility committee to identify the new issues. The committee could develop "white papers" and corporate positions on new issues and help to decide what to do about them.
- Hold in-company seminars for employees to pass on information and generate new ideas on social-responsibility problems.

After his interviews Dan Wilson recommended to the president that the Washington, D.C., office manager and the manager of the charitable and educational trusts should report to the office of the vice president for social responsibility. The Washington office manager should also be made a regional vice president; this would give him higher stature in his contacts with members of Congress and others.

His next recommendation was the appointment of a social-responsibility and public-affairs committee with decision-making powers to replace the *ad-hoc* committee. Membership on the committee would consist of the regional vice president for the Washington office, public relations director, law department representative who was responsible for legislative matters, tax department director, personnel director, general manager for U.S. pharmaceutical operations, general manager for Europe, general manager for Asia-Pacific, the president, and the vice president of public affairs as chairman.

The committee would meet quarterly or more frequently at the discretion of the chairman. The purpose of the committee would be to identify major social and political problems, issues, and opportunities and to decide on courses of action and adoptions of policy.

Wilson decided that the agenda for the first committee meeting should include the following:

1   Development of a manual for use by the committee and other executives in the company that would provide uniform, accurate information on the following:

- Minority employment.
- Ecological expenditures.
- Charitable contributions, including the historical record of the amounts for various causes and total contributions as a percent of income.
- Actions by the corporation, if any, to support minority businesses.
- Salaries of females compared with salaries of males at the same salary grade level.
- The number of males versus females at each salary grade level.
- White papers identifying corporate stands on major social-responsibility and public-affairs issues.
- Overseas employment by area and expatriate employment as a percentage of total employment in the area.
- Total exports broken down into exports for resale and exports for further processing (value added) by overseas entities.
- Imports back into the United States from overseas entities.
- Internal "balance of payments" for company operations country by country.
- Internal training and educational programs concerned with social, political, and economic subjects.

2   Identification and agreement on a list of specific issues and problems. The list would be broken down into two parts; the first part would contain those issues that were of sufficient immediate importance for ongoing programs now; the second list would be a "watch list"—things that may

develop into major issues but that are not sufficiently clear at the moment to justify any significant effort. Wilson decided that this item should appear on every agenda of the committee.

3 Consideration and decision on new policies or changes in present policies and activities. Some examples would be the following:

- Blacks on the board of directors.
- Support of minority businesses.
- Targets for percent of minority groups in total employment.
- Percent of income that should be provided for charitable contributions; guidelines on causes to support.
- Worldwide charitable giving policy versus policy for U.S. headquarters location.
- Ecology.
- Educational training programs.
- Involvement in political and social issues in foreign countries.

4 Consideration of specific programs to be undertaken and their priorities.
5 Consideration of a 1–2-day seminar to communicate and sell the need for greater social responsibility.

Wilson considered beginning the first meeting with a presentation by a recognized consultant who could outline all the major sociological, economic, and political trends that were important to the future of the corporation.

The final recommendation by Wilson was that social responsibility be included as an integral part of the company's strategic planning process. To accomplish this result, he proposed:

- Appropriate requests for new capital expenditures that are submitted to the president and board for approval should have a section covering any social-responsibility problems, including ecological problems, pertinent to the request, along with ways they could be handled.
- Strategic planning procedures prescribed by corporate planning should require that each operating division plan and each overseas area plan have a section on social responsibility that outlines the problems and identifies the strategies and plans that will be followed to solve them.

The president accepted Wilson's recommendations, but he was concerned about how he was going to measure the success of Wilson's efforts. He discussed the matter with Wilson, and they agreed that studies should be made in the United States, the United Kingdom, France, Germany, Belgium, Italy, Canada, Brazil, and Japan to reach conclusions on the present image of the company so that later studies carried out could identify progress or slippage.

The Major Points of the Case

Notice the public-affairs strategies in the case dealt with three points: (1) the increased demands that society has placed on business for social responsibility, (2) the likelihood that these demands will not be met unless organizational and planning steps are taken to make certain that proper attention is given, (3) the proposal that business could benefit from anticipating changes in the demands and attitudes of society and taking action.

The first point was covered early in this chapter.

The second point has been recognized by a large number of companies, and they have established offices. In a survey conducted by Henry Eilbirt and I. Robert Parket of the City University of New York, 90% of 96 responding firms from a survey of 400 large companies showed formal organizational structuring of public-affairs activity. Relatively few companies, however, include public affairs as an integral part of their strategic planning process. This is probably the next phase of the evolution of the function.

The third point covered the need to anticipate social issues and deal with them before they become critical, the case of the U.S. automobile industry being a good example. A strong argument can be made that industry and the public would have been better off if the air pollution problem from automotive exhaust, the safety problems, and the shift in demand to smaller cars had been anticipated and action taken by industry before public and government demands forced the issue. Solutions to the technical problems would probably have been more effective and efficient. The public and the industry would have benefited from having the smaller cars and by not having to rely heavily on imported small cars.

CHAPTER 10

DEVELOPING THE PLANNING SYSTEM

In this final chapter we discuss key issues involved in developing a planning system—the major things to consider in organizing, staffing, and evaluating effectiveness.

At the outset top management must decide on:

1   The role of planning.
2   The most suitable planning system.
3   The role of staff planners.

THE ROLE OF PLANNING

Definitions of the role of planning abound. Here are some:

- Planning is the process of determining a desirable future condition and deciding how to proceed from an existing to the desired state.
- Long-range planning is a continuous process of making risk-taking decisions *systematically* and with the best possible knowledge of their futurity. It is systematically organizing total efforts needed to carry out these decisions. It is measuring results of decisions against expectations by means of systematic feedback.
- Strategic planning is concerned with determining objectives and selecting the most attractive combination of alternatives for achieving those objec-

tives. Tactical planning is concerned with determining the most efficient use of resources that have already been allocated to achieving a stipulated objective. Hence, tactical planning follows strategic planning. A third kind of planning is operating or budget planning, which is concerned with developing a control mechanism to ensure the most efficient and effective implementation of the action specified in the strategic and tactical plans and to provide the basis for measuring and controlling actual performance relative to plans. Strategic planning is quite gross, quite broad. Tactical planning is more specific, more directed. And operating or budget planning is extremely detailed.

- Planning in general is the conscious determination of courses of action to achieve preconceived objectives. It is deciding in advance what is to be done, when it is to be done, by whom it is to be done, and how it is to be done.

- Strategic planning guides the choice among the broad directions in which the company seeks to move and concerns the general planned allocations of the firm's managerial, financial, and physical resources over future specified periods of time. Operational planning, on the other hand, focuses on the ways and means by which each function may be programmed for optimum progress in attainment of strategic objectives.

These definitions say about the same thing. A composite definition might look like this:

Planning is a systematic step-by-step procedure. The first step consists of setting long-range goals and objectives. The second step (strategic planning) consists of deciding on routes with alternatives for reaching goals and objectives. The third step (tactical planning) consists of determining actions that must be taken to implement the strategies. The fourth step consists of deciding on detailed actions that must be taken "today" to implement tactical plans. The last step consists of evaluating results and when necessary revising and adjusting previous steps.

THE MOST SUITABLE PLANNING SYSTEM

Once the role of planning has been resolved, the next step is to decide on the most suitable planning system. The key issues are:

- To what extent should top-down (authoritative) or bottom-up (participative) planning be used?
- For what parts of a business should separate strategies and plans be developed?

- How many staff planning groups are needed?
- Where should the staff planning groups be located in the organization?

Top-Down and Bottom-Up Planning

As we have previously stated, with top-down planning, top executives do all the planning. The chief executive officer (CEO) and the immediate staff set goals and objectives and develop the forecasts, strategies, and action plans. Lower levels are informed only of the strategies and plans that they are to implement.

In bottom-up planning, forecasting, setting of goals and objectives, and developing of strategies and action programs occur at the lower levels of the company—at the "planning unit" levels. The company plan is the total of all of the individual plans. Bottom-up planning helps to generate more sound ideas and to improve morale and loyalty.

Usually, both types of planning are used. Interaction occurs between the top and the bottom until a decision is reached. Top executives begin by providing the lower level managers with future business environment assumptions and policy decisions on which plans are to be based. Still, there may be considerable give-and-take before conclusions are reached. If the company is a U.S. multinational, for instance, forecasts of the U.S. economy are usually decided at the top, but those for other world areas are usually made by area management groups. Even when these forecasts are made at the top, they are subjected to modification by area management groups.

For What Parts of a Business Should Separate Plans and Strategies Be Developed?

The answer to this question is easy for a company that has a single line or a very narrow line of businesses. For companies like General Electric, however, the answer is harder. A decision is needed on which products or businesses require most of top management's attention.

Obviously, some standards must apply. We like General Electric's use of "strategic business units" (SBUs), which are defined as follows:

- An SBU must have a unique mission, independent of the business mission of any other SBU.
- An SBU must be a full-fledged competitor in the external market.
- An SBU must be able to accomplish integrated strategic planning in products, markets, facilities, and organization—relatively independently of other SBUs.

● An SBU manager must be able to make decisions within approved plans on technology, manufacturing, marketing, asset management, and other areas crucial for success.

Notice that with SBUs the less important products and businesses are slighted by top management and become the total responsibility of lower levels of management.

HOW MANY STAFF PLANNING GROUPS ARE NEEDED?

The answer to this question depends on top management's thinking about planning and the kind of operations.

A top-level corporate planning group is usually needed in large corporations. But large corporations can do without a centralized corporate planning staff—as long as operating results are favorable. Take DuPont, for example. Although in existence since 1802, it did not establish a corporate planning staff until 1975. At that time the company was having planning problems. The need for a central planning staff to assist top management to improve and direct the planning system became clear.

Organizations and situations determine whether other planning groups are needed. Product divisions with worldwide responsibility will probably have their own planning staffs, and so will important geographic-area management groups.

Companies that have an international division and product divisions with wordwide responsibility have three principal choices: (1) have the product divisions do all the planning; (2) have an international planning group (a) assist the product divisions, (b) plan for foreign businesses for which product divisions are not responsible, and (c) plan for overseas affiliates that work with more than one product division; (3) have the corporate planning staff do the work of the international planning group.

Special groups are sometimes needed to handle special needs. Take diversification, for example; some companies have created an entire division or department and called it the "new enterprise division" or "central development department."

Companies that have diversification by acquisition as a major goal will often have an acquisition specialist on its corporate planning staff. In fact diversification by acquisition is such an important activity in some companies that the head of corporate planning may be the acquisitions expert.

WHERE SHOULD STAFF PLANNING GROUPS
BE LOCATED IN THE ORGANIZATION?

To be effective, planning must be considered by the line manager as the manager's role. Staff planners merely assist.

A corporate planning group will report to the CEO or to a senior vice president immediately below the CEO. Even when reporting to a senior vice president, the head of the corporate planning group still must have frequent contacts with the CEO. An international planning group should report to the head of international; a product division planning group should report to the chief executive in charge of the product division; new products and new businesses planning groups should report either to the CEO of the company or to the person in charge of new products and new businesses.

THE ROLE OF STAFF PLANNERS

Once the roles of planning have been construed and the most suitable planning systems resolved, the role of staff planners can be defined. By "planners," we mean staff planners, like the corporate planning director or corporate planning vice president, not line planners.

We discuss first typical "planner" roles and then others more controversial.

Develop the Planning System

Planners assist the line by developing the planning system. They determine what actions must be taken to prepare a total corporate plan, who will take these actions, when they will be taken, and what methods of followup will be used.

The planning system is usually made known to those who need to know by means of a planning manual, or a planning guide, or a memo that explains procedures, formats, and time schedules. Meetings with concerned groups permit questions to be raised on parts of the planning manual or memos that are unclear or have not been covered.

Guide and Assist

Planners should guide and assist the line so that well-thought-out plans are completed on time.

Planners gather information and analyze the internal and external environment, with greater emphasis given to the latter. For instance, planners typically analyze profitability and share of market by product lines to help establish objectives and goals of the corporation. They compare a company's record of capital expenditures with future plans to assist in establishing new objectives and goals. They may also conduct surveys of their company's and competition's technology to compare strengths and weaknesses. They might compare the level and availability of technical personnel with normal attrition rates to project possible critical shortages.

Planners analyze capital expenditure proposals. The CEO or "executive committee" seldom has the time to analyze these project requests thoroughly. Staff help being needed, the corporate planning group can evaluate the project to ensure that it fits corporate strategies and plans.

Planners often forecast business conditions. They assess competition and the company's competitive position and provide information on new opportunities for the company.

Sometimes planners analyze strategies and plans submitted by product divisions or area groups. As pointed out in Chapter 7, plans are frequently incomplete or inconsistent, and the planner must play the devil's advocate.

Planners also train and innovate. They can train by transmitting new planning techniques and information to others through memos, newspaper articles, books, or seminars. They can innovate by developing new techniques or by using known techniques in new ways, for example, by using the learning curve to predict competitor's costs.

The corporate planner will sometimes serve as secretary to the top executive decision-making or advisory committee. This role keeps the planner well informed of important decisions and events affecting the company. The planner can advise the committee of actions that are inconsistent with desired strategies and plans.

Finally the planner should make major contributions in assisting top management to prepare goals, objectives, and policies.

Gather and Evaluate Information

In guiding and assisting, planners are committed to gather and evaluate information continually. They must decide *what* information is needed; *how* to obtain it, for example, the services, periodicals, and networks to use; and how to present it and put it to use.

Prepare the Corporate Long-Range Plan

Planners prepare the corporate long-range plan by consolidating unit plans. This consolidation undergoes "top-down" analysis. Are unit goals, objectives, and policies consistent with corporate? Are the necessary resources available? What are the key assumptions of the plan?

Preparing the corporate long-range plan is a multiphase operation. Product divisions and other planning units discuss and review the first consolidation. Some revisions and changes are made. Deliberations continue. Finally a general agreement is reached.

When operating divisions and an international division with an area management structure have worldwide product responsibility, preparing a long-range plan becomes complex. The operating divisions prepare worldwide strategies and plans. The international planner extracts the international segments and prepares an international consolidation. This consolidation is reviewed with the area managers, who may then be asked to prepare their own area plans. The area plans may differ from the consolidated plans of the operating divisions.

Now the international staff planner must consolidate the area plans into an international plan to be reviewed by top management and perhaps modified before finally approved.

Followup

Followup is necessary at all stages of planning. In the initial stages the planner may help top management follow up on corporate objectives by preparing long-range plans. Later the planner may help top management follow up on long-range plans by initiating action programs. Then the planner sees whether the action plans were performed on schedule.

Followup on fixed-capital investments is another job of the planner. Evaulations are needed on the extent capital investment appropriation requests have met expectations; reasons must be given for variances.

Planning

Should planners plan, as well as help others to plan? There are strong divergent views in answer to this question. Some top managers believe that "planning is too important to have a planner tinker with it"; others believe that, unless staff planners are made accountable for planning, they will become too theoretical to be helpful.

The latter view seems wiser. Primarily planners should, of course, help line managers plan, but unless they are doing some of the planning, they cannot see problems as line managers see them.

On acquisitions, corporate planners are frequently deeply involved with planning. Planners will search for and identify companies to be acquired. After receiving the CEO's approval, planners frequently make the initial contacts for preliminary negotiations. After a tentative agreement has been reached, planners are involved in the final negotiations.

Top-Level Decision Maker

Should a staff planner be a top-level decision maker? Usually, the planner is not, at least not formally. For instance, planners are not usually members of an executive committee or top committee making major policy and operating decisions. Sometimes, however, a planner serves as a secretary to the committee. That position or a close relationship with the CEO and other top-level executives in the organization enables the planner to *influence* decisions.

Qualifications

Stated qualifications for a planner are often overexaggerated; they are meant for gods, not people. Here are some examples:

- A planning coordinator should be a person qualified to be a good operating manager.
- A successful planner should have a good measure of creativity.
- The planner should be a keen analyst and be effective in working with others.
- The staff planner should be someone already enjoying a measure of respect among key executives.
- The planner should be a super diplomat able to move about unobtrusively within an organization, getting things done by suggestion rather than by decree.
- The planner is usually highly trained and educated; tends to be systematic, logical, methodical, and intellectual in approach; and is conditioned by education to be factual.

- The planner is both philosopher and realist, theoretical and practical politician, soothsayer and salesperson.
- The planner must be oriented toward the future.
- The planner must not be an ivory tower theorist.
- The planner should have wide experience, breadth of vision, and depth of understanding; should be a good persuader; should be familiar with all aspects of the business; should have an analytical bent of mind and the ability to call the shots as they are seen; should be able to say "no"; needs a working knowledge of economics and of world politics; should have an extensive background in the industry or in the company; should have been with the company 10 years or more and be acceptable to top-management group.

In "An Open Letter to the President on Hiring a Corporate Planner," Joe O'Donnell continued with the theme that the person to head up his new formal corporate planning function, if not a god, should at least be a superman or superwoman. Observe his list:

- Strong integrity. The person will need it to stand up to you.
- Strong determination to succeed. Must have a record of having succeeded in almost everything tried.
- Strong belief in planning. Must be an evangelist and therefore must also understand it.
- Strong intelligence. Must be capable of thinking conceptually and seeing the overall picture. Must be philosophical but at the same time highly practical.
- Strong leadership qualities. Has to act as a catalyst to get you and your entire organization heading in the right direction. Has to do this without any command authority whatsoever.
- Try to find someone in your own organization:
    - It will take an outsider a long time to get the feel of how fast your organization is capable of changing.
    - The outsider adds to the threat inherent in changes that formal planning will bring about.
- He should not be a perfectionist. Hot-rod planners can destroy a corporation because they try to force it to move too fast. It requires a lot of emotional maturity to accept a lot less than perfection.
- Hard working. Must study, attend courses, and think a great deal.

● In addition to these essentials, O'Donnell added these:

- Be likeable.
- Be mature and discreet.
- Have a strong desire to help others.
- Be a corporate-minded person.
- Be one who doesn't need to receive credit.

Enough searching for the impossible, let us consider qualifications more realistically. They include acceptance of the organization, an excellent analytical mind, sensitivity to others, a sense of diplomacy, and good communication skill. Finally planners must have the full support and confidence of the CEO or organization support will wither.

In the past controllers were frequently made the corporate planning director or served as controller and head of long-range planning. Recently this practice has changed for several reasons. First, controllers emphasize numbers, the quantitative. Having more experience with planning, companies now concentrate more on strategies than on numbers. Second, as pointed out by E. Kirby Warren of Columbia University, there are "basic conflicts between need for the controller to be guardian of corporate resources and the need for a planning designer who can gain the confidence of line and staff participants in planning."

Quantification in planning should be the third step, not the first. Identifying possible strategies and deciding on one is the first step. Translating strategies into detailed plans is the second.

All planning is oriented toward the future, but too many controllers rely on projections of past history. This approach is incompatible with the times. There are too many discontinuities, like supply shortages, too many new innovations. The long-range planner must recognize these things or the plans will go awry.

Training

Some companies assign executives to head a planning group merely for training. Such a practice is unwise, since these executives lack the experience and expertness required to launch a successful formalized long-range planning program. As we have implied earlier, planning is a special art that requires special abilities and talents.

Rotating Organization Structure (ROS), developed by Ronald J. Ross, is designed to improve planning rather than to train executives and therefore has value.

The ROS applies to planning at the product group and functional group level (engineering, research, purchasing, etc.) Managers are rotated in and out of planning so that those who plan must also implement. Since planning and implementation are done sequentially, each planning unit must have two managers. When one manager is planning, the other is implementing.

In addition to believing that planners should be implementers, Ross believes, and we agree, that orientation to change is vital for sucessful planning. The ROS provides an atmosphere favorable to change.

Measuring Effectiveness

Planning effectiveness must be measured continuously if plans and strategies are to be in accord with the times. There are two ways to measure effectiveness.

1   Determine whether action programs have been implemented.
2   Determine whether quantitative projections have been achieved.

Usually, telephone calls, discussions, and memos disclose the degree of implementation. But keep in mind that, if action programs contain enough detail to make accountability clear and schedules definite, measurement is easy.

If the period for evaluating quantitative results is short, say 1 or 2 years, figures may reflect only temporary economic conditions. If the quantitative measurement covers many years, which it should, it is easy to tell whether corporate strategies are succeeding or failing. If strategies are failing, obviously proper indicators were lacking.

Now quantitative measurements are necessary. One result of quantitative measurement is the insights gained that can lead to action programs. For instance, a formalized system for submitting capital expenditure proposals and reviewing actual performance can show where the most critical mistakes have been made, for example, capital costs, operating costs, sales volume, prices, start-up costs, and so forth, and signal, therefore, where attention should be focused on *future* capital request proposals. Still, quantitative measures represent one type of indicator that is usually less effective than well-prepared action reports.

While systems for measuring planning effectiveness differ for different companies, all include regular reviews of plans. Success depends on how often they are reviewed and the reviewing techniques used, who does the reviewing, and how well the subjects for review are selected.

Whether the plans are of divisions, of units, or simply of "key issues," top management must be the ultimate reviewer with assistance from a corporate planning staff. The assistance of the planning staff is necessary because top managers are faced with the change from handling day-to-day operating problems to long-range ones.

One successful way to separate operating problems from strategic formulation is to prepare an agenda solely on strategy and stick to it. Sometimes reviewing plans at locations miles away from the general offices discourages interruptions and makes it easier for top-management groups to concentrate only on plans.

How often reviews should be carried out depends on circumstances and the feelings of the CEO and top-management committee. Some companies have reviews once a month, others every 2 months, and still others only once a year. At times, also, when a company is facing a particularly critical situation, reviews are held much more often than normally.

Techniques used in review sessions also vary with the peculiarities of management. Some companies prefer the use of charts, others do not. Typically, individuals responsible for plans make the presentation. The techniques they use are as varied as their personalities, their likes, and skills.

Tolerance To Change

As mentioned in Chapter 2, research conducted by the Stanford Research Institute on the growth of U.S. corporations makes plain the importance of careful planning for long-term growth. The study showed that the most important single contribution to success is the ability of companies to visualize the impact of change and take advantage of it.

We believe that ways to measure companies' tolerance to change would provide a fruitful field of study. At present all we have is fragmentary individual experiences. Sears Roebuck and Montgomery Ward, both mass merchandisers, are classic examples. In 1945 both companies had sales of about $1 billion a year. Ten years later, Sears had quadrupled sales, but Ward's sales stayed almost the same. Why did Sears grow robustly? Why did Montgomery Ward stagnate?

Most people who have seriously studied these two companies agree Montgomery Ward's Sewell Avery refused to bet on American expansion and change. Under Avery, Ward's strategy was to have small stores in small towns supplied by a distribution center, hoard cash, and not expand. On the other hand, Sears was the first major retailer to move to the suburbs and to provide telephone shopping, night hours, self-service, and computerization of physical distribution.

In the thirties Sewell Avery kept Ward solvent by cutting costs and firing personnel. After World War ll he had the idea that postwar inflation would end in another crash. He failed to see that conditions in the fifties were different from those of the thirties. In short he exhibited a low tolerance to change.

Under John A. Barr, Ward still had troubles. He decentralized, started a market research department, and hired competent middle managers, but he still could not overcome the troubles created by old stores in poor locations.

The next president, Robert Brooker, a former president of Whirlpool and vice president and director of Sears, knew that mass merchandising required planning. He brought in an able top-management team, including Jim Lutz of McCrory's and Ed Donnell from Sears, to stress big-city mass merchandising. He, too, had a setback in 1967 in the company's Chicago operations in converting Fair Store department stores to Ward. The reason was low tolerance to change of department store people to mass-merchandising procedures. Brooker admitted that he should have trained a team and brought them in to run the stores.

Even Sears is not immune to a lowering of tolerance to change. Its profits dropped 28% during the first 9 months in 1975 compared with a rise of 7.4% in profits for Montgomery Ward. In addition to its subsidiary Allstate Insurance Company, which lost more than $200 million in 1975, Sears ran into headaches with its attempts to upgrade soft-goods merchandise. Arthur Wood, the president, conceded that, in moving to higherpriced women's wear, the company turned over a $5 billion budget apparel market to competitors. In 1976 Sears moved back to the middle market. Sears' sales of $15 billion and profits of $695 million in 1976 both set records.[1]

Unquestionably Sears management has a high tolerance to change. "We never stop watching, listening, and reacting to the customer no matter how high we go in the company," said one executive.

On the other hand, Sears' gigantic size—900 stores, 1700 catalog and tele-

---

[1] "At the Top of the Tower," *Time*, November 21, 1977, p. 80.

phone sales offices, 13 large distribution centers, and 124 warehouses—and chain operations with their long lead times between ordering and delivery lower tolerance to change. For they prevent the company from keeping pace with smaller companies on fast-changing fashions.

It is safe to say that the size of a corporation, the nature of the industry, and the "mentality" of the CEO, the other top managers, and the line executives are important ingredients in tolerance to change. Without doubt, companies in high-technology growth industries, like electronics, exhibit a higher tolerance to change than low-growth and low-technology industries like the railroads—perhaps because they must do so to survive. Moreover, large corporations react slower to change than small companies because typically more people and more levels of organization are involved in the decision. Because of its precision of measurement, research on tolerance to change can lead to the formulation of standards and laws.

The extent to which a company tolerates change compared with its theoretical maximum could be expressed as a coefficient placed on a scale between zero and one. The rate at which a company can absorb change would require not only an understanding of the company and its external environment but also of the tools used to evaluate them. At the outset all the important variables would have to be recognized and defined. Even if our search for quantitative value were not utterly precise, the differences in tolerance to change coefficients by companies and industries would offer considerable gain. At least one measure of evaluating growth potential would be available.

Now it should not be construed that all companies should have high coefficients of change. Certainly companies in low-growth and low-technology industries could have high earnings and return on investment without it. On the average, however, companies with high tolerance to change should have higher earnings in the long run than companies in their industry that do not. Or put in another way, companies that intelligently observe and evaluate change in the internal and external environment and develop and implement sound strategies to account for these changes will be the most successful. We are emphatic about this point; after all, wasn't it the basis for this book?

INDEX